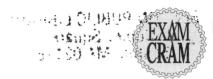

The Sair Linux/GNU Installation and Configuration Cram Sheet

This Cram Sheet contains the distilled, key facts about the Sair Linux/GNU Installation and Configuration Level 1 certification exam 3X0-101. Review this information last thing before entering the test room, paying special attention to those areas where you feel you need the most review. You can transfer any of the facts onto a blank piece of paper before beginning the exam.

LINUX HISTORY AND LICENSES

1. The last open source version of Unix was version 6, developed by AT&T. Minix, Xinu, and Linux were developed as clones of Unix version 6.

2. Most of Linux was developed by Richard Stallman's Free Software Foundation (FSF). Linus Torvalds developed the kernel.

3. The two major licenses behind Linux software are the General Public License (GPL), also known as *copyleft*, and the Open Source License from the Open Source Initiative (OSI).

4. You can copy and sell GPL and OSI software without a warranty.

5. GPL software is considered to be higher quality because of the community development model. Linux modularity allows developers to work separately.

6. Because GPL software does not come with a warranty; you can "fix" it yourself by modifying code, installing drivers, and relying on the community for help.

7. The costs associated with open source/GPL software is the time and skill required to maintain, modify, and update the open source code.

LINUX DOCUMENTATION

8. Linux command documentation can be found through the **man**, **xman**, **info**, **xinfo**, and **tkinfo** commands. In most distributions, you can search through the titles of manual (man) pages with the **man -k** or **apropos** commands.

9. The Linux Documentation Project has an extensive Linux library online, including HOWTOs and book-length guides at **www.linuxdoc.com**.

10. When troubleshooting, use the **www.deja.com** Web site to look through the newsgroups. It's a great database of Linux problems and solutions.

THE STRUCTURE OF LINUX

11. Linux can be divided into six basic modules:

- *Kernel*—Communicates directly with hardware. Kernel versions are set up in the major.minor.patch format; odd minor numbers represent beta versions of the kernel, which are not suitable for production.

- *Init*—Starts the shell, watches for shutdown signals. Only the root or superuser can run init. Init is the first program, with a PID of 1. Unlike others, init has no parent program.

- *Daemons*—Watch for data. Resident in memory.

- *Network*—Works for client/server communication. Like the kernel, network modules are stored in protected mode memory.

- *User Mode*—Includes login, shell, and utility programs. The login and shell programs are started by init. Other utilities are started by the shell.

- *X Window*—Programs associated with the Linux GUI.

59. You can reprioritize specific programs with the **nice** and **renice** commands.

60. You can run a program in the background with the **&** switch. If the program is already running, press Ctrl+Z and then type "bg".

X WINDOW

61. The two main configuration utilities for the X Window are the graphical XF86Setup and text-based xf86config utilities.

62. Other related X Window utilities are SuperProbe for your graphics card; Red Hat's Xconfigurator, mouseconfig; and kbdconfig, and S.u.S.E.'s SaX.

63. When Linux starts the X Server, log in (if required) at a display manager such as **xdm**. Then Linux starts window managers such as GNOME or KDE.

64. Two ways to enter the X Window are the **startx** and **xdm** commands. The **xdm** command starts a graphical login display manager.

65. Key components of window managers are known as *widgets*.

66. Several typesetting languages process text files with the fonts and graphics that you need, including nroff, groff, TeX, LaTeX, and HTML.

67. To copy in the X Window, highlight desired text, move the cursor to the paste location, and press the middle mouse button. (You can configure a two-button mouse to simulate the middle button by pressing both buttons.)

TROUBLESHOOTING

68. In FTP, the **mget *.*** command downloads only those files with a dot in the name. The **mget .** command downloads all files from a specific FTP directory.

69. If you see **LI** instead of the LILO **boot:** prompt, your BIOS may have trouble reading your hard disk, or Linux can't find your secondary boot loader /boot/boot.b.

). If you don't see the LILO **boot:** prompt, your MBR may be missing. Boot into Linux with a rescue disk, and run **/sbin/lilo** to restore the /etc/lilo.conf file.

. If you forget a root password, run the **linux single** command at the LILO **boot:** prompt to start single-user mode. Then you can edit the /etc/passwd file.

72. Create a boot or rescue floppy disk: in MS-DOS, use the **rawrite** command; in Linux use the **dd if=/mnt/cdrom/images/boot.img of=/mnt/floppy** command.

73. The **/sbin/kbdrate -r 30** command sets the keyboard repeat rate to 30 cps.

74. Turn on the Num Lock for a virtual terminal with the **setleds +num < /dev/tty***x* **> /dev/null** command, where *x* is a virtual terminal number.

75. Use the Network Time Protocol to synchronize the time on your computer. For example, the **ntupdate clock.isc.org** command synchronizes the time on your computer with the Internet Software Consortium server.

76. Log files are set up in facility.level format, as defined in the /etc/syslog.conf file. For example, lpd.err collects print-related errors.

77. For the *cannot open display:0.0* error, run **DISPLAY=localhost:0.0**.

78. If you have a printer problem, check physical connections, error logs, lock files, spools, the /etc/printcap file, and then try sending text files to your printer.

79. If you hear "thrashing" characteristic of high activity on your hard disk, you probably need more RAM.

) CORIOLIS™
Certification Insider Press

29. Interactivity lets you use the HISTORY of previous commands. Review and reuse old commands with the up arrow or ! and the first letters of the previous command.

30. You can apply shell variables to other shells with the **export** command.

31. There are three basic data streams: standard input (stdin), standard output (stdout), and standard error (stderr).

32. You can redirect data streams in five different ways:
    - >—Redirects standard output from the left of the arrow to a file to the right of the arrow. It overwrites the file if it already exists.
    - >>—Redirects and appends standard output to a file or script to the right of the arrow.
    - 2>—Redirects standard error to a file or script to the right of the arrow.
    - <—Directs the contents of a file from the right of the arrow to a program or script to the left of the arrow. Commonly used for data files.
    - Pipe (|)—Used between two commands or scripts. It redirects the standard output from the left of the pipe as standard input to the script or command to the right of the pipe.

33. There are two different wildcards. The * represents 0 or more characters. Each ? represents a single character.

34. Use the backslash (\) to escape special characters like wildcards and spaces.

35. Commands inside back quotes (') are executed by the shell.

CRITICAL COMMANDS

36. The **cd ~** command changes to your home directory.

37. Key file manipulation commands include **cp**, **mv**, **rm**, and **ln**. The **rm -rf** command removes all specified files, directories, and subdirectories, even if not empty, without prompting.

38. Key commands to review your files include **ls -ltr**.

39. Key commands to review the contents of a file include **less**, **more**, **head**, and **tail**.

40. You can create and delete directories with the **mkdir** and **rmdir** commands.

41. You can search through the contents of a file with the **grep** command.

42. You can use the **mdir**, **mmove**, and **mcopy** commands to access unmounted MS-DOS drives.

43. You can use commands like **alias dir="ls -l"** to create new commands.

44. You can create and extract and zip and unzip from archives with the **tar**, **gzip**, and **gunzip** commands.

45. The **file** command shows file types.

46. The **find** and **locate** commands search for files. The **locate** command is faster because it searches through a database, although the database may be out of date.

47. The **wc** command returns a count of lines, words, and characters in a file.

48. While the **df** command specifies space on each mounted volume, the **du** command specifies the space used by each file.

SYSTEM AND NETWORK ADMINISTRATION

49. The printer is governed by the **lpd** daemon. The default printer, as shown in the /etc/printcap file, is **lp**. Related commands include **lpr**, which prints a file; **lpq**, which checks the print queue; **lprm**, which removes jobs from the print queue; and **lpc**, which lets you administer the line printer system.

50. The print spool is stored in the /var/spool/lpd directory.

51. Two common printer languages are PostScript and PCL.

52. You can manage driver modules with the **lsmod** (list modules), **rmmod** (remove module), and **insmod** (install module) commands.

53. Three steps to create a new user: modify the /etc/passwd file, create a home directory, and copy default configuration files from the /etc/skel directory.

54. Change the default shell for a user by modifying the /etc/passwd file.

55. Four commands that help automate the process of creating new users: **adduser**, **useradd**, **userdel**, and **newusers**.

56. Files and directories are owned by users and groups. You can change ownership with the **chown** and **chgrp** commands.

57. You can find logged-on users with the **who** and **w** commands. Local logins are associated with gettys or terminals of ttyx. Network logins have gettys like ttypx.

58. If you want to kill a program named gone, open a second virtual terminal. Use the **ps aux | grep gone** command, and then find the process identifier (PID) number associated with gone. Use the **kill** command to terminate that PID.

12. Linux is a multitasking, multiterminal, multiuser system.
    - *Multitasking*—Runs more than one process at a time. Each program may need more than one process, or task.
    - *Multiterminal*—Allows simultaneous logins. You can open another terminal from the GUI with the Ctrl+Alt+F*x* command, where *x* is between 1 and 6. Each terminal is also known as a getty.
    - *Multiuser*—Multiple users can log on to the same computer simultaneously.

13. Linux configures peripherals on different buses, usually to request service from your memory or CPU: IRQ, PCI, I/O, and DMA. IRQ conflicts can be a problem. A plug-and-play BIOS may not work well with Linux.

14. The Filesystem Hierarchy Standard (FHS) governs the files and directories on Linux. Important directories include:
    - */*—The root directory
    - */boot*—Essential startup utilities, often including the Linux kernel
    - */dev*—Device drivers
    - */etc*—Basic configuration files
    - */home*—Home directories for all users except root
    - */proc*—Kernel processes that are currently active; a "pseudofile" system
    - */sbin*—System administration commands
    - */var*—Log files, print spools

INSTALLATION STEPS

15. There are 10 basic common installation steps: boot media; set up language, mouse, and keyboard; set up LILO for single or dual-boot; format partitions; install software; set up default operating system; enter network settings (IP address, network mask, gateway, DNS, domain); set up X Window configuration (controller and monitor); and create rescue disks.

16. To make room on a Microsoft Windows computer for Linux, check the hard disk for errors with ScanDisk, consolidate data with Defrag, back up current data, then use a partition-splitting utility like fips.

17. Linux only boots from partitions below cylinder 1024. Depending on the hard drive, this may be as low as 512MB.

18. The first and second disks on a controller are a *master* and a *slave*. The master and slave on the first IDE controller are known as *hda* and *hdb*; on the second IDE controller, they are *hdc* and *hdd*.

STARTUP AND SHUTDOWN

19. Use the **append** command in the lilo.conf file to specify IRQ, I/O, and amount of RAM. Use the same commands without "append" at the LILO **boot:** prompt.

20. The **lilo** command restores lilo.conf to your Master Boot Record (MBR).

NETWORK CONFIGURATION

21. Almost any network installation, through NFS, Samba, FTP, or a modem, is slower than a direct installation from CD-ROM.

22. Four network components set up your computer on a TCP/IP network:
    - *IP address*—Four numbers between 0 and 255, divided by decimals, such as 192.168.0.26. This convention is known as dotted decimal or dotted quad format. IP addresses may be stored in the /etc/hosts file. DHCP servers can assign IP addresses for you.
    - *Network mask*—A special IP address that determines the range of usable IP addresses on your LAN. Also known as a *subnet mask*.
    - *Gateway address*—The IP address of a computer on your LAN that's also connected to another network such as the Internet.
    - *DNS*—Also known as a *nameserver*, which has a database of domain names such as www.coriolis.com and IP addresses such as 38.187.128.10.

23. Computers use the loopback address, 127.0.0.1, to communicate with themselves on a TCP/IP network.

24. Major network applications include Netscape for Web pages, FTP clients such as gFTP for files, and Telnet to connect to remote Linux computers.

SHELL MANAGEMENT

25. Linux users believe in the superiority of the command-line interface. GUI tools such as LinuxConf are not as reliable.

26. The absolute path to a file is based on the root (/) directory. The relative path is based on the current or present working directory.

27. The shell checks all directories listed in $PATH for scripts or programs. If you include the dot (.) in the $PATH variable, the shell also checks the current directory, but this leaves you vulnerable to Trojan horses.

28. Three commands allow you to exit from a command-line interface shell: **logout**, Ctrl+D, and **exit**.

Sair Linux/GNU Installation and Configuration

Michael Jang

Sair Linux/GNU Installation and Configuration Exam Cram

Limits of Liability and Disclaimer of Warranty

The author and publisher of this book have used their best efforts in preparing the book and the programs contained in it. These efforts include the development, research, and testing of the theories and programs to determine their effectiveness. The author and publisher make no warranty of any kind, expressed or implied, with regard to these programs or the documentation contained in this book.

The author and publisher shall not be liable in the event of incidental or consequential damages in connection with, or arising out of, the furnishing, performance, or use of the programs, associated instructions, and/or claims of productivity gains.

Trademarks

Trademarked names appear throughout this book. Rather than list the names and entities that own the trademarks or insert a trademark symbol with each mention of the trademarked name, the publisher states that it is using the names for editorial purposes only and to the benefit of the trademark owner, with no intention of infringing upon that trademark.

The Coriolis Group, LLC
14455 N. Hayden Road
Suite 220
Scottsdale, Arizona 85260

(480)483-0192
FAX (480)483-0193
www.coriolis.com

Jang, Michael H.
    Sair Linux/GNU installation and configuration / Michael Jang.
        p.   cm. -- (Exam cram)
    Includes index.
    ISBN 1-57610-953-4
    1. Electronic data processing personnel--Certification.   2. Operating systems (Computers)--Certification.   3. Linux.   I. Title.   II. Series.
QA76.3.J345   2001
005.4'32--dc21
                                    00-065697
                                    CIP

Printed in the United States of America
10 9 8 7 6 5 4 3 2 1

President and CEO
Keith Weiskamp

Publisher
Steve Sayre

Acquisitions Editor
Sharon Linsenbach

Development Editor
Deb Doorley

Product Marketing Manager
Brett Woolley

Project Editor
Jennifer Ashley

Technical Reviewer
Leon Joannis

Production Coordinator
Wendy Littley

Cover Designer
Jesse Dunn

Layout Designer
April Nielsen

QA76.3
.J345
2001

The Coriolis Group, LLC • 14455 North Hayden Road, Suite 220 • Scottsdale, Arizona 85260

ExamCram.com Connects You to the Ultimate Study Center!

Our goal has always been to provide you with the best study tools on the planet to help you achieve your certification in record time. Time is so valuable these days that none of us can afford to waste a second of it, especially when it comes to exam preparation.

Over the past few years, we've created an extensive line of *Exam Cram* and *Exam Prep* study guides, practice exams, and interactive training. To help you study even better, we have now created an e-learning and certification destination called **ExamCram.com**. (You can access the site at **www.examcram.com**.) Now, with every study product you purchase from us, you'll be connected to a large community of people like yourself who are actively studying for their certifications, developing their careers, seeking advice, and sharing their insights and stories.

I believe that the future is all about collaborative learning. Our **ExamCram.com** destination is our approach to creating a highly interactive, easily accessible collaborative environment, where you can take practice exams and discuss your experiences with others, sign up for features like "Questions of the Day," plan your certifications using our interactive planners, create your own personal study pages, and keep up with all of the latest study tips and techniques.

I hope that whatever study products you purchase from us—*Exam Cram* or *Exam Prep* study guides, *Personal Trainers*, *Personal Test Centers*, or one of our interactive Web courses—will make your studying fun and productive. Our commitment is to build the kind of learning tools that will allow you to study the way you want to, whenever you want to.

Visit ExamCram.com now to enhance your study program.

Help us continue to provide the very best certification study materials possible. Write us or email us at **learn@examcram.com** and let us know how our study products have helped you study. Tell us about new features that you'd like us to add. Send us a story about how we've helped you. We're listening!

Good luck with your certification exam and your career. Thank you for allowing us to help you achieve your goals.

Keith Weiskamp

Keith Weiskamp
President and CEO

Look for these other products from The Coriolis Group:

LPI General Linux I Exam Cram
by Emmett Dulaney

LPI General Linux II Exam Cram
by Emmett Dulaney and Christopher Hare

Sair Linux/GNU Security, Ethics, and Privacy Exam Cram
by Dee-Ann LeBlanc and Evan Blomquist

General Linux I Exam Prep
by Dee-Ann LeBlanc

Linux System Administration Black Book
by Dee-Ann LeBlanc

Linux Install and Configuration Little Black Book
by Dee-Ann LeBlanc and Isaac-Hajime Yates

About the Author

Michael Jang (LCP, MCSE) is currently a full-time writer on Linux and Microsoft operating systems. His experience with computers goes back to the days of jumbled punch cards. He has recently coauthored *Linux Networking Clearly Explained* (Morgan Kaufmann Publishers, 2000) and has also written *MCSE Windows 98 Exam Prep* (The Coriolis Group, 1999) as well as *MCSE Guide to Microsoft Windows 98* (Course Technology, 1998). He has also served as technical editor for several Microsoft Help Desk books, including those on Windows NT Workstation 4, Windows 98, and Office 2000.

In his previous life as a Boeing engineer, Michael worked a variety of jobs, including project manager for the first FAA type certified In-Seat Video systems.

Acknowledgments

Computer books are a group effort. The acquisitions editor, Sharon Linsenbach, moved quickly to organize the team behind the book. The developmental editor, Deb Doorley, gave this project a great start. The technical editor, Leon Joannis, acted as a partner to make sure everything worked. The copyeditor, Anne-Marie Walker, took the time to learn about Linux before getting into the details. And the project editor, Jennifer Ashley did a great job making sure everything went as planned. I'd also like to thank Wendy Littley, the production coordinator; Jesse Dunn, cover designer; and April Nielsen, layout designer, for putting everything together.

I'd like to thank the president of Sair, Tobin Maginnis, who spent the time to help me understand the motivations behind his exams. Tobin, next time we meet, remember to keep me away from the Krispy Kremes. I'd also like to thank John Muster, who taught me to use Linux, and gave me perspective on its historical impact.

Thank you Nancy, for all your love and support. Writing a book and buying a house at the same time would not be possible without you. And thanks to the bears from Momma Bears' Bears, who surround me and make my workspace much more pleasant.

Finally, thanks to the Linux community of developers, who with their selfless devotion to better software, are proving that a community can compete effectively with a monopoly.

Contents at a Glance

Table of Contents

. . . .

Chapter 6
Startup and Shutdown 95

. . . .

Chapter 7
Commanding the Shell 115

Introduction

Welcome to *Sair Linux/GNU Installation and Configuration Exam Cram*! This book aims to help you get ready to take—and pass—the Sair Linux/GNU Installation and Configuration Level 1 certification exam 3X0-101. This Introduction explains Sair's certification programs in general and talks about how the *Exam Cram* series can help you prepare for Sair's certification exams.

Exam Cram books help you understand and appreciate the subjects and materials you need to pass Sair certification exams. *Exam Cram* books are aimed strictly at test preparation and review. They do not teach you everything you need to know about a topic (such as the ins and outs of building your own RPMs). Instead, I present and dissect the questions and problems I've found that you're likely to encounter on a test. I've worked from Sair's own training materials, preparation guides, and tests. My aim is to bring together as much information as possible about Sair Linux/GNU certification exams.

Nevertheless, to completely prepare yourself for any Sair Linux/GNU exam, you should begin by taking the Self-Assessment included in this book (immediately following this Introduction). This tool will help you evaluate your knowledge base against the requirements for an LCA or LCP under both ideal and real circumstances.

Based on what you learn from that exercise, you might decide to begin your studies with some classroom training, or you might pick up and read one of the many Linux guides available from Sair or third-party vendors. I strongly recommend that you also install and configure at least *four* versions of Linux, because nothing beats hands-on experience and familiarity when it comes to understanding the questions you're likely to encounter on a certification test. Book learning is essential, but hands-on experience is the best teacher of all.

You can find more information on the benefits associated with Linux Certification at **www.linuxcertification.com/reasons.php**.

The Linux Certified Administrator (LCA) Program

Each LCA exam consists of 50 questions. The candidate must receive a score of 74 percent on the exam, which corresponds to 37 correct questions.

The best place to keep tabs on the LCA program and its various certifications is on the Linux Certification Web site. The current URL for this program is **www.linuxcertification.com**. Details of the LCA program change frequently; make sure to monitor the "News" and the "Exams" links often for the latest and most accurate information about the LCA programs.

The Linux Certified Professional (LCP) Program

Passing either the Installation and Configuration Level 1 exam 3X0-101 or the System Administration Level 1 exam 3X0-102 also qualifies you as a Linux Certified Professional (LCP). You'll receive a card in the mail along with your certificate once you pass one of these two exams that lists your LCP status, name, and serial number.

Taking a Certification Exam

Alas, testing is not free. Your exam will cost $99, and is administered by Prometric/Thomson Learning (formally known as Sylvan Prometric). To reach the people behind the Sair Linux/GNU exams, email **questions@sairinc.com**.

You can sign up for a test through Prometric's Web site at **www.prometric.com**. Or, you can register by phone at 800-755-3926 (within the United States or Canada) or at 410-843-8000 (outside the United States and Canada).

To sign up for a test, you must possess a valid credit card, or contact either company for mailing instructions to send them a check (in the United States). Only when payment is verified, or a check has cleared, can you actually register for a test.

To schedule an exam, call the number or visit either of the Web pages at least one day in advance. To cancel or reschedule an exam, you must call before 7 P.M. pacific standard time the day before the scheduled test time (or you may be charged, even if you don't appear to take the test). When you want to schedule a test, have the following information ready:

➤ Your name, organization, and mailing address.

➤ Your Test ID. (Inside the United States, this means your Social Security number; citizens of other nations should call ahead to find out what type of identification number is required to register for a test.)

➤ The name and number of the exam you wish to take.

➤ A method of payment. (As we've already mentioned, a credit card is the most convenient method, but alternate means can be arranged in advance, if necessary.)

All exams are completely closed-book. In fact, you will not be permitted to take anything with you into the testing area, but you will be furnished with a blank sheet of paper and a pen or, in some cases, an erasable plastic sheet and an erasable pen. We suggest that you immediately write down on that sheet of paper all the information you've memorized for the test. In *Exam Cram* books, this information appears on a tear-out sheet inside the front cover of each book. You will have some time to compose yourself, record this information, and take a sample orientation exam before you begin the real thing. We suggest you take the orientation test before taking your first exam, but because they're all more or less identical in layout, behavior, and controls, you probably won't need to do this more than once.

How to Prepare for an Exam

Preparing for any Linux exam requires that you obtain and study materials designed to provide comprehensive information about the specific exam for which you are preparing. The following list of materials will help you study and prepare:

➤ Online documentation can be found on the Linux Certification Web site (**www.linuxcertification.com**).

➤ The Linux Documentation Project (online resource can be found on **www.linuxdoc.org**).

In addition, you may find training courses from Sair's Accredited Centers of Education (ACE) useful in your quest for Sair Linux/GNU expertise. Training has been available on a limited basis for free at past Linux World Expo conferences in the San Francisco Bay Area as well as in New York. If you can get to one of these conferences, monitor the **www.linuxcertification.com** and **www. linuxworldexpo.com** Web sites for news. You may get lucky. In addition, you may also find the following series useful:

➤ *Study guides*—Several publishers—including The Coriolis Group—offer Linux titles. The Coriolis Group series includes the following:

  ➤ *The Exam Cram series*—These books give you information about the material you need to know to pass the tests.

> ➤ *The Exam Prep series*—These books provide a greater level of detail than the *Exam Cram* books and are designed to teach you everything you need to know from an exam perspective. Each book comes with a CD-ROM that contains interactive practice exams in a variety of testing formats.

Together, the two series make a perfect pair. Check **www.examcram.com** for additional products from Coriolis.

You'll find that this book will complement your studying and preparation for the exam, either on your own or with the aid of the previously mentioned study programs. In the section that follows, I'll explain how this book works and why this book counts as a member of the required and recommended materials list.

About This Book

Each topical *Exam Cram* chapter follows a regular structure, along with graphical cues about important or useful information. Here's the structure of a typical chapter:

> ➤ *Opening hotlists*—Each chapter begins with a list of the terms, tools, and techniques that you must learn and understand before you can be fully conversant with that chapter's subject matter. The hotlists are followed by one or two introductory paragraphs to set the stage for the rest of the chapter.

> ➤ *Topical coverage*—After the opening hotlists, each chapter covers a series of topics related to the chapter's subject. Throughout this section, I highlight important topics or concepts as Exam Alerts, like this:

 This is what an Exam Alert looks like. Normally, an Exam Alert stresses concepts, terms, software, or activities that are likely to relate to one or more certification test questions. For that reason, any information found offset in Exam Alert format is worthy of unusual attentiveness on your part. Indeed, most of the information that appears on the Cram Sheet appears as Exam Alerts within the text.

Pay close attention to material flagged as an Exam Alert; although all the information in this book pertains to what you need to know to pass the exam, I flag certain items that are really important. You'll find what appears in the meat of each chapter to be worth knowing, too, when preparing for the test. Because this book's material is very condensed, I recommend that you use this book along with other resources to achieve the maximum benefit.

In addition to the Exam Alerts, I have provided tips that will help build a better foundation for Sair Linux knowledge. Although the information might not be on the exam, it is certainly related and will help you become a better test taker.

This is how tips are formatted. Keep your eyes open for these, and you'll become a Linux guru in no time.

➤ *Practice questions*—This section presents a series of mock test questions and explanations of both correct and incorrect answers.

➤ *Details and resources*—Every chapter ends with a section titled "Need to Know More?", which provides direct pointers to third-party resources offering more details on the chapter's subject. If you find a resource you like in this collection, use it, but don't feel compelled to use all the resources. On the other hand, I recommend only those resources that I use on a regular basis, so none of my recommendations will be a waste of your time or money. (But purchasing them all at once probably represents an expense that many network administrators and would-be LCAs or LCPs might find hard to justify.)

Additionally, you'll find a glossary that explains terms, and an index that you can use to track down terms as they appear in the text.

Finally, the tear-out Cram Sheet attached next to the inside front cover of this *Exam Cram* book represents a condensed and compiled collection of facts and tips that I think you should memorize before taking the test. Because you can dump this information out of your head onto a piece of paper before answering any exam questions, you can master this information by brute force—you need to remember it only long enough to write it down when you walk into the test room. You might even want to look at it in the car or in the lobby of the testing center just before you walk in to take the test.

How to Use This Book

If you're prepping for a first-time test, keep in mind that I've structured the topics in this book to build on one another. Therefore, some topics in later chapters make more sense after you've read earlier chapters. That's why I suggest you read this book from front to back for your initial test preparation. If you need to brush up on a topic or you have to bone up for a second try, use the index or table of contents to go straight to the topics and questions that you need to study. Beyond the tests, I think you'll find this book useful as a tightly focused reference to the requirements behind installing and configuring Linux.

Given all the book's elements and its specialized focus, I've tried to create a tool that will help you prepare for—and pass—the Level 1 Installation and Configuration exam. Please share your feedback on the book with me, especially if you have ideas about how I can improve it for future test-takers.

Please send your questions or comments to The Coriolis Group at **learn@examcram.com**. Please remember to include the title of the book in your message. Also, be sure to check out the Web page at **www.examcram.com**, where you'll find information updates, commentary, and certification information.

Thanks, and enjoy the book!

Self-Assessment

I included a Self-Assessment in this *Exam Cram* book to help you evaluate your readiness to tackle Linux Certified Administrator (LCA) or Linux Certified Professional (LCP) certification. This Self-Assessment should also help you understand what you need to master the topic of this book—namely, Sair Linux/GNU Installation and Configuration Level 1 certification exam 3X0-101. But before you tackle this Self-Assessment, let's talk about concerns you may face when pursuing an LCA or LCP and about what an ideal LCA candidate might look like.

LCAs in the Real World

In the next section, I describe an ideal LCA candidate, knowing full well that only a few real candidates will meet this ideal. In fact, my description of that ideal candidate might seem downright scary. But take heart: although the requirements to obtain an LCA might seem formidable, they are by no means impossible to meet. However, you should be keenly aware that getting through the process takes time, requires some expense, and consumes substantial effort.

Introduced in the fall of 1999, the LCA program is very young. Demand for this certification is growing, and the limited seating for the testing makes the LCA even more valuable. However, if you're willing to tackle the process seriously and to do what it takes to obtain the necessary experience and knowledge, you can take—and pass—all the certification tests involved in obtaining an LCA. In fact, Coriolis has designed its *Exam Crams* and companion *Exam Preps* to make it as easy for you as possible to prepare for certification exams. We've also greatly expanded our Web site, **www.examcram.com**, to provide a host of resources for various certifications.

The Ideal LCA Candidate

Just to give you some idea of what an ideal LCA candidate is like, following are some relevant statistics about the background and experience such an individual might have. Don't worry if you don't meet these qualifications—this is a far from ideal world, and where you fall short is simply where you'll have more work to do.

➤ Academic or professional training in network theory, concepts, and operations. This training includes everything from networking hardware and software to the Linux operating system, services, and applications.

➤ Two or more years of professional networking experience, including experience with Ethernet, modems, and other networking media. This experience must include installation, configuration, upgrading, and troubleshooting.

➤ Two or more years in a networked environment with hands-on experience with four of the following Linux distributions: Caldera, Corel, Debian, Mandrake, Red Hat, S.u.S.E., Stampede, Slackware, Storm Linux, or TurboLinux. A solid understanding of each system's architecture, installation, configuration, maintenance, and troubleshooting is also essential.

➤ Familiarity with key Linux-based TCP/IP-based services, including HTTP (Web servers), DHCP, and DNS, plus familiarity with one or more of the following: FTP, Samba, Squid, NFS, iptables, or ipchains.

Put Yourself to the Test

The following series of questions and observations is designed to help you figure out how much work you must do to pursue Sair Linux/GNU certification and what kinds of resources you might consult on your quest. Be absolutely honest in your answers, or you'll end up wasting money on exams you're not yet ready to take. There are no right or wrong answers, only steps along the path to certification. Only you can decide where you really belong in the broad spectrum of aspiring candidates.

Two things should be clear from the outset, however:

➤ Even a modest background in computer science will be helpful.

➤ Hands-on experience with Linux, Linux products, and Linux technologies is an essential ingredient to certification success.

Educational Background

1. Have you ever taken any computer-related classes? [Yes or No]

   If Yes, proceed to question 2; if No, proceed to question 4.

2. Have you taken any classes on Unix operating systems? [Yes or No]

   If Yes, you'll probably be able to handle discussions on commands, architecture, and system components. If you're rusty, brush up on basic Unix concepts, especially virtual memory, multitasking regimes, user mode versus superuser mode operation, filesystems, and general computer security topics.

If No, consider some basic reading in this area. I strongly recommend a good general book on Unix, such as *Unix Made Easy*, by John Muster (Osborne/ McGraw-Hill, 1996, ISBN 0-07882-173-8). If this title doesn't appeal to you, check out reviews of other, similar titles at your favorite online bookstore.

3. Have you taken any TCP/IP-based networking concepts or technologies classes? [Yes or No]

   If Yes, you'll probably be able to handle Linux's networking terminology, concepts, and technologies (brace yourself for frequent departures from normal usage). If you're rusty, brush up on basic networking concepts and terminology, especially networking media, transmission types, the OSI reference model, and networking technologies such as Ethernet and WAN links.

   If No, you might want to read one or two books in this topic area. The two best books that I know of are *Computer Networks*, *3rd Edition*, by Andrew S. Tanenbaum (Prentice-Hall, 1996, ISBN 0-13-349945-6), and *Linux Network Administrator's Guide*, by Olaf Kirch and Terry Dawson (O'Reilly and Associates, 2000, ISBN 1-56592-400-2).

   Skip to the next section, "Hands-on Experience."

4. Have you done any reading on the Linux operating system or networks? [Yes or No]

   If Yes, review the requirements stated in the first paragraphs after questions 2 and 3. If you meet those requirements, move on to the next section.

   If No, consult the recommended reading for both topics. A strong background will help you prepare for the Sair Linux/GNU exams better than just about anything else.

Hands-on Experience

The most important key to success on all types of certification exams is hands-on experience. If I leave you with only one realization after you take this Self-Assessment, it should be that there's no substitute for time spent installing, configuring, and using Linux and its components, upon which you'll be tested repeatedly and in depth.

5. Have you installed, configured, and worked with:

   ➤ At least one Linux distribution? [Yes or No]

   ➤ Four or more Linux distributions? [Yes or No]

   If Yes, make sure you understand the different methods used to configure, install, and work with different Linux distributions.

If No, you'll want to obtain a copy of at least four different Linux distributions and learn how to install, configure, and maintain them. If you don't have the facilities to download these distributions onto CD-ROMs, you can purchase them inexpensively from Linux e-tailers such as **www.cheapbytes.com** or **www.linuxmall.com**. You can use this book to guide your activities and studies.

6. For any specific Linux product that is not itself an operating system (for example, the X Window System or Apache), have you installed, configured, used, and upgraded this software? [Yes or No]

If the answer is Yes, skip to the next section. If it's No, you must get some experience. Read on for suggestions on how to do this.

With various Sair Linux/GNU exams, experience is a must, be it something as simple as installing a game from an RPM or as challenging as NFS or Apache.

Before you even think about taking any exam, make sure you've spent enough time with the related software to understand how it can be installed and configured, how to maintain such an installation, and how to troubleshoot that software when things go wrong. This will help you in the exam as well as in real life.

Testing Your Exam-Readiness

Whether you attend a formal class on a specific topic to get ready for an exam or use written materials to study on your own, some preparation for the Sair Linux/GNU Certified Administrator exam is essential. You want to do everything you can to pass the exam on your first try. That's where the importance of studying comes in.

For any given subject, consider taking a class if you've tackled self-study materials, taken the test, and failed anyway. The opportunity to interact with an instructor and fellow students can make all the difference in the world if you can afford that privilege. For information about Sair Linux/GNU classes, visit their Accredited Centers of Education (ACE) Web site at **ace.linuxcertification.com**.

Onward, through the Fog!

After you've assessed your readiness, undertaken the right background studies, obtained the hands-on experience that will help you understand the products and technologies at work, and reviewed the many sources of information to help you prepare for a test, you'll be ready to take a round of practice tests. When your scores come back high enough to get you through the exam, you're ready to go after the real thing. If you follow this assessment regime, you'll know not only what you need to study but also when you're ready to make a test date. Good luck!

Sair Linux/GNU
Certification Exams

. . . .

Terms you'll need to understand:

✓ Radio button

✓ Checkbox

✓ Multiple-choice question formats

✓ Careful reading

✓ Process of elimination

Techniques you'll need to master:

✓ Preparing to take a certification exam

✓ Practicing (to make perfect)

✓ Making the best use of the testing software

✓ Budgeting your time

✓ Saving the hardest questions until last

✓ Guessing (as a last resort)

Exam taking is not something that most people anticipate eagerly, no matter how well prepared they might be. In most cases, familiarity helps to lessen test anxiety. In plain English, this means you probably won't be as nervous when you take your fourth or fifth certification exam as you'll be when you take your first one.

Whether it's your first exam or your tenth, understanding the details of exam taking (how much time to spend on questions, the environment you'll be in, and so on) and the exam software will help you concentrate on the material rather than on the setting. Likewise, mastering a few basic exam-taking skills should help you recognize—and perhaps even outfox—some of the tricks and gotchas you're bound to find in some of the exam questions.

This chapter, besides explaining the exam environment and software, describes some proven exam-taking strategies that you should be able to use to your advantage.

The Exam Situation

When you arrive at the testing center where you scheduled your exam, you'll sign in with an exam coordinator. He or she will ask you to show two forms of identification, one of which must be a photo ID, and both should have your signature. After you've signed in and your time slot arrives, you'll be asked to deposit any books, pagers, cell phones, bags, and other items you brought with you. Then, you'll be escorted into a closed room. Typically, the room will be furnished with anywhere from one to half a dozen computers, and each workstation will be separated from the others by dividers designed to keep you from seeing what's happening on someone else's computer.

You'll be furnished with a pen or pencil and a blank sheet of paper or, in some cases, an erasable plastic sheet and an erasable felt-tip pen. You're allowed to write down any information you want on both sides of this sheet. Before the exam, you should memorize as much of the material that appears on the Cram Sheet (inside the front cover of this book) as you can so you can write that information on the blank sheet as soon as you are seated in front of the computer. You can refer to your rendition of the Cram Sheet anytime you like during the test, but you'll have to surrender the sheet when you leave the room.

Most test rooms feature a wall with a large picture window. This permits the exam coordinator standing behind it to monitor the room, to prevent exam takers from talking to one another, and to observe anything out of the ordinary that might happen. The exam coordinator will have preloaded the appropriate Sair Linux/GNU certification exam—for this book, that's the Installation and Configuration Level 1 certification exam 3X0-101—and you'll be permitted to start as soon as you're seated in front of the computer.

All Sair Linux/GNU certification exams allow a certain maximum amount of time in which to complete your work. (This time is indicated on the exam by an on-screen counter/clock, so you can check the time remaining whenever you like.) The exam consists of randomly selected questions, and you may take up to 60 minutes to complete the exam.

The Installation and Configuration Level 1 certification exam 3X0-101 is computer generated and uses a multiple-choice format. Although this might sound simple, the questions are constructed not only to check your mastery of basic facts and figures about Linux technologies, but also to require you to evaluate one or more sets of circumstances or requirements. You might be asked to select the best or most effective solution to a problem from a range of choices, all of which technically are correct. Taking the exam is quite an adventure, and it involves real thinking. This book shows you what to expect and how to deal with the potential problems, puzzles, and predicaments.

Exam Layout and Design

Some exam questions require you to select a single answer, whereas others ask you to select multiple correct answers. The following multiple-choice question requires you to select a single correct answer. Following the question is a brief summary of each potential answer and why it is either right or wrong.

Question 1

Which command can be used with the appropriate parameters or switches to count the number of lines in a text file?

○ a. **grep**

○ b. **wc**

○ c. **lc**

○ d. **cat**

The correct answer is b. The command **wc -1** will count the number of lines within a file. **grep** can be used to find strings, **lc** does not exist, and **cat** is used to display files. Therefore, all answers except b are incorrect.

This sample question format corresponds closely to the Sair Linux/GNU certification exam format; the only difference on the exam is that questions are not followed by answer keys. To select an answer, position the cursor over the radio button next to the answer. Then, click the mouse button to select the answer.

Let's examine a question that requires choosing multiple answers. This type of question provides checkboxes rather than radio buttons for marking all appropriate selections.

Question 2

> Which of the following are valid GUI configuration utilities? [Check all correct answers]
>
> ❑ a. XF86Setup
>
> ❑ b. xf86setup
>
> ❑ c. xf86config
>
> ❑ d. XF86Config

The correct answers are a and c. XF86Setup is the standard GUI configuration utility from the XFree86 project. xf86config is the command line version of the XF86Setup utility. The other two options are not valid commands or configuration utilities.

For this type of question, more than one answer is required. Such questions are scored as wrong unless all the required selections are chosen. In other words, a partially correct answer does not result in partial credit when the test is scored. If you are required to provide multiple answers and you do not provide the number of answers that the question asks for, the testing software will mark the question for you and indicate at the end of the test that you did not complete that question. For Question 2, you have to check the boxes next to items a and c to obtain credit for a correct answer. Notice that picking the right answers also means knowing why the other answers are wrong!

Although these two basic types of questions can appear in many forms, they constitute the foundation on which all the Sair Linux/GNU certification exam questions rest. At any time, Sair can choose to include other questions involving exhibits, charts, or network diagrams to help document a Web site scenario that you'll be asked to troubleshoot or configure. Paying careful attention to such exhibits is the key to success.

Using Sair's Exam Software Effectively

A well-known principle when taking exams is to first read over the entire exam from start to finish while answering only those questions you feel absolutely sure of. On subsequent passes, you can dive into more complex questions more deeply, knowing how many such questions you have left.

Fortunately, Sair's exam software makes this approach easy to implement. At the top-left corner of each question is a checkbox that permits you to mark that question for a later visit.

Note: Marking questions makes review easier, but you can return to any question if you are willing to click the Forward or Back button repeatedly.

As you read each question, if you answer only those you're sure of and mark for review those you're not sure of, you can keep working through a decreasing list of questions as you answer the trickier ones in order.

There's at least one potential benefit to reading the exam completely before answering the trickier questions: Sometimes, information supplied in later questions sheds more light on earlier questions. Other times, information you read in later questions might jog your memory about networking facts, figures, or behavior that will help with earlier questions. Either way, you'll come out ahead if you defer those questions about which you're not absolutely sure.

Keep working on the questions until you're certain of all your answers or until you know you'll run out of time. If questions remain unanswered, you'll want to zip through them and guess. Not answering a question guarantees you won't receive credit for it, and a guess has at least a chance of being correct.

At the very end of your exam period, you're better off guessing than leaving questions unanswered.

Exam-Taking Basics

The most important advice about taking any exam is this: Read each question carefully. Some questions are deliberately ambiguous, some use double negatives, and others use terminology in incredibly precise ways. I have taken numerous exams—both practice and live—and in nearly every one I have missed at least one question because I didn't read it closely or carefully enough.

Here are some suggestions on how to deal with the tendency to jump to an answer too quickly:

➤ Make sure you read every word in the question. If you find yourself jumping ahead impatiently, go back and start over.

➤ As you read, try to restate the question in your own terms. If you can do this, you should be able to pick the correct answers more easily.

➤ When returning to a question after your initial read-through, read every word again; otherwise, your mind can quickly fall into a rut. Sometimes, revisiting a question after turning your attention elsewhere lets you see something you missed, but the strong tendency is to see what you've seen before. Avoid that tendency at all costs.

➤ If you return to a question more than twice, try to articulate to yourself what you don't understand about the question, why the answers don't appear to make sense, or what appears to be missing. If you chew on the subject for a while, your subconscious might provide the details that are lacking or you might notice a "trick" that will point to the right answer.

Above all, deal with each question by thinking through what you know about installation and configuration essentials. By reviewing what you know (and what you've written down on your information sheet), you'll often recall or understand things sufficiently to determine the answer to the question.

Question-Handling Strategies

Based on exams I've taken, some interesting trends have become apparent. For those questions that take only a single answer, usually two or three of the answers will be obviously incorrect, and two of the answers will be plausible; of course, only one can be correct. Unless the answer leaps out at you (if it does, reread the question to look for a trick; sometimes those are the ones you're likely to get wrong), begin the process of answering by eliminating those answers that are most obviously wrong.

Things to look for in obviously wrong answers include nonexistent commands, incorrect utility names, inconsistent conditions, and terminology you've never seen. If you've done your homework for an exam, no valid information should be completely new to you. In that case, unfamiliar or bizarre terminology probably indicates a totally bogus answer.

Numerous questions assume that you understand the inner workings of Linux utilities inside and out. If your knowledge in these areas is well grounded, it will help you cut through many otherwise confusing questions.

Budget your time by making sure you've completed one-quarter of the questions one-quarter of the way through the exam period and three-quarters of them three-quarters of the way through.

If you're not finished when 55 minutes have elapsed, use the last 5 minutes to guess your way through the remaining questions. Remember, guessing is potentially more valuable than not answering because blank answers are always wrong, but a guess can turn out to be right. If you don't have a clue about any of the remaining questions, pick answers at random, or choose all a's, b's, and so on. The important thing is to submit an exam for scoring that has an answer for every question.

Mastering the Inner Game

In the final analysis, knowledge breeds confidence, and confidence breeds success. If you study the materials in this book carefully and review all the practice questions at the end of each chapter, you should become aware of those areas where additional learning and study are required.

Next, follow up by reading some or all of the materials recommended in the "Need to Know More?" section at the end of each chapter. The idea is to become familiar enough with the concepts and situations you find in the sample questions that you can reason your way through similar situations on a real exam. If you know the material, you have every right to be confident that you can pass the exam.

After you've worked your way through the book, take the practice exam in Chapter 15. This will provide a reality check and help you identify areas you need to study further. Make sure you follow up and review materials related to the questions you miss on the practice exam before scheduling a real exam. Only when you've covered all the ground and feel comfortable with the whole scope of the practice exam should you take a real one.

Armed with the information in this book and with the determination to augment your knowledge, you should be able to pass the certification exam. However, you need to work at it, or you'll spend the exam fee more than once before you finally pass. If you prepare seriously, you should do well. Good luck!

Additional Resources

A good source of information about Sair certification exams comes from Sair itself, and the best place to go for exam-related information is online. If you haven't already visited the Sair Web site, do so right now at **www. linuxcertification.com.**

The menu options on the home page point to the most important sources of information in the Web pages. Here's what to check out, in order of importance:

➤ *Knowledge Matrix*—Use this area to review the skills and knowledge that will be tested on the exam.

➤ *Online Quizzes*—This area includes sample questions for the four Sair Linux Certified Administrator exams. These questions are mostly useful for getting used to the question formats. They will not appear on the actual exam.

➤ *Exams*—This page fully explains the certification process and contains links to objectives, sample questions, and the certification structure.

➤ *FAQ*—This page lists frequently asked questions with answers about the exams.

➤ *Our Team*—This page holds links to the Industry leaders and Sair personnel behind the exam.

These are just the high points of what's available in the Linux Certification pages. As you browse through them—and I strongly recommend that you do—you'll probably find other informational tidbits mentioned that are every bit as interesting.

Coping with Change on the Web

Sooner or later, all the information I've shared with you about the Linux Certification pages and the other Web-based resources mentioned throughout the rest of this book will go stale or be replaced by newer information.

There's always a way to find what you want on the Web if you're willing to invest some time and energy. Most large or complex Web sites offer a search engine. Feel free to use general search tools—such as **www.google.com**, **www.lycos.com**, and **www.excite.com**—to search for related information. Although Sair offers the best information about its certification exams online, plenty of third-party sources offer information, training, and assistance in this area. The bottom line is this: If you can't find something where the book says it lives, start looking around. If worst comes to worst, you can always email us at Coriolis. We just might have a clue.

A Short History
of Linux

Terms you'll need to understand:

✓ Open source

✓ Free software

✓ Free Software Foundation (FSF)

✓ GNU's Not Unix (GNU)

✓ General Public License (GPL)

✓ Copyleft

✓ Halloween Documents

Techniques you'll need to master:

✓ Understanding the background behind Linux

✓ Explaining different styles of software licensing and
documentation

✓ Describing the use and development of "free software"

✓ Getting Linux documentation over the Internet

✓ Finding documentation inside Linux

A sense of history is important on the Sair Linux/GNU Level 1 Installation and Configuration exam. As a Linux administrator, you need to explain the benefits and obligations of using open source software to nontechnical users. In this chapter, you'll learn some of the basic premises behind the development, licensing, and documentation of Linux.

Although you may not agree with some of the assumptions or analyses in this chapter, they are nonetheless some of the more important premises behind the development of Linux software and important for you to know.

Unix and Open Source Development

Linux was developed as a clone of Unix. In other words, the developers of Linux built their system without using the programming instructions, also known as the source code, used to build Unix. Because Linux is a Unix clone, you can use most of the same commands and applications on either operating system.

Although it would have been easier to adapt Unix for the personal computer, there are important historical reasons behind the development of Linux. And the way Linux was developed drives the way Linux developers, companies, and users work today.

AT&T and Unix Development

When Unix was developed in 1969, the American Telephone and Telegraph (AT&T) Company was a regulated monopoly in the United States. Although Unix was developed at AT&T's Bell Labs, various court and regulatory rulings kept AT&T out of the computer business. So AT&T kept the license for Unix and distributed the operating system with source code to universities for a nominal fee. Because AT&T wasn't making money from Unix, its lawyers insisted that the license explicitly state that Unix comes with no warranty. This release technique became known as *open source*.

The timing was good. Various universities adapted the Unix source code to work with three different kinds of computers available at the time: mainframes, minicomputers, and microcomputers. One key to this adaptation was the C programming language.

At about the same time, the U.S. Department of Defense's Advanced Research Project Agency (ARPA) wanted to set up a nationwide communications network that could survive a nuclear war. Most universities on this ARPA network used Unix. TCP/IP was built on Unix and eventually became the communication protocol for the ARPANET. The ARPANET eventually developed into the Internet that you know today. Unix and derivative clones, like Linux, are critical tools in the Internet.

The last freely distributed Unix system, popular in the mid-1970s, is known as Version 6. All Unix variants and clones, including Linux, Minix, Xinu, Solaris, and the Berkeley Standard Distribution (BSD), were cloned or developed from Unix Version 6.

Not Quite Free Software

AT&T retained the license to Unix through the 1980s. When the U.S. government settled the AT&T antitrust suit in 1982, one of the conditions allowed AT&T to go into the computer business. At that point, AT&T was able to sell the Unix operating system and source code with all the protections associated with a copyright.

The programmers who used Unix wanted to keep the advantages of an open source operating system. Unix programmers wanted the ability to customize the software. As academics, they wanted to share the results. The Unix users of the time had the high level of knowledge that made open source software worthwhile.

 Open source software is a double-edged sword. If you want to use open source software, you often need to pay the costs associated with maintaining open source code. Not everyone has the high level of knowledge required to modify Unix or Linux source code. Those with the knowledge can reap great rewards.

To this end, Douglas Comer developed Xinu in 1983 to illustrate operating system structures in a classroom setting. In 1986, Andrew Tannenbaum developed Minix as a Unix clone and alternative. Like Linux, Minix does not use Unix's source code, and therefore does not infringe on any of AT&T's Unix copyrights.

The Free Software Foundation

Richard Stallman started work on the GNU (GNU's Not Unix) project in 1984. One of Stallman's statements used in his introductory Usenet message might help to summarize the thrust of this program: "I consider that the golden rule requires that if I like a program I must share it with other people who like it." Stallman's purpose was to set up a group where the free sharing of software would be strongly encouraged. Although he wanted GNU to run Unix programs, he also wanted to improve on Unix. Before he could do that, however, he needed to create GNU with all of the components of a Unix operating system including a kernel.

Note: Some of the believers in Stallman's way of thinking shared the software of others, with or without their permission. One item that they shared in the mid-1970s (without permission) was an operating system crafted by two Harvard students named Bill Gates and Paul Allen. As most of you know, these students eventually started Microsoft.

These efforts coalesced around a group known as the Free Software Foundation (FSF) (**www.fsf.org**). They developed the General Public License (GPL) to build a body of free software protected from those who would use it to create proprietary closed source systems. By 1990, they had cloned most of the major components of Unix except the kernel.

The Open Source Initiative

A group closely related to the FSF is the Open Source Initiative (OSI). This group was started in 1998 by Eric Raymond to define and defend *free software*.

When Netscape released the source code for its core Mozilla system, it set up its own license loosely modeled on the GPL. A number of prominent people in the open source community were not satisfied with Netscape's efforts. The OSI was created to set criteria to qualify open source software, which includes a license that is even less restrictive than the GPL. Unlike software under the GPL, you can package OSI software with other proprietary products.

You can find more information on the OSI at **www.opensource.org**.

The General Public License (GPL)

Richard Stallman developed the General Public License (GPL) to bring the advantages previously available with Unix to the general software community. He wanted to develop a license that would protect software from anyone who would hide its source code. GNU software is licensed under the GPL. There are three basic principles behind the GPL:

➤ All GPL software must be distributed with a complete copy of the source code. The source code must include clear documentation.

➤ Any software added to GPL software must also be clearly documented. If the new software interacts with the GPL software, the package as a whole must be distributed as GPL software.

➤ Any GPL software comes without a warranty.

Legal interpretations of the actual license are covered under the copyright laws and are thus beyond the scope of this book. The following sections describe the GPL and the development of Linux in more detail.

Copyleft Requirements

The GPL is sometimes known as *copyleft*. Although copyrights typically keep others from copying and selling a work, copyleft uses the copyright laws to preserve the rights of others to use, copy, modify, and distribute software free of charge.

Anyone can sell GPL software. For example, vendors such as LinuxMall (www.linuxmall.com) sell most Linux distributions with source code. None of the profits go to packagers like Red Hat. If you buy Red Hat Linux from LinuxMall, you can copy the entire CD and sell it to others, and you are limited only by the conditions of the GPL. If you improve the software, you can resell that too, as long as you include the additional source code under the conditions of the GPL.

Documentation

One gray area in the GPL and open source licenses is documentation. Good programs include clear documentation embedded in the source code. But clarity in documentation is subjective. Should open source documentation on a Java program be clear to COBOL programmers? What about network engineers or even the general public?

Not all documentation associated with GNU or open source software is clear. In some cases, Linux programmers have suggested that some companies provide less than adequate documentation on purpose to hide the secrets behind their software.

The GPL and open source licenses don't require that program authors develop books or manuals outside of the source code. Yet some developers do include the manuals and books with their GPL or open source software. Some third-party books on Linux and Linux applications are also published under the GPL or related licenses.

Linux Development

By 1990, the FSF had put together every fundamental component they needed for an operating system except the kernel, which is the code that allows an operating system to communicate with computer hardware. Linus Torvalds was not happy with the operating systems available at that time for computers with the 386 CPU, so he started experimenting with a kernel. By 1995, several companies had assembled Linus's kernel with the GNU software of the FSF to produce the first Linux distributions.

Richard Stallman and the people behind the FSF believe that the Linux operating system is more properly known as GNU/Linux because it combines a large number of GNU programs with one Linux kernel.

Linux and most Linux applications are released under the GPL. Some applications are released under even less restrictive licenses, such as that sponsored by the OSI. Other Linux applications are protected by more conventional copyrights. The battle between these various philosophies on licensing will continue well into the future.

The Open Source Business

Unlike Microsoft, Linux distributors can't rely on earnings from the sales of Linux software for most of their revenue. Anyone who can download large files can obtain Linux free of charge from any number of sites on the Internet. Anyone who can also use a CD-writer can easily resell Linux to others.

The following sections discuss how GNU and open source software are developed, how Linux-related companies make money, the paradigm shifts required to work without a warranty, and Microsoft's view of this phenomenon.

The Community Development Model

Linux made the cover of *Forbes* magazine on August 10, 1998. The cover story acknowledged the community of developers who thrive not on money, but on the status that they get from creating better software. As these "Freeware Children" from all over the world work together as a community, they create a better product.

One good example of community development is what Red Hat did with its beta software. For example, when Red Hat released Red Hat Linux 7, it took the following steps in the spirit of community development:

1. It created a beta version of the software. With source code and program documentation, it licensed Red Hat 7 beta under the GPL and posted it to various FTP sites for downloading.

2. The beta release was announced on various newsgroups including the **linux.redhat.announce** newsgroup. Users were invited to try the software and submit comments, bug reports, and bug patches.

3. Once appropriate revisions were made, Red Hat stopped further changes and set up final packages for release by download and on CD.

4. Red Hat offered the final version of Red Hat Linux 7 for sale.

5. Red Hat also included detailed documentation, including installation instructions, in a book format for sale with its CDs.

Red Hat has just a few hundred employees. However, through the community development process, Red Hat receives the help of thousands of developers who want Red Hat to succeed.

Other Linux businesses use this same community development model to help perfect their software. The Linux community believes that this results in higher quality software.

Making Money through Free Software

Even though Linux is free, Linux companies make money from the software they develop. Linux developers are among the best paid workers in the software industry.

The expertise of authors and companies who produce higher quality software is valued in the industry. Although they might not make much money from sales of the software, they can make money from documentation, support contracts, and the consulting services required to make Linux work for individual companies.

Companies that sell proprietary software compete in part by guarding their secrets. Companies that distribute GPL and open source software have no software secrets. They cooperate with each other to create the highest quality product. You may not agree that these premises are true, but they are key to the Linux business model.

 The Sair Linux/GNU exams assume that you accept the premises of cooperative software development.

Working without a Warranty

Some decision makers fear Linux because it does not come with a warranty. Because Linux software is developed by the "community," there is nobody to hold responsible for problems. Working without a warranty requires a paradigm shift. If you have a problem, you can't badger a Linux distributor to help you because they probably did not develop the particular software that caused the problem.

 The cost of Linux is not in the price of the operating system, but in the cost of the support you need for the operating system.

However, the open source nature of Linux allows you to look at your problems in a different way. If you can't get a Linux application to work, you can rewrite the source code. If you find a security problem, someone probably already has a patch on the Internet, ready to download. If you can't get Linux support for your hardware, someone may have developed and posted an appropriate Linux driver on the Internet. The developers get the credit, and you get the software that you need quickly.

Note: You may also find patches and drivers on the Internet for proprietary operating systems, like Microsoft Windows. However, the availability of these proprietary downloads depends on cooperation between Microsoft and other software and hardware vendors. The availability of Linux patches and drivers depends on need; if enough people need it, someone will want to write it. Whether or not this works for you depends on your own experience.

In other words, when you use open source software, you are given the freedom to fix any problems that may arise. You don't have to wait months or years for the next release by a proprietary software company to solve your problems. But debugging and rewriting code takes a lot of skill. If you need additional help, you can always hire Linux developers or support groups to get the job done.

 Linux advocates suggest that the open source model results in higher quality software. Because no company controls GNU software like Linux, users are free to modify it to meet their own needs. GNU software like Linux thus evolves in this free market of ideas, protected by licenses like the GPL.

The Microsoft Analysis

The first of two reported Microsoft memos on GPL and open source software was leaked on Halloween eve, 1998. Hence, these documents are referred to as the *Halloween Documents.*

 Responses like the Halloween Documents are sometimes associated with a campaign of fear, uncertainty, and doubt, also known as FUD.

In the Halloween Documents, the authors acknowledge superior quality in GPL software based on the open source development model and standard GNU software tools and libraries. They also consider the GNU GPL as the most robust software license available based on how it promotes development in the longer term. These documents focus in part on Linux as a potential threat to Microsoft revenue.

The GPL, Open Source, and Free Software

Many people in the Linux world use the terms *GPL, open source,* and *free software* interchangeably. Although these concepts are closely related, they are not identical, at least according to Stallman and Raymond.

The GPL doesn't apply to all Linux software. For example, the XFree86 Project develops its Graphical User Interface (GUI) software, the X Window, under a less restrictive license more closely associated with Raymond's OSI. Under their license, you can modify and sell XFree86 software without the limitations associated with the GPL as long as you pass on this license in whatever product you create.

Although GPL software can be used and modified, the authors retain some control of the source code. They can require that any changes be made as patches to the original source code. Meanwhile, free software can be copied, redesigned, and shared with others with or without the source code. The distinctions are subtle but significant to many who are emotionally attached to Linux.

Internet Resources

One of the striking facts about Linux is the amount of documentation available on the Internet. There are several comprehensive libraries of Linux documentation on just about every Linux application. Software and documentation are created and updated constantly. There are a number of Linux newsgroups and news sites that provide the latest development information. Linux problems of all kinds, from all kinds of users, are documented in a number of different newsgroups. This effectively provides a database for all but the most obscure problems. You can search through this "database" using the tools available at the Deja.com Web site (**www.deja.com**).

Linux Libraries

Among the number of excellent sources of information on Linux, one of the most important is the Web site of the Linux Documentation Project (**www.linuxdoc.org**). This Web site includes:

➤ *Guides*—Book-length documents on everything from network and system administration to the Linux kernel. Although several of these guides are available (for a price) at many bookstores, you can download them from this Web site free of charge.

➤ *HOWTOs*—Subject-specific documents with detailed installation and troubleshooting instructions for almost all commonly used GNU/Linux programs and applications.

➤ *man pages*—Manual pages for each Linux command. If you're using an older version of Linux, you may be able to find a more current manual page.

➤ *FAQs*—Also known as *frequently asked questions*. FAQs are available for some Linux programs. The key FAQ is entitled "Linux Frequently Asked Questions with Answers."

Other prominent Linux resources include Web sites of the companies that create the major Linux distributions, as well as sites like the Linux Online Web site at **www.linux.org**.

Linux News Sites

As you start to configure and maintain Linux computers, you'll need to keep up with the latest developments. Even if you don't use the latest Linux releases, you should monitor at least one major Linux news site for new security problems (and available fixes) that may occur on your system. And with the right news site, you may be able to find help with the problem that you're having or the application that you need to improve your business's productivity. A few important Linux news sites include:

➤ *Fresh Meat*—The latest Linux releases for every imaginable Linux program and application (**www.freshmeat.net**).

➤ *Linux Today*—News releases that cover developments in Linux software, security, and business events (**www.linuxtoday.com**).

➤ *Wide Open News*—An e-zine of Linux sponsored by Red Hat (**www.wideopen.com**).

Detailed Linux Searches

If you have a problem making Linux work for you, chances are good that someone has already discussed the problem online. If you can't find a solution in the libraries of the Linux Documentation Project, the next step is to search the newsgroups. The easiest way to search multiple newsgroups is by searching the discussions list at the Deja.com Web site noted earlier. This site automatically indexes every relatively recent message in Usenet and many other newsgroups. View an example of a search for installing Apache (the Linux Web Server) on Caldera Linux in Figure 2.1.

Command Resources

Another set of resources is available when you boot Linux on your computer. At the command line, you can get help for almost any Linux command, read through manual pages for most commands, or search through information pages for a number of applications. Graphical versions of the **man** and **info** commands are also available.

help

When you want more information about a Linux command, go to **help** first. When you use the **help** switch for a Linux command, more information about

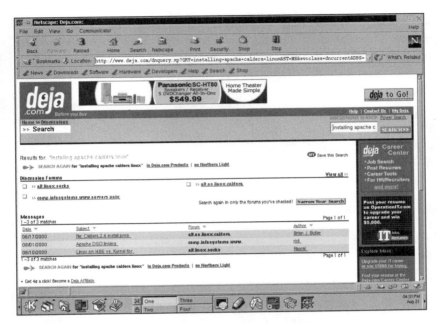

Figure 2.1   Deja.com search results for installing Apache on Caldera Linux.

the options available for that command is displayed. For example, if you want more information on the **mkdir** command, open a command line interface and type the following:

```
mkdir --help
```

You can see an example of the result in Figure 2.2.

In some Linux distributions, you can substitute -**h** or -**?** for --**help**.

man

Just about every Linux command comes with a manual, also known as a *man page*. Each Linux manual includes a complete description of the command as well as a

```
[mj@linuxtester mj]$ mkdir --help
Usage: mkdir [OPTION] DIRECTORY...
Create the DIRECTORY(ies), if they do not already exist.

  -m, --mode=MODE    set permission mode (as in chmod), not rwxrwxrwx - umask
  -p, --parents      no error if existing, make parent directories as needed
      --verbose      print a message for each created directory
      --help         display this help and exit
      --version      output version information and exit

Report bugs to <bug-fileutils@gnu.org>.
[mj@linuxtester mj]$ 
```

Figure 2.2   Getting command help.

description of the function of each available command switch. For example, if you want to see the manual for the **ls** command, open a command line interface and type the following:

```
man ls
```

If you want to review commands related to a specific topic, you can search through the available manuals. For example, if you want to view the Linux commands that are used for Ethernet, type:

```
man -k ethernet
```

The output for this particular command is something like the following:

```
arpsnmp (8)   - keep track of ethernet/ip address pairings
ethers (5)    - Ethernet address to ip number database
pcnet_cs (4)  - Generic NS8390-based PCMCIA Ethernet driver
```

Your output varies with your Linux distribution and the modules you have installed. The previous aren't the only commands you can use to configure an Ethernet network. But they are the commands with the word *ethernet* in their headers.

Another way to search for man page headers is with the **apropos** command, which is equivalent to **man -k**.

*Note: If you're running some versions of Red Hat Linux, the **man -k**, **apropos**, and* **whatis** *commands don't work as shown. But they do work in most Linux distributions, including Debian, Corel, and Caldera, and are consistent with the manual pages available even in Red Hat Linux.*

The number shown in parentheses corresponds to the Linux category for that command. There are nine different categories of Linux man pages, which are described in Table 2.1.

One of the special features of the File Formats category (5) is how it documents each field in critical control files. For example, if you want to know the function of each field in the encrypted password file /etc/shadow, type the following command:

```
man 5 shadow
```

If you want to list the title of a specific manual page, use the **whatis** command. For example, the following command returns the title of the **apropos** man page:

```
whatis apropos
```

Table 2.1   Manual page categories.

Section	Description
1	User Commands
2	System Calls
3	Subroutines
4	Devices
5	File Formats
6	Games
7	Miscellaneous
8	System Administration
9	New

info

The **info** command sets up a structured way to look through different manual pages. When you type the **info** command, you'll see the set of options shown in Figure 2.3. Move your cursor using your keyboard arrow keys to the option or command of your choice, and press Enter. In most cases, the info utility then takes you to a subsequent screen containing a set of subsidiary options. Continue to choose the desired option until you get to the command manual section that you need.

```
File: dir      Node: Top      This is the top of the INFO tree

   This (the Directory node) gives a menu of major topics.
   Typing "q" exits, "?" lists all Info commands, "d" returns here,
   "h" gives a primer for first-timers,
   "mEmacs<Return>" visits the Emacs topic, etc.

   In Emacs, you can click mouse button 2 on a menu item or cross reference
   to select it.

* Menu:

Texinfo documentation system
* Standalone info program: (info-stnd).    Standalone Info-reading program.
* Texinfo: (texinfo).          The GNU documentation format.
* install-info: (texinfo)Invoking install-info. Update info/dir entries.
* makeinfo: (texinfo)makeinfo Preferred.      Translate Texinfo source.
* texi2dvi: (texinfo)Format with texi2dvi.    Print Texinfo documents.
* texindex: (texinfo)Format with tex/texindex. Sort Texinfo index files.

Miscellaneous
* As: (as).                    The GNU assembler.
* Autoconf: (autoconf).        Create source code configuration scripts.
* Bfd: (bfd).                  The Binary File Descriptor library.
* Binutils: (binutils).        The GNU binary utilities.
* CVS: (cvs).                  Concurrent Versions System
* CVSclient: (cvsclient).      The client/server protocol used by CVS
* File utilities: (fileutils). GNU file utilities.
* Finding Files: (find).       Listing and operating on files
                                 that match certain criteria.
* GIT: (git).        GNU Interactive Tools
* Gdb: (gdb).                  The GNU debugger.
-----Info: (dir)Top, 299 lines --Top-----------------------------------
ESC ESC-
```

Figure 2.3   Getting structured command help.

Unfortunately, not all commands are available through the info utility. Most newer commands only include a man page.

Graphical Help Utilities

There are three graphical versions of the **man** and **info** commands: **xman, tkman,** and **xinfo**. These utilities are suitable for use in a GUI such as GNOME (GNU Network Object Model Environment) or KDE (K Desktop Environment). Unfortunately, not all of these commands are standard on the latest Linux distributions. If you want to try them out, open a GUI, start a command-line shell window, and enter one of these commands. The commands include the following characteristics:

➤ *xman*—As shown in Figure 2.4, this command includes a fairly simple interface. When open, press Ctrl+S to activate a search screen. Type a command in the search screen, press Enter, and **xman** takes you to the man page for that command.

➤ *tkman*—This command allows you to search through manual page headers.

➤ *xinfo*—This command adds menu buttons to the info screen. Unfortunately, it has the same limitations as the info utility.

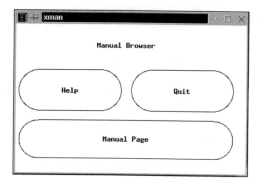

Figure 2.4 Getting command help in a graphical interface.

Practice Questions

Question 1

> Which of the following operating systems was developed before the others?
>
> ○ a. Linux
>
> ○ b. Unix System 6
>
> ○ c. Minix
>
> ○ d. Xinu

Answer b is correct. Unix System 6 was the last Unix system freely licensed by AT&T to universities in the 1970s and 1980s. Xinu, Minix, and Linux were developed after AT&T entered the computer business and started selling Unix on a commercial basis. Therefore, answers a, c, and d are incorrect.

Question 2

> Who started the FSF?
>
> ○ a. Linus Torvalds
>
> ○ b. Eric Raymond
>
> ○ c. William Gates
>
> ○ d. Richard Stallman

Answer d is correct. Richard Stallman founded the FSF in 1983. Linus Torvalds developed the Linux kernel. Eric Raymond launched the OSI. William Gates is the founder of Microsoft. Therefore, answers a, b, and c are incorrect.

Question 3

> Which of the following statements best describes open source software?
>
> ○ a. Linux or any application used on Linux
>
> ○ b. Software that is released with its commented programming code
>
> ○ c. Software that is protected by the GPL
>
> ○ d. b and c

Answer b is correct. Open source software is released with a copy of its source code. At a minimum, open source software includes a clear set of comments within the source code. Not all applications used on Linux are open source; therefore answer a is incorrect. Not all open source software is protected by the GPL; therefore, answers c and d are incorrect.

Question 4

> Which of the following are benefits of GPL software? [Check all correct answers]
>
> ❏ a. You can change the source code to meet your needs.
>
> ❏ b. You can improve on the software and sell it for a profit.
>
> ❏ c. It is easy to use.
>
> ❏ d. Many companies and individuals are working to improve it.

Answers a, b, and d are correct. Because GPL software like Linux focuses on its advanced customers, it may not include features to help beginners. Therefore, answer c is incorrect.

Question 5

> Which of the following describe the differences between copyright and copyleft? [Check all correct answers]
>
> ❑ a. You can repackage copyleft software without permission from the original developers.
>
> ❑ b. You can add to copyleft software and sell it for a profit.
>
> ❑ c. You can modify copyleft software, release it, and keep your changes secret.
>
> ❑ d. You cannot modify copyleft software.

Answers a and b are correct. You can add to copyleft software without permission. Even though you're required to allow users to obtain your software free of charge, you can still sell it for a profit. Companies like Red Hat offer their Linux distributions free of charge over the Internet and sell the same software in stores. But you can't sell or release modified copyleft software if you keep the changes to the source code secret. Therefore, answer c is incorrect. Licenses like the GPL allow you to modify copyleft software. Therefore, answer d is incorrect.

Question 6

> If you own a company that develops free GPL software, how can you make money?
>
> ○ a. Sell the software in computer stores or over the Internet.
>
> ○ b. Sell service contracts to help your customers work with your software.
>
> ○ c. Sell documentation that helps others use your software.
>
> ○ d. All of the above.

Answer d is correct. Even though GPL software is free, you can still sell it. A number of manufacturers, including Red Hat, Caldera, and Corel, sell their Linux distributions in computer stores and over the Internet. These companies, among others, offer service contracts to support their Linux distributions. One of the benefits of buying their software packages is that they often include book-length documentation as well as limited service contracts.

Question 7

Which of the following commands perform the same functions? [Check all correct answers]

- ❑ a. **apropos man**
- ❑ b. **man apropos**
- ❑ c. **man --help**
- ❑ d. **man -k man**

Answers a and d are correct. The **apropos** command is synonymous with **man -k**. The **man apropos** command returns the manual page for the **apropos** command. Therefore, answer b is incorrect. The **man --help** command returns the options that you can use with the **man** command. Therefore, answer c is incorrect.

Question 8

Why is the quality of GPL software considered to be higher than the quality of proprietary software?

- ⭕ a. It is supported by smarter developers.
- ⭕ b. Users have control of GPL software and can modify it to meet their needs.
- ⭕ c. Companies like Red Hat and Caldera have superior business models when compared to Microsoft.
- ⭕ d. The U.S. Department of Justice declared that GPL software is superior.

Answer b is correct. Unlike with proprietary software, users have effective control of GPL software and can modify it to meet their needs without waiting for the development cycle of any particular company. Although open source developers like to think of themselves as "smarter," this is not necessarily true. Some of the best developers do work for companies like Microsoft. Therefore, answer a is incorrect. Although open source developers do like to believe they have superior business models, as of this writing, few Linux distributors make money from Linux. Therefore, answer c is incorrect. Because the U.S. Department of Justice has made no pronouncement on the quality of GPL software, answer d is incorrect.

Question 9

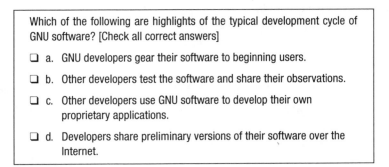

Which of the following are highlights of the typical development cycle of GNU software? [Check all correct answers]

- ❑ a. GNU developers gear their software to beginning users.
- ❑ b. Other developers test the software and share their observations.
- ❑ c. Other developers use GNU software to develop their own proprietary applications.
- ❑ d. Developers share preliminary versions of their software over the Internet.

Answers b and d are correct. GNU software is constantly released over the Internet, even in preliminary forms. Interested developers download and test this software and share their observations with the software authors. One of the characteristics of GNU software is that it is geared to higher-level users. Therefore, answer a is incorrect. One of the conditions of GNU software, under the GPL, is that others can't use its source code in their own (or anyone else's) proprietary applications. Therefore, answer c is incorrect.

Question 10

Which of the following statements most accurately describes some of the advantages and disadvantages of GPL software?

- ○ a. You have and can modify the source code, but the manufacturers don't provide a warranty.
- ○ b. You can resell GPL programs, but you have to provide a warranty.
- ○ c. Because you have the source code, you can clone GPL software and sell it for a profit.
- ○ d. When you purchase a GPL program, you purchase the right to warranty support.

Answer a is correct. GPL software includes the source code. You can modify the source code to meet your needs. But GPL software offers no warranty. Because the GPL states that you do not have to provide a warranty, answers b and d are incorrect. Because you don't need to clone GPL software to resell it, answer c is incorrect.

Need to Know More?

 McHugh, Josh. "For the Love of Hacking." *Forbes*. 10 August 1998. This cover story in the self-described "Capitalist Tool" of magazines describes the reasons behind the success and perceived superiority of open source software.

 Explore the Web site for the FSF, the governing body for the GNU project, at **www.fsf.org**. This site includes a history of the FSF as well as descriptions of free and open source software.

 Browse the Web site of the Linux Documentation Project at **www.linuxdoc.org**, which is the central repository for Linux manuals, HOWTOs, FAQs, and a number of other book-length documents.

 Investigate the Web site for the OSI at **www.opensource.org**, which defines the essential limitations on open source software. This site includes an annotated version of the so-called Microsoft Halloween Documents, which are internal Microsoft white papers on the open source movement.

Linux Structure

Terms you'll need to understand:

✓ Kernel

✓ Network

✓ Init

✓ Daemons

✓ User mode

✓ X Window

✓ Multitasking

✓ Multiuser

✓ Virtual console

✓ Hardware compatibility list

✓ Winmodem

✓ Video Adapter

✓ ISA, BIOS, PCI

✓ IRQ, I/O, DMA, shared memory address

Techniques you'll need to master:

✓ Describing the main Linux modules

✓ Using multitasking and multiuser features

✓ Understanding the benefits of the command-line interface (CLI)

✓ Working with the interaction between Linux and computer hardware

✓ Planning memory for different Linux installations

Linux is a structured operating system. Its components can be divided into six kinds of modules. Linux allows you to run multiple programs simultaneously with multiple terminals for multiple users working from one or more computers. Although Linux graphical tools are available, command-line tools still provide more reliable results. The modularity of Linux makes it important for you to understand the different ports your hardware uses to communicate with components inside your computer as well as with your peripherals.

Modular Linux

One of the strengths of GNU/Linux is its modularity. Because the modules are covered under the General Public License (GPL), developers can work independently. They can reuse and reconfigure these modules to achieve different results. GNU/Linux can be divided into at least six categories of modules: kernel, network, init, daemons, user mode, and the X Window.

Kernel

The kernel is the most important part of any operating system. It allows Linux to communicate with computer hardware. The kernel communicates with your hardware through dedicated device drivers. For example, when you mount a floppy drive, a specific kernel driver sends and receives messages to and from the floppy drive.

If you install new hardware, and it isn't detected when you start Linux, you can add a driver module to your kernel with the **insmod** command. If you have to download a driver for your new hardware, you should also add that driver module to the kernel.

Other parts of the kernel manage the Linux file system as well as any data stored in such areas as your disk cache. The kernel is loaded into protected-mode memory when you start Linux.

Network

In a client/server network, clients ask servers for items they need, like files or applications. In a Linux network, clients can even ask for X Window information. In other words, you can set up terminals on Linux clients that access their graphical user interface (GUI) data from a Linux server.

Note: In principle, this client/server relationship for the GUI is operationally similar to Microsoft's Terminal Server.

The network modules of the Linux operating system are designed to keep client/server communication running as smooth as possible. Ideally, the connection between client and server is seamless.

Because network modules are loaded in the same area as the kernel, their failure may mean that you have to reboot Linux.

Init

If you're familiar with the output of the **ps** command, you know that the only way to start a Linux program is with another Linux program. But there has to be a starting point. When you boot Linux on your computer, the kernel loads and starts init, which is also a daemon. The init program then mounts your drives, opens your terminals, and starts your command-line interface (CLI) shell. After Linux boots on your computer, init modules watch for anything that might shut down your computer, such as a power failure signal from an uninterruptible power supply (UPS) or a reboot command, as shown in Figure 3.1.

Init works at several different run levels, primarily through the /etc/inittab file, as well as associated scripts in the /etc/rc.d directory. Depending on your distribution, the programs that init starts may be divided into run levels 0 through 6. Most distributions leave one or more of these levels unused. In general, run levels are divided into the following categories, usually in the following order:

➤ *Shutdown/halt*—The init program stops all services currently running on your computer.

```
#
# inittab      This file describes how the INIT process should set up
#              the system in a certain run-level.
#
# Author:      Miquel van Smoorenburg, <miquels@drinkel.nl.mugnet.org>
#              Modified for RHS Linux by Marc Ewing and Donnie Barnes
#
# Default runlevel. The runlevels used by RHS are:
#   0 - halt (Do NOT set initdefault to this)
#   1 - Single user mode
#   2 - Multiuser, without NFS (The same as 3, if you do not have networking)
#   3 - Full multiuser mode
#   4 - unused
#   5 - X11
#   6 - reboot (Do NOT set initdefault to this)
#
id:3:initdefault:

# System initialization.
si::sysinit:/etc/rc.d/rc.sysinit

l0:0:wait:/etc/rc.d/rc 0
l1:1:wait:/etc/rc.d/rc 1
l2:2:wait:/etc/rc.d/rc 2
l3:3:wait:/etc/rc.d/rc 3
l4:4:wait:/etc/rc.d/rc 4
l5:5:wait:/etc/rc.d/rc 5
l6:6:wait:/etc/rc.d/rc 6

# Things to run in every runlevel.
ud::once:/sbin/update

# Trap CTRL-ALT-DELETE
ca::ctrlaltdel:/sbin/shutdown -t3 -r now

# When our UPS tells us power has failed, assume we have a few minutes
# of power left.  Schedule a shutdown for 2 minutes from now.
# This does, of course, assume you have powerd installed and your
# UPS connected and working correctly.
pf::powerfail:/sbin/shutdown -f -h +2 "Power Failure; System Shutting Down"
```

Figure 3.1   Run levels and reboot options in the /etc/inittab file.

➤ *Single User*—Init starts just the programs needed to allow one user to log in to your Linux system. When you have a major problem with your system, you can go into single-user mode (sometimes with a special recovery floppy) to fix whatever is wrong. If a critical file is damaged, you may be able to restore it with a backup on a floppy disk.

Note: Some distributions have an additional run level, known as "S" for Single-user mode.

➤ *Multiuser*—At the multiuser level, init starts the programs that allow multiple users to log in to your Linux system simultaneously.

➤ *Multiuser with networking*—The multiuser with networking level starts the network daemons on your computer after the multiuser run level.

➤ *Multiuser with the X Window*—Because X Window programs can also be split between client and server, the multiuser with the X Window level can only start after init starts your network programs.

➤ *Reboot*—At the reboot level, init runs the programs at the Shut down/halt level, and then restarts your computer at one or more of the multiuser levels.

Some distributions may combine or further divide some of these categories. You can actually run the init program at any time. You can review how Red Hat Linux organizes run levels in Figure 3.1.

 Because init can affect every user currently logged on to a Linux system, only the root or superuser can run the **init** command.

Daemons

Linux services are known as *daemons*. In Linux, several dozen daemons can run simultaneously, standing at the ready to start your network, serve Web pages, print your files, or connect you to other Linux or Windows computers. Typical daemons include:

➤ *Apache*—The Linux Web server, also known as **httpd**

➤ *Printer*—The printer daemon, also known as **lpd**, that manages communication with your printer

➤ *Samba*—The network program that allows Linux to talk to Microsoft Windows computers, also known as **smbd**

When started, a daemon is loaded into your RAM, where it waits for requests for service.

User Mode

Any Linux program or utility that talks to the kernel is a user mode program. Because user mode programs don't communicate directly with your hardware (a job for the kernel), these programs can crash without affecting the basic operation of the Linux operating system. There are three basic categories of user mode programs:

➤ *Login*—This program associates a user id with a user's shell and other personalized settings, such as with the X Window and Netscape.

➤ *Shell*—The Linux command interpreter. The most common Linux shell is known as *bash* (for Bourne Again SHell), which was developed from the original Unix Bourne shell.

➤ *Utilities*—Any command used inside a shell.

X Window

Linux builds the X Window from program modules needed to build a graphical user interface (GUI). GUI window managers, such as GNOME and KDE as well as all GUI applications, are built on the foundation of the X Window.

Sharing Resources

Linux meets the fundamental requirements of a server. In part, this is because Linux is a multitasking, multiuser, multiterminal system. Because it can share its resources among multiple programs, it is a multitasking system. It is a multiuser system because you can set up multiple user accounts. And different users can log in to the same Linux computer at the same time, making it a multiterminal system.

Multitasking

There are a lot of programs that demand attention from your computer. Some programs are commands like **ls** or daemons like Apache, the Linux Web server. Others are device drivers that interpret activity like keystrokes, data coming through a network card, or the processing of information that your monitor needs for its display. Multitasking is the way your operating system manages these demands.

Linux uses preemptive multitasking, which means that it dedicates specific resources to different programs based on a hierarchy of priorities. Linux manages these priorities to ensure that each current program gets its share of computer resources. Preemptive multitasking forces all programs to share the use of your computer resources.

 When Linux manages multiple tasks, it is really managing multiple processes. A *process* is the current status of a program. As you run a program, you're running libraries associated with that program. As the program requests services from components such as your hard drive or printer, it interacts with the Linux kernel.

Other programs make demands on your computer constantly. For example, when you type a keystroke, your keyboard sends an interrupt service routine (ISR) that travels through interrupt request (IRQ) ports.

Multiple Users

One factor that differentiates Linux as a server is its capability to manage the demands of multiple users and accounts simultaneously. As a multiuser system, Linux requires you to log in to access your files.

 On a true multiuser system, multiple users can log in to the same Linux computer simultaneously. In contrast, on a single sequential user system like Windows 98/ME, only one user can log in to that computer at a time.

Multiple Terminals

Users can log in to a Linux computer through a number of virtual consoles. On the local Linux computer, you can log in through four or more virtual consoles and one X Window. The actual setup depends on your Linux distribution, available communications hardware, and the way you manage the /etc/inittab file. You can also log in remotely through serial, modem, or network connections. A list of possible virtual consoles is shown in Table 3.1.

You can log in to any number of these consoles with one or more accounts. You can even log in multiple times with the same account. If you have the appropriate hardware, you can add more consoles in the /etc/inittab file. The command that starts different consoles is known as a *getty*. The six **mingetty** commands shown in Figure 3.2 correspond to six different command-line consoles.

If your Linux system boots to the command line, Linux first takes you to console tty1. If you're booting directly to the X Window, it takes you to console tty7. If you started in a command-line window, you can access the other consoles by pressing Alt and the corresponding function key shown in Table 3.1.

Table 3.1	Typical login consoles.*		
Console	**Type**	**Access Method**	**Comments**
tty1	Local command line	Alt+Ctrl+F1	Default
tty2	Local command line	Alt+Ctrl+F2	Default
tty3	Local command line	Alt+Ctrl+F3	Default
tty4	Local command line	Alt+Ctrl+F4	Default
tty5	Local command line	Alt+Ctrl+F5	Default
tty6	Local command line	Alt+Ctrl+F6	Default
tty7	Local GUI	Alt+Ctrl+F7	Assumes X Window is configured
ttyx	Serial connection	Modem or cable	Various terminals available (sometimes shown as *ttysx*)
ptyx	Network connection	Remote terminal	Any remote terminal (also known as a pseduo-terminal; sometimes shown as *ttypx*)

These consoles can be used only if properly configured through the /etc/inittab file. Additional consoles can be configured through this file as well. By default, on many Linux systems, six terminal consoles are available. You need to use the Alt, Ctrl, and Function keys to access a different console only from the X Window. You can skip the Ctrl key from a command-line window.

```
# Trap CTRL-ALT-DELETE
ca::ctrlaltdel:/sbin/shutdown -t3 -r now

# When our UPS tells us power has failed, assume we have a few minutes
# of power left.  Schedule a shutdown for 2 minutes from now.
# This does, of course, assume you have powerd installed and your
# UPS connected and working correctly.
pf::powerfail:/sbin/shutdown -f -h +2 "Power Failure; System Shutting Down"

# If power was restored before the shutdown kicked in, cancel it.
pr:12345:powerokwait:/sbin/shutdown -c "Power Restored; Shutdown Cancelled"


# Run gettys in standard runlevels
1:2345:respawn:/sbin/mingetty tty1
2:2345:respawn:/sbin/mingetty tty2
3:2345:respawn:/sbin/mingetty tty3
4:2345:respawn:/sbin/mingetty tty4
5:2345:respawn:/sbin/mingetty tty5
6:2345:respawn:/sbin/mingetty tty6

# Run xdm in runlevel 5
# xdm is now a separate service
x:5:respawn:/etc/X11/prefdm -nodaemon
```

Figure 3.2 Consoles configured in the /etc/inittab file.

Gettys are also known as *consoles* or *login ports*. The tty7 console is available only if you've configured the X Window on your Linux system. If you're already in a command-line window, you don't need to press the Ctrl key to switch consoles.

There are several advantages to multiple consoles. You can log in to multiple ports to run several programs from the command line. If the program you're running goes out of control, you can log in to a different console to kill that program.

Command Management

Command management deals with the tools that you need to administer Linux. With the latest distributions, you can choose between CLI and GUI administration tools. Linux GUI administration tools are often less than complete. Some Linux GUI commands may override settings that you've edited into your configuration files. Also, most Linux GUI commands do not report the details of success and failure, which can be critical when you're troubleshooting a problem.

For these reasons, many experienced Linux users prefer the CLI.

 When you study Linux commands, focus on command-line interface (CLI) tools.

Linux GUI tools are based on add-ons to standard command-line utilities. So when you use a GUI tool, like Red Hat's LinuxConf, you're actually using a GUI control for different command-line utilities. Not all of LinuxConf's controls work. There are, however, a number of shortcuts built into the CLI. Linux administrators who learn these shortcuts often do their work more quickly than administrators who try to use a GUI tool.

The apparent superiority of CLI tools may not last forever, but CLI superiority is a key assumption of the Sair Linux/GNU exams.

Hardware Compatibility

Hardware compatibility is sometimes a problem for the Linux administrator. When first released, newer hardware may not always include a Linux driver.

A special problem is the "winmodem," which is a telephone modem that substitutes Microsoft Windows driver libraries for some hardware controllers.

To deal with these issues, you need to know the kinds of hardware to avoid, alternate locations for Linux drivers, and the way Linux communicates with different types of hardware.

Hardware Compatibility Lists

Before installing Linux on a computer, you should check two different lists. You can find the main Linux hardware compatibility list (HCL), the "Hardware-HOWTO," on the Linux Documentation Project Web site at **www.linuxdoc.org**. Many Linux distributors keep their own HCLs on their Web sites. These lists are more up-to-date. If you see your hardware on your distribution's HCL, you'll probably find the appropriate Linux driver packaged with the distribution.

If you don't see your hardware on the HCL, there is no need to panic. There is a way to configure just about any device that isn't in the "Linux Incompatible Hardware" section of the "Hardware-HOWTO." Many manufacturers provide Linux drivers on disk or through their Web sites. These sites may also list Linux compatible products that your hardware can emulate. For example, many network cards can emulate a Novell 2000 adapter, and thus can work with its Linux driver.

Modems

One of the banes of the Linux administrator is the winmodem. A winmodem substitutes Microsoft Windows software drivers and libraries for the hardware that controls a regular modem. Because the source code for Microsoft Windows is currently unavailable, it is difficult to create Linux drivers for a winmodem.

Some Linux gurus believe that it would be wrong to try to create drivers for winmodems. Devices like winmodems, which use your computer's Central Processing Unit (CPU), affect the performance of the entire system.

Although some Linux developers have developed techniques for working with some winmodems, the prevailing attitude in the Linux community is to avoid winmodems because of the interaction with the CPU.

Video Adapters

Another common hardware problem is the video adapter, sometimes known as the graphics card. Although you may not require graphics if you do your work at the command line, most users demand a high level of performance from video hardware.

When possible, the XFree86 project creates Linux drivers for video adapters. But this work takes time, and not all video adapter manufacturers release the design information required for a Linux driver. Although you can set up standard VGA settings on almost any card, standard 16-color VGA graphics are not enough for anyone who uses a graphical application. So before you install Linux, check the XFree86 Web site for the latest list of supported video adapters.

Printers

The other major hardware uncertainty is printers. As shown in the "Hardware-HOWTO" on the Linux Project Documentation site, some ink- and bubble-jet printers don't have Linux drivers. However, if you have a new PostScript or generic text printer, you may be able to set it up with generic Linux drivers.

Alternately, check your printer manufacturer's Web site. As the popularity of Linux grows, more hardware manufacturers are creating Linux drivers for their equipment. Most manufacturers post their drivers for download on their Web sites.

Driver Development

There are several sources of new drivers. Many manufacturers release Linux drivers when they release a new product. Some Linux companies and nonprofit groups develop drivers under the GPL or related licenses. Many developers create their own drivers that they post on various Internet (Web and FTP) sites.

At the time of this writing, a major hole in the Linux hardware driver library includes peripherals that connect through a Universal Serial Bus (USB). This issue should be addressed, at least for keyboards, mice, and sound cards, by the release of the Linux kernel version 2.4 around the beginning of the year 2001. For the latest information, refer to the Linux USB Web site at **www.linux-usb.org**.

Hardware Management

Most users don't have hardware problems when they install Linux on their computers. In general, users with the latest Linux distributions but *not* the "latest and greatest" hardware usually have the least amount of trouble. Choosing hardware at least a few months old generally insures that all of the components are effectively listed on the Linux HCL, or at least have Linux drivers.

As an administrator, you're more likely to run into hardware problems. For the Sair Linux/GNU exam, you need to know about several different categories of conflicts.

Just about every part of your computer needs processing power and memory. Each component uses a specific port to ask for processing power from your CPU. While it waits for this processing power, each component stores its request and data in a dedicated address in your random access memory (RAM). If two parts of your computer try to use the same port or the same area in memory, you generally get a hardware conflict.

 Ports are conceptually similar to television channels; two different pieces of hardware generally can't use the same channel.

Conceptually, the solution is fairly simple: Change the port or designate a different area in memory. But to understand how these ports and areas work, you need to know a bit about the architecture inside your personal computer.

The backbones of computer architecture are known as *buses*. A bus is a communication highway inside your computer. Different buses regulate communication for ISA adapters, PCI cards, and RAM. If you're using Linux with kernel 2.2

or later, the ports used on each bus may depend on the settings in a Plug-and-Play BIOS.

ISA Bus

When you install an ISA adapter, there is potential for conflict on four different kinds of ports:

➤ *IRQ*—Computer components use IRQ ports to ask the CPU for processing time. Computers generally have 16 IRQ ports. Basic computer components, like keyboards, hard drives, modems, BIOS clocks, and so forth, already occupy most IRQ ports.

➤ *Input/output (I/O)*—I/O addresses are dedicated locations in RAM that work like a cache. For example, information that comes through a network card waits in a specific range of I/O addresses for processing.

➤ *Direct Memory Address (DMA)*—A DMA bypasses your CPU. For example, some sound cards have a specific DMA because they can independently process an audio file directly from a hard drive. DMA conflicts are relatively rare.

➤ *Shared memory address*—Adapters that can't use a DMA use a shared memory address. Adapters can use a DMA or a shared memory address but not both.

The Linux command to reconfigure Plug-and-Play ISA adapters is **isapnp**. For more information, refer to its man page.

PCI Bus

When choosing a PCI adapter, consider the following three issues. First, there are fewer Linux drivers available for PCI adapters. Second, older PCI cards may not work in newer computers. Third, many PCI cards also rely on IRQ ports to communicate with the CPU, so they may conflict with your ISA cards.

 If one PCI card is more important than the others, you can improve its performance by installing it in the slot furthest from your ISA cards. Closer slots get lower priority when they compete for CPU time. PCI SCSI adapters often need higher priority slots.

BIOS

The BIOS (Basic Input/Output System) on your motherboard is the first program that runs when you turn on your computer. It includes a routine in its read-only memory (ROM) that checks your buses for new and existing hardware.

Plug-and-Play BIOSes also set the communication ports (IRQ, DMA, I/O, shared memory address) used by each component.

However, Plug-and-Play BIOSes are not perfect. The ports that are assigned in Linux may still conflict. You may need to set the ports manually. If you have a lot of conflicts, you may even have to deactivate Plug-and-Play in your BIOS.

Solutions

When you have a conflict, you need to assign different ports. You can make changes with commands, such as **isapnp** or **ifconfig**. In some cases, you can even use your Linux distribution's GUI configuration tools; I've used Red Hat's LinuxConf and S.u.S.E.'s YaST with some degree of success in this area.

Sometimes, you can change the port or address on the card itself. Some newer cards come with driver floppies that change the software embedded in the card. If you don't have the floppy available, you may be able to download the program from the manufacturer's Web site.

Alternately, some older adapter cards work with jumpers, which are connectors on the card that you can physically remove and install on different combinations of metal pins. The port or memory address used by your card depends on the pins connected by the jumper.

Note: If you have to work with components inside your computer, take precautions. Turn off your computer before taking it apart. Be sure to touch some large metal object (such as a metal computer case) to dissipate static electricity before you touch anything inside your computer. Be gentle when you remove or install anything (cards, chips, and so on).

Memory

The amount of RAM that you need for Linux depends on what you want to do with your computer. Linux doesn't require a lot of RAM. The Linux kernel needs about 1MB of space. The programs for which you need to set up a CLI require another 2MB to 3MB. In other words, if you're just setting up a Linux computer as a network firewall, 4MB of RAM may be enough.

The following sections describe four possible installation scenarios for Linux.

Network Firewall

You can set up a Linux computer as a dedicated firewall to protect the rest of your network. A properly installed firewall is the only path between your local area network (LAN) and another network, such as the Internet. All you need on this computer is the Linux kernel, network card drivers, network daemons, and a script based on a Linux firewall program, such as ipchains or iptables. You can set up this firewall using 4MB to 8MB of RAM.

Because so little computing power is required, one popular option is to set up network firewalls on an older system, like a PC with a 386 CPU. This is a great use for an older computer.

Command-Line Network Server

If you're setting up Linux just for the command-line interface (CLI), you don't need the power required by a graphical workstation. In this case, 16MB to 32MB of RAM should be sufficient, even if you share your system with multiple users. If any of your users run memory intensive programs, such as scientific models, the amount of RAM should be increased.

You should also set up a reasonable amount of virtual memory, which allows Linux to move or swap infrequently used programs to a dedicated location on your hard drive. This is also known as *swap space* and is usually set up in a dedicated Linux swap partition. Generally, a swap partition should be twice the size of your RAM.

GUI Workstations and Servers

Graphics is perhaps the biggest driving force in the ever increasing demand for computing power. To use a few graphical programs in the X Window efficiently, you need at least 32MB to 64MB of RAM. The amount of RAM needed can easily increase a great deal if you use more graphic-intensive applications.

You should also set up a larger swap partition when working with graphics. However, at these higher levels of RAM, swap partitions need not exceed 100MB. After all, it takes time for your computer to exchange the information in your swap partition with the information in your RAM.

If you're setting up a GUI server, 64MB to 128MB of RAM is a practical minimum. If your GUI server has to coordinate the graphic design efforts of several users, this amount of RAM should also be increased.

If you can afford to install enough RAM to handle every function and application that you and your users might perform, you may not need a swap partition. In fact, if you have very large amounts of RAM (e.g., over 1GB), accessing a swap partition in Linux will slow you down.

Special Memory Issues

Memory requirements increase as you allow more users and more graphics on your system. Unless you have an older computer or older Linux kernel, extra RAM is helpful:

➤ If you have an older Linux kernel, earlier than version 2.2.1, you need to configure the Linux Loader (LILO) to tell the kernel to look for memory above 64MB. For example, if you have 128MB of RAM, add an **append= "mem=128M"** line to your /etc/lilo.conf file.

➤ If you have a computer with memory speed of 60 nanoseconds (ns: one ns = 10^{-9} seconds) or less, you need RAM cache, which is also known as L2 cache. Generally, you need at least 512KB of L2 cache per 64MB of memory. If your RAM and motherboard are rated at PC100 or better, this issue is generally not significant.

When you're setting up a graphical workstation, another memory issue relates to your video card. As you'll see in Chapter 4, graphic resolution depends on the amount of memory on your video card.

Practice Questions

Question 1

Which of the following are characteristics of the Linux kernel? [Check all correct answers]

❑ a. The kernel allows the Linux operating system to communicate with your computer hardware.

❑ b. It includes a series of device drivers. You can load additional device drivers as you add more hardware to your computer.

❑ c. It includes a series of device drivers. You can configure your computer's BIOS to manage your hardware ports and memory addresses through the kernel.

❑ d. It is the first program that starts when you boot Linux.

Answers a and b are correct. Linux device drivers are the part of the kernel that allow the operating system to communicate with your hardware. You can load additional drivers into the kernel as needed. The computer BIOS does not interact with the Linux kernel. Therefore, answer c is incorrect. Even though the Linux kernel starts before init, the init program is the first program that starts when you boot Linux. Therefore, answer d is incorrect.

Question 2

Which of the following processes are normally part of various init run levels?

○ a. The X Window manager and the **ls** command

○ b. Multiuser programs and shutdown signals from a UPS

○ c. Reboot and networking

○ d. Single-user mode and the Linux kernel

Answer c is correct. The **reboot** command has its own init run level. Another run level is used to start network utilities. The X Window is started at an init run level. Although init starts the shell, it does not start the **ls** command that is run through the shell. Therefore, answer a is incorrect. Multiuser programs are set up in an init run level. Although UPS signals are part of the /etc/inittab file, these signals themselves are not part of any init run level. Therefore, answer b is incorrect.

Recovery disks can be used to start the programs associated with the single-user mode run level, but the Linux kernel is not part of any specific run level. Therefore, answer d is incorrect.

Question 3

> If you haven't configured your X Window, how can you start your GUI?
>
> ○ a. **startx**
>
> ○ b. **X**
>
> ○ c. **xdm**
>
> ○ d. Alt+Ctrl+F7
>
> ○ e. None of the above

Answer e is correct. If you haven't configured the X Window, you can't use any of the standard ways to start the X Window: **startx**, **X**, and **xdm**. Therefore, answers a, b, and c are incorrect. Although you can return to an X Window with the Alt+Ctrl+F7 command, if you have already started it you can't start it in this way. Therefore, answer d is incorrect.

Question 4

> Which of the following statements is a valid example of single sequential user multitasking?
>
> ○ a. Several users are logged in to a Linux computer, but Linux can only handle their programs in sequence, one at a time.
>
> ○ b. There are multiple user accounts on a Microsoft Windows 98 computer. All users can log in simultaneously. Each user can run several programs simultaneously.
>
> ○ c. Several users are logged in to a Linux computer, but Linux can run several of their programs simultaneously.
>
> ○ d. There are multiple user accounts on a Microsoft Windows 98 computer. Each user can run several programs simultaneously. Only one user can log in at a time.

Answer d is correct. Only one user can log in at a time on a single sequential user operating system like Windows 98. While logged on to Windows 98, that user can run several programs simultaneously, which is called *multitasking*. Linux is a multitasking operating system. Therefore, answer a is incorrect. All users cannot log in simultaneously to a Microsoft Windows 98 computer. Therefore, answer b is incorrect. Although everything in answer c is true, it is a description of a multiuser system. Therefore, answer c is incorrect.

Question 5

> Which of the following statements most accurately describes preemptive multitasking?
>
> ○ a. While multiple programs are running, one program controls the CPU and other computer resources for as long as it needs them. If it doesn't need the resources for a few moments, it can let other programs use these resources. When that program is done, the kernel assigns these resources to the program with the next highest priority.
>
> ○ b. While multiple programs are running, several programs receive dedicated slices of time with the CPU and other computer resources. Other programs or drivers can request access while other programs are running. The kernel can choose to stop whatever is running and adjust priorities accordingly.
>
> ○ c. While multiple programs are running, they share simultaneous access to the CPU and other computer resources for as long as they need them. If these programs don't need the resources for a few moments, they can let other programs use these resources. When all of the running programs are done, the kernel assigns these resources to the program with the next highest priority.
>
> ○ d. While multiple programs are running, they share simultaneous access to the CPU and other computer resources. When other programs or drivers request access, the resources are shared among all programs simultaneously.

Answer b is correct. In preemptive multitasking, the CPU divides its time between several programs. When another program needs access, the kernel decides whether to stop a currently running program by lowering its priority. Answer a is a description of cooperative multitasking, and is therefore incorrect. Even in multitasking, different programs share time on the resources. They can't use the resources at the exact same time because their data would become jumbled. Therefore, answers c and d are incorrect.

Question 6

In a multiuser system like Linux, which of the following considerations limit the number of times that you can log in to one Linux operating system simultaneously? [Check all correct answers]

❑ a. Number of computers on your network

❑ b. Users set up on your computer

❑ c. Availability of a modem and a network card

❑ d. Parameters defined in the /etc/inittab file

Answers a, c, and d are correct. You can set up the /etc/inittab file with as many virtual consoles as you need through modems, network connections, or the appropriate keys on the local computer. As a user, you can log in to all available virtual consoles simultaneously. Creating additional users does not affect the number of times that you can log in to that computer. Therefore, answer b is incorrect.

Question 7

Which of the following is an advantage of GUI administration tools when compared to corresponding CLI tools?

○ a. GUI tools are built on a foundation of CLI tools.

○ b. GUI tools provide more information.

○ c. GUI tools are more reliable.

○ d. Experienced Linux users prefer GUI tools.

○ e. None of the above.

Answer e is correct. Although GUI tools add source code to a foundation of CLI tools, that itself does not give the GUI an advantage. In fact, the additional code required means that there is more that can go wrong. Therefore, answer a is incorrect. A number of messages from a CLI command are usually not shown in the corresponding GUI command. In other words, GUI tools provide less information. Therefore, answer b is incorrect. Because GUI tools require more source code than corresponding CLI tools, there is more that can go wrong. Therefore, answer c is incorrect. Although answer d is most subjective, the current bias of experienced Linux users is towards CLI tools. Therefore, answer d is incorrect.

Question 8

> You just installed an internal modem in an ISA slot on your computer. When you start Linux, you find that both your ISA modem and your PCI sound card do not work. You conclude that there is a conflict of some sort. Which of the following is the most likely place for conflict?
>
> ○ a. Another PCI card
>
> ○ b. DMA
>
> ○ c. IRQ
>
> ○ d. Memory bus

Answer c is correct. Both PCI and ISA cards communicate with the CPU through IRQ ports or channels. Although PCI cards get priority based on where they're installed on your computer, that doesn't affect their priority relative to an ISA card. Therefore, answer a is incorrect. DMA conflicts are relatively rare. Therefore, answer b is incorrect. The memory bus connects your RAM to your CPU and is not closely related to your ISA or PCI buses. Therefore, answer d is incorrect.

Question 9

> Which of the following are major types of modules of the Linux operating system? [Check all correct answers]
>
> ❑ a. X Window
>
> ❑ b. Kernel
>
> ❑ c. Run levels
>
> ❑ d. Init
>
> ❑ e. Network
>
> ❑ f. Daemons
>
> ❑ g. Login and shells

Answers a, b, d, e, f, and g are correct. They correspond to the different modules of the Linux operating system. Run levels are the programs that are started by init. But run levels are themselves not modules of the Linux operating system. Therefore, answer c is incorrect.

Question 10

You're setting up a computer for a user who does a lot of intense graphics development work. If you include 128MB of RAM on that computer, how big of a swap partition do you need?

○ a. 128MB

○ b. 192MB

○ c. 256MB

○ d. 100MB

Answer d is correct. As RAM increases beyond 64MB, swap space beyond 100MB does not enhance performance significantly. The recommended size of a swap partition may vary. A few years ago, you might have been satisfied with a swap partition equal to your installed RAM. Current practice is to set up a swap partition twice the size of your RAM. However, because you're setting up a computer that already has over 100MB of memory, the basis for the other answers is not relevant. Therefore, answers a, b, and c are incorrect.

Need to Know More?

 LeBlanc, Dee-Ann. *General Linux I Exam Prep.* The Coriolis Group, Scottsdale, AZ, 2000. ISBN 1-57610-567-9. Chapter 4 includes a good description of the different run levels available in Red Hat and S.u.S.E. Linux.

 Explore the Web site for the Linux Documentation Project at **www.linuxdoc.org,** which is the central repository for Linux manuals, HOWTOs, and a number of other book-length documents. Important HOWTOs for this chapter include the "Hardware-HOWTO" with the general Linux HCL and the "Plug-and-Play-HOWTO," which describes the interaction of Plug-and-Play BIOS and hardware in detail.

 Check out the Web site for the PC Guide at **www.pcguide.com,** an online resource of every major component inside a standard personal computer.

 Check out the Web site for the XFree86 project at **www.xfree86.org,** which is a nonprofit organization dedicated to creating video drivers for Linux, Unix, and related operating systems. Before you install Linux, review the latest list of supported video adapters on this Web site.

Hardware Configuration

Terms you'll need to understand:

✓ Partition

✓ Volume

✓ Swap partition/disk

✓ Filesystem Hierarchy Standard

✓ CD-ROM and controller

✓ Video controller

✓ Resolution

✓ Graphic mode

Techniques you'll need to master:

✓ Managing partitions and volumes

✓ Setting up a drive for multiple operating systems

✓ Describing the Filesystem Hierarchy Standard

✓ Setting up a drive for separate Linux volumes

✓ Understanding different CD-ROM options

✓ Describing configuration options available for video
controllers and monitors

This chapter covers the configuration of four key hardware components: hard drives, CD-ROM drives, video cards, and monitors. When you manage partitions on your hard drive, you can set up multiple operating systems on your computer. When you set up separate volumes on your hard drive, you can manage the major file systems within Linux. Current Linux installations almost always require a CD-ROM drive, so you need to know the potential problems with setting up this type of drive. To set up Linux graphics, you need to know how to set up your video card. And you need to make sure that the settings you create on your video card do not damage your monitor.

Multiple Operating Systems

It usually takes time for a Microsoft Windows user to convert to Linux. Not all of the programs used on Windows are immediately available on Linux. Consequently, it is useful to have both operating systems available during the transition period.

The standard way to configure side-by-side operating systems is through a *dual-boot*. In a dual-boot configuration, you can select the operating system of your choice (Linux or Windows) when you start your computer.

In general, Linux, Windows, and other operating systems must be set up on different partitions or logical drives. Once you know your options for partitioning, you can make room on a Windows computer to install Linux. Once you have enough room, there are several tools available to split partitions.

Hard Disk Partition Management

Generally, you need different drive volumes to set up different operating systems on the same computer. With different drives, you can accommodate different file systems, such as Microsoft's FAT16 and Linux's second extended file system (ext2fs). You can then set up a different operating system on each volume.

Hard drives can be divided into the following:

➤ *Primary partition*—You can have up to four different primary partitions on a hard drive. One primary partition must be marked as "active" and can include a boot loader, such as the Linux Loader (LILO). If you mount a Linux directory on a primary partition, it is also known as a *volume*.

➤ *Extended partition*—If four partitions are not enough, you can convert one of the primary partitions into an extended partition. You can then subdivide the extended partition into as many logical volumes or drives as you need. Because you can't mount a Linux directory in an extended partition, it is not a volume.

➤ *Logical drive*—You can subdivide an extended partition into as many logical drives as you need. Although you can't set up a Linux directory in an extended partition, you can set up Linux directories on logical drives. Therefore, logical drives are volumes.

➤ *Swap partition*—In Linux, it's common to set up a swap partition as an exclusive area on your hard drive. You can set up a swap partition on any volume.

A volume is any logical division on your hard drive, which includes all of the preceding categories except the extended partition. In Microsoft operating systems, you can assign a drive letter, such as C:, D:, or E:, on each volume. In the Linux operating system, you can mount different directories on each volume.

When you start your computer, your Basic Input/Output System (BIOS) identifies the first hard disk on your system. The first area it reads on your hard disk is the Master Boot Record (MBR), which then identifies the primary and extended partitions, as well as any other volume configured on your disk. Unless you have a boot loader, your computer then moves on to the active primary partition to boot your operating system.

If you have a boot loader in your MBR, you generally get a menu that allows you to choose from the various operating systems loaded on your computer.

You can also set up partitions on two or more hard drives inside your computer.

Making Room on Windows

You may already have a separate partition, empty and ready for Linux. However, with the variety of computers that you'll encounter, you'll need to know how to split a hard disk with just one partition that is currently dedicated to Microsoft Windows.

If you want to set up a computer with Microsoft Windows and Linux, install Windows first. Linux installation programs are designed to accommodate Microsoft Windows. Linux setup programs give you the option to set up a boot loader like LILO, which allows you to choose from the operating systems that are available on your computer. On the other hand, the Windows setup program eliminates any startup reference to Linux by overwriting the MBR on your hard disk.

Assume that you have a computer where the only operating system is Microsoft Windows. You need to do some groundwork before you can start the Linux installation process:

1. Check the integrity of your disks. Before you install Linux, you want to isolate and mark any bad areas on your hard disk. The Windows and/or MS-DOS ScanDisk utilities do this job well.

2. Reorganize the data on your drive. The Defrag utility, sometimes known as the Disk Defragmenter, organizes the files on your drive into one contiguous area at the beginning of your drive. (Defragmentation is much less of a problem on Linux.)

3. Back up your system. If something goes wrong during the next step, you could lose all the information on your hard drive.

4. Split your current partition. The standard Linux partition-splitting utility for MS-DOS is known as fips (First Interactive Partition Splitter). Third-party partition splitters include Partition Magic (**www.powerquest.com**) and System Commander (**www.v-com.com**). These third-party tools also include boot loaders that take the place of LILO on the MBR.

If you don't mind backing up and restoring all of your data, you can use a tool known as fdisk. Different versions are available for Microsoft and Linux operating systems. Because fdisk does not split partitions, you would have to delete your current partition (and all of its data), and then create two different partitions in the area that you just cleared.

 Know the basic steps to make room on a Microsoft Windows partition for Linux.

Splitting Partitions

This section contains a brief guide to fips. Read and print the fips documentation before you split your current partition, and make sure you know how much room you want for Linux.

Once you've prepared your hard drive as stated in the previous section, you can use fips. It's available on most Linux distribution CDs in the \dosutils directory. It's also available online from the fips Web site at **www.igd.fhg.de/~aschaefe/ fips**. Because fips is released under the General Public License (GPL), it is free and comes without a warranty. Therefore, use it at your own risk.

You can only run fips in MS-DOS mode. You can't run it from inside Microsoft Windows. In addition, you should run it from a bootable floppy. Copy at least the fips.exe, restorrb.exe, and errors.txt files to a bootable MS-DOS floppy disk. When you run fips, let it analyze your disk. When prompted, let fips make a backup copy of your root and boot sectors. This saves your current partition information in a rootboot.000 file on your floppy (if you run fips and back up your root and boot sectors again, the rootboot.000 file is incremented to rootboot.001, rootboot.002, and so forth). Fips then goes to work. If you have a partition that it can split, you'll be able to use your arrow keys to adjust the size of the two partitions that you just created.

Note: If fips does not work, you may have data at the end of your partition. The Windows Defrag utility may not move certain "unmovable" data, such as hidden or system files. You can check to see if there is data by viewing the Windows Defrag utility map of free and filled sectors. Generally, you can make this data "movable" by undoing the hidden and system attributes of these files.

 Linux only boots from partitions that end at or below cylinder 1024. In some cases, this can be as low as 512MB. If you can reset disk addressing in your BIOS to large block addressing (LBA), you can sometimes get around this limitation. Don't make the change unless you have a complete backup; you could very well lose all data on that drive. Alternately, you can set up Linux to boot from your floppy drive. If you have a dual-boot system, your floppy would include the LILO program, which lets you select one of your loaded operating systems. A third option is to set up a small separate boot partition that ends below cylinder 1024.

If fips does not provide the desired result, use the restorrb.exe utility. It restores the root and boot sectors of your disk through the rootboot.000 file that fips stored on your bootable floppy.

Note: As of this writing, the fips manual appears to be in error. The only file created from using fips to back up your MBR is rootboot.00x. If you need to restore your original MBR, you can do it with the restorrb.exe command and rootboot.000.

Volume and Drive Names

The Linux naming convention for hard disk volumes is straightforward. The naming system also applies to any CD that isn't installed on a sound card. The first two letters of the name depend on the kind of disk that you have. If you have a regular hard disk, the letters are *hd*. If you have a Small Computer Systems Interface (SCSI) hard disk, the letters are *sd*.

The third letter depends on your hard disk's position. The first hard disk is designated as *a*, the second disk is designated as *b*, and so on. In other words, if you have two different physical hard disks, the second disk is known as *hdb*. For naming purposes, CD-ROM drives are also categorized as hard disks.

 The first and second disks on a computer are often installed as a "master" and a "slave."

The character in the fourth position depends on how you've partitioned that disk. Because you can have up to four primary partitions, they are designated as 1, 2, 3, and 4. The first logical drive that you create is in position number 5, even if you have only 1 primary partition.

You can see some examples of how this naming convention works in Table 4.1.

Other Means

If you want to keep your MS-DOS or Microsoft Windows programs, you don't have to set up Windows and Linux in a dual-boot configuration. And if you do have both operating systems in a dual-boot, you don't have to reboot to go from one to the other.

Linux includes DOS emulators, known as DOSEMU utilities. These utilities allow you to use different commands to directly read, write, and execute MS-DOS files. Linux also includes emulators that can run some Microsoft Windows 3.1 and 9x programs, which are based on the work of the Windows Is Not an Emulator (WINE) project. Unfortunately, emulators like WINE are still "alpha" software. In other words, because development work is still in progress, they are not suitable for general use. As of this writing, you cannot reliably run key applications like Microsoft Word through WINE.

Another option is the commercial product known as VMware, which allows you to run any current Windows or Linux operating system inside Linux or Windows NT/2000. VMware can set up a virtual machine in a large file or access either operating system in other local disk volumes. One significant drawback is that it requires a lot of RAM: a minimum of 64MB on Linux and 96MB on Windows NT/2000.

The Filesystem Hierarchy Standard

When you install Linux, you can set up one big volume or separate volumes for the directories of your choice. The advantage of setting up several volumes is that

Table 4.1	Typical partition names.
Name	**Description**
hda3	The third primary partition on the first hard disk.
sdb6	The second logical drive on the second SCSI hard disk.
hda8	The fourth logical drive on the first hard disk.
hdb	Because this has no number, it refers to a CD-ROM. And because it is in the second position, it suggests that you have only one regular hard drive on your computer.

it limits certain risks to your system. For example, if you have log files that usually grow until they fill your disk, a special volume for log files prevents any overflow from affecting other data or programs on your system. To decide how you want to divide partitions on Linux, you first need to know about the different available file systems.

In Linux, the way you can set up directories in different volumes is based on the Filesystem Hierarchy Standard (FHS).

Major Directories

The FHS is designed to serve as a common template for directories in Linux and other related operating systems. As an administrator, it makes your job easier if you can always find the same directories in the same place on every Linux computer, irrespective of distribution.

Every Unix-type system starts with a root directory. In general, Linux mounts other directories as shown in Table 4.2 on the root directory.

Table 4.2	Typical Linux directories.*
Volume	**Description**
/	Represents the root directory. All other directories are under this directory in the file system hierarchy. Any directory that is not mounted in a separate volume is included in the root directory's volume.
/bin	Includes essential command-line utilities. Do not mount this volume separately. If you ever need to use your recovery disk, you won't be able to get to these utilities.
/boot	Contains Linux startup utilities. Includes almost everything that Linux needs to start, before it moves on to other directories for configuration files. Usually includes the Linux kernel. A separate boot partition generally does not have to be over 10MB.
/dev	Lists all device drivers available to the system. For example, when you mount a floppy drive, you are typically mounting /dev/fd0 onto another directory. Do not mount this volume separately.
/etc	Includes basic configuration files for the computer, such as password files, daemon settings, and X Window requirements.
/home	Contains home directories for specific users. If you mount this volume separately, be sure to leave enough room for all of the users that you need now and in the future.
/lib	Includes program libraries needed by the kernel and essential command-line utilities. Do not mount this volume separately.
/mnt	Lists the mount point of removable media, such as floppies and CD-ROM drives.

(continued)

Table 4.2	Typical Linux directories *(continued)*.
Volume	**Description**
/opt	Includes any applications, such as WordPerfect or Star Office, that you might add after installing Linux.
/proc	Contains all currently running kernel-related processes.
/root	Contains the home directory for the root user. Do not mount this directory separately.
/sbin	Includes many system administration commands.
/tmp	Stores any temporary files. Generally, all files in this directory should be deleted whenever you reboot Linux. This is also a good location for down-loaded files.
/usr	Contains any small programs and data for all users. Includes many subdirectories.
/var	Contains variable data; includes log files and print spools.

For more detailed information on the standard components of the FHS, refer to the governing Web page at www.pathname.com/fhs.

 Know your Linux volumes. The root directory (/) stands above the others and is different from the /root volume. Be able to cite the kinds of files that are stored in each volume.

You may choose to mount several subdirectories on their own volumes. Linux swap space is generally set up in its own volume. You can set up volumes to keep log files in your /var directory from crowding out all of your other Linux files and directories. You may also want to set up partitions for users' home directories (/home) and larger programs (/opt), so you don't overwrite them in the future when you upgrade your Linux system.

 Volumes in Linux include any primary partition or logical drive that you've formatted for Linux. Unlike a Microsoft system, volumes do not have names like "Desktop Drive". However, you can mount a directory on a specific volume.

You can even mount subdirectories on a specific volume. For example, if you want to make sure that the owner of the mj account doesn't increase his Netscape disk cache to an unreasonable size, you can set up a volume for the /home/mj/.netscape/cache directory.

Path Management

When you describe the location of a file, there are absolute paths and relative paths. An absolute path describes the location of a file relative to the root (/)

directory. For example, you can type the following command to get to the scripts that start a number of Linux daemons:

```
cd /etc/rc.d/init.d/
```

The forward slash in front of the first directory makes this the absolute path. You can type this command from anywhere in Linux to get to this directory. Sometimes, you may accidentally type the command without the forward slash:

```
cd etc/rc.d/init.d/
```

In this case, Linux looks for these directories under your home directory. For example, if your home directory is /home/mj, this command makes Linux look for the /home/mj/etc/rc.d/init.d directory. Unless you keep a copy of these files deep in your home directory, Linux won't find anything.

 A directory listing with the first forward slash is an absolute path; without the first forward slash, it is a relative path.

Linux has many directories and subdirectories. If you need to know where you are in the filesystem hierarchy, type the following command:

```
pwd
```

The **pwd** (present working directory) command returns your current directory.

Mounted Drives as Directories

Removable drives are by definition located on different partitions. Because you don't always have a floppy or a CD in their drives, Linux generally does not mount these drives when you start or reboot your computer. Mounted drives can be read-only or read/write. If you want to mount your floppy drive, put a floppy in the drive, and then type the following command:

```
mount /dev/fd0 /mnt/floppy
```

The /dev/fd0 parameter is the name of the device driver assigned to your floppy drive. If you have two floppy drives, you may have to use /dev/fd1. The /mnt/floppy parameter is the directory from where you can access files on your CD-ROM.

*Note: The **mount** commands shown in this section are not complete. The proper commands are **mount −t vfat /dev/fd0 /mnt/floppy** and **mount −t iso9660 /dev/cdrom /mnt/cdrom**. But the extra switches are unnecesary based on settings in most /etc/fstab configuration files.*

Although you can mount your floppies or CD-ROM on any available directory, a number of programs refer to distribution-specific directories, such as /floppy. If you want to mount a regular ATAPI CD-ROM, put a CD in your CD-ROM drive, and then type the following command:

```
mount /dev/cdrom /mnt/cdrom
```

The purists among you may prefer to use the name of the actual CD-ROM driver. When you boot, you may see a message that states that hdc is assigned to your CD-ROM drive. In other words, you can also type the following command:

```
mount /dev/hdc /mnt/cdrom
```

Alternately, you can review your Linux boot messages through the **dmesg** command. When you've mounted your drives, you can review the result with the **mount** command, which returns the result in Figure 4.1.

In Figure 4.1, you can see how different directories are mounted on this particular system. The root (/) and boot directories are mounted on Linux's second extended file system (ext2) as well as a floppy drive using Microsoft's VFAT file system, and a CD-ROM is mounted through the standard CD-ROM ISO9660 file system.

You can unmount your drives with the **umount** command (that's right, no *n*). For the situation shown in Figure 4.1, the following command dismounts your floppy drive:

```
umount /mnt/floppy
```

```
[mj@linuxtester mj]$ mount
/dev/hda5 on / type ext2 (rw)
none on /proc type proc (rw)
/dev/hda1 on /boot type ext2 (rw)
none on /dev/pts type devpts (rw,gid=5,mode=620)
/dev/hdc on /mnt/cdrom type iso9660 (ro)
/dev/fd0 on /mnt/floppy type vfat (rw)
[mj@linuxtester mj]$ ▮
```

Figure 4.1　Currently mounted drives.

If you previously moved files to or from your floppy drive, there may be a delay while Linux finishes dismounting the drive.

Pseudofile Systems

There are several file systems on Linux that really aren't file systems at all. In other words, Linux sets up several volumes that represent items like kernel routines or device managers. A pseudofile system is sometimes known as a *system abstraction*.

Typical Linux pseudofiles and file systems include the following:

➤ */proc*—Processes currently running through the kernel

➤ */dev/xyz*—Files that are names of device drivers

➤ */dev/null*—An output file that ignores output from a utility or a script

Alternatives to Partitioning

Customizing volumes and partitions for Linux can be a lot of work. But it can help you optimize the space that you use on your hard disk.

Alternately, you can let your Linux setup programs make the decisions for you. For example, several Linux distributions allow you to set up "Servers" or "Workstations" that use your entire hard disk for Linux. Depending on the size of your drive, you may end up with just a root volume and a swap disk.

CD-ROM and Controller

Until the development of the ATAPI interface, CD-ROM configuration was a difficult matter for any operating system.

Audio CD-ROMs were introduced prior to data CD-ROMs. As they were adapted for the computer, the first data CD-ROMs required another driver to send information through a sound card. SCSI CD-ROMs came later; they first came with special controllers. This section discusses these internal CD-ROM drives.

Today, external CD-ROM drives are available for the parallel port and Universal Serial Bus (USB) interfaces. If you have a parallel port interface, use the parallel port driver. More information on parallel port interfaces should be available on the Linux Parallel Port Home Page at **www.torque.net/parport**. If you have a USB CD-ROM, you'll need a Linux distribution with kernel 2.4 or later. For the latest information on installing USB drives and other peripherals, refer to the Linux USB Web site at **www.linux-usb.org**.

Sound Card CD-ROM Drives

Linux administrators will inevitably need to accommodate older equipment, especially when companies cut costs. CD-ROM drives were originally connected to systems through sound cards. There are about a dozen different sound card drivers available, and each is associated with a specific card. Review the "CD-ROM-HOWTO" for details of available drivers.

The problem with sound card based CD-ROM drivers is that many manufacturers claim that their cards are Sound Blaster compatible. Unfortunately, this claim is usually not good enough for the Linux Sound Blaster CD-ROM driver.

As a result, finding the right sound card device for a CD-ROM is usually accomplished through a trial-and-error process. In other words, you can try loading a device driver to the kernel. If it works for your CD-ROM, you'll be able to mount that device. For example, if the following command actually mounts a CD-ROM, then you know to add the sbpcd.o driver to your kernel:

```
mount /dev/sbpcd /mnt/cdrom
```

 If you want sound and CD-ROM functionality from this kind of system, you need a driver that interfaces with your CD-ROM and a driver for your sound card.

Regular CD-ROM Drives

Current CD-ROM drives are connected to your computer through SCSI and ATAPI interfaces.

Working with a SCSI CD-ROM drive is similar to working with a regular partition. Linux should recognize most SCSI CD-ROMs when you boot your computer. Your boot messages or the **dmesg** command will indicate if the drive is recognized. Linux may also associate a SCSI CD-ROM drive with the /dev/ cdrom device. Check the status of this device with the following command:

```
ls -l /dev/cdrom
```

You may see the following result:

```
lrwxrwxrwx   1   root   root   3   Dec 15 19:30 /dev/cdrom -> sdc
```

If you see this result, Linux has associated the /dev/cdrom device with the sdc driver, which also means that you have at least two other SCSI disks or CD-ROMs on your computer.

Current CD-ROM drives, built to the ATAPI standard, typically work just as well as SCSI drives. Unfortunately, there are some older ATAPI CD-ROMs with problems, such as difficult manufacturer-specific drivers. If you have this problem, look through the "CD-ROM-HOWTO" for help.

A Video Controller

A video controller is almost like an independent computer. It has a processor and memory, and it sends messages and data to your monitor.

The graphic mode that you set through your video controller determines the number of colors and picture elements that you see on your monitor. Picture elements are more commonly known as *pixels*. You can set your graphic mode, processor type, and video memory in tools like XF86Setup from the XFree86 Project. The details are illustrated in Figure 4.2.

As you can see near the top of Figure 4.2, there are a number of available processors, also known as *Video Servers*. Each processor corresponds to a specific type of card. Some cards are generic, such as Mono and SVGA. Others are associated with specific processors, such as ATI's Mach64. If your card is not shown on XFree86's card list, but is similar to one of the listed Video Servers, you may be able to configure it yourself using the options shown in Figure 4.2.

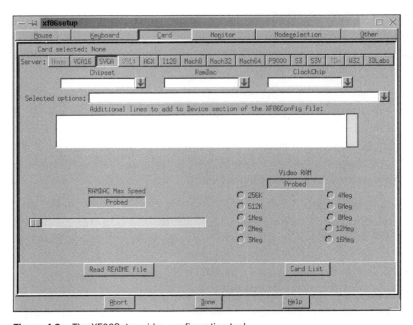

Figure 4.2   The XF86Setup video configuration tool.

The other major video configuration tool is the xf86config command-line tool. A number of distributions have their own video configuration tools. For example, Red Hat's Xconfigurator and S.u.S.E.'s SaX also allow you to change the settings on your video card and monitor.

Video Memory

Your screen resolution and number of colors you want to use depends on the video memory that you have available. The memory you need depends on the following equation:

```
Horizontal Resolution × Vertical Resolution × Color in bits /
(8 bits / byte) = Required Memory in bytes
```

For example, if you want a 1024×768 resolution screen with 32-bit color, you need just over 3MB of memory:

```
1024 × 768 × 32 / 8 = 3.1 MB
```

In other words, you can set this graphic mode if you have a video card with 4MB of memory. The Linux X Window uses any leftover video memory for its other virtual screens.

Video Graphic Modes

The graphical resolution of your screen depends on your horizontal and vertical pixel rows as well as the number of colors required. The graphic mode shown in the last section was 1024×768×32 bits.

The graphic mode of your video card depends on your graphical resolution along with the refresh rate of your picture. The horizontal refresh rate is the number of times per second that your card sends data to each line. Horizontal refresh rates typically range from 31 to 80kHz and higher. The vertical refresh rate is the number of times your whole screen is refreshed per second. Vertical refresh rates typically range from 60 to 80 hertz and higher.

If you set a high graphical resolution, you need a fast horizontal refresh rate. Although higher vertical refresh rates are typically easier on the eyes, the vertical rate that you set depends on the capabilities of your monitor and what looks best to you.

Monitor Management

Monitors have limits. The picture you set cannot exceed the physical size of your screen. Also, the number of pixels you set cannot significantly exceed the number of physical pixels available on the screen. Although you generally want to set horizontal and vertical refresh rates as high as possible, you don't want to exceed the capabilities of your monitor.

Most new monitors won't let you exceed their capabilities. With most monitors, if you set rates higher than they can handle, you'll receive a screen message such as "Out of Range." But with a few monitors, a refresh rate that's too high can burn out the monitor. If you set the resolution too high, the refresh rate increases, which can also cause trouble.

You can use the XF86Setup or xf86config tool to manage the settings on your monitor. If you're using Red Hat or S.u.S.E., you can also use Xconfigurator or SaX, respectively. XF86Setup seems to be the preferred tool that is covered on the Sair exam.

Monitor Graphic Modes

You can change the graphic modes on most monitors. In other words, you can change the number of pixels shown on your screen and the number of colors used for each pixel. Even if you thought you configured this setting with your video card, you have to do it again with your monitor. After all, they are separate components with separate drivers.

Older monitors support only one or two graphic modes. The multisync monitors of today support several modes. To make sure that you keep your monitor working, you need to balance its capabilities against the settings you create for your video card.

The graphical capability of a monitor depends on its screen size and dot pitch. Larger screens and smaller dot pitch sizes allow you to set up more detailed graphic modes on your monitor.

If you set your graphic mode to the maximum resolution of your monitor, you may be disappointed. Monitors let you set graphic modes with more pixels than are physically available on the monitor. For example, one 14-inch monitor with a .25mm dot pitch has a maximum screen size of 240mm×180mm. In other words, it has 960 horizontal dots in a row and 720 vertical dots in a column. Yet this monitor allows you to set a graphic mode of 1024×768 pixels. When your monitor tries to fit 1024×768 pixels on a screen that has only 960×720 dots, some pixels don't quite make it. The result is a blurry monitor.

Monitor Refresh Rates

The refresh capability of a monitor depends on the technology inside. Check your monitor's documentation for its allowable horizontal and vertical refresh rates, and then go back to the tool that you used to configure your video card and monitor. Make sure that the settings for both systems do not exceed the capabilities of your monitor.

 If you configure more than one graphic mode, you can normally switch between these modes with the Ctrl+Alt+Num+ or Ctrl+Alt+Num- keys. (This key combination only works with the plus and minus keys on the numeric keypad.)

Practice Questions

Question 1

> Which of the following ways can you set up five volumes on a single hard disk?
>
> ○ a. Set up five primary partitions.
>
> ○ b. Set up two primary partitions, one extended partition, and three logical drives.
>
> ○ c. Set up three primary partitions and two logical drives.
>
> ○ d. Set up one primary partition, one extended partition, and three logical drives.

Answer b is correct. You can only set up a logical drive within an extended partition. Because you can't set up more than four primary partitions in a hard disk, answer a is incorrect. You cannot set up a logical drive without an extended partition; therefore, answer c is incorrect. Because an extended partition is not a volume, answer d is incorrect.

Question 2

> You have a computer with Microsoft Windows installed. It is set up on one primary partition. There are no other partitions or logical drives available. Which of the following steps should you take before you split this partition to accommodate Linux? [Check all correct answers]
>
> ❑ a. Run the fips utility to rearrange the data on your drive.
>
> ❑ b. Run the Windows Defrag utility to consolidate the data on your drive.
>
> ❑ c. Run the Windows ScanDisk utility to make sure your drive has no errors.
>
> ❑ d. Back up your hard disk.

Answers b, c, and d are correct. The Windows Defrag utility consolidates the data on your drive. The Windows ScanDisk utility checks for errors on your drive. Because splitting partitions can be a dangerous business, you should always back up the data on your disk. The fips utility is used to split partitions; therefore, answer a is incorrect.

Question 3

> You used the fips utility to split your partition, and then you realized that you made a mistake. Which of the following actions should you take?
>
> ○ a. Back up your hard drive, and then run fips again.
>
> ○ b. Run fips again, and then use the restorrb utility. Make sure that you have the rootboot.000 file that fips created and saved on your floppy drive.
>
> ○ c. Use fdisk to rebuild the partitions on your hard drive. Run the restorrb utility to re-create your original partitions.
>
> ○ d. Run the restorrb utility. Make sure that you have the rootboot.000 file that fips created and saved on your floppy drive. Run fips again.

Answer d is correct. Assuming you had saved your root and boot sectors, you should have a rootboot.000 file on a bootable floppy drive. You should be able to use the restorrb utility to use this file to rewrite your original root and boot information. If you made a mistake with fips, you don't want to back up the result. Therefore, answer a is incorrect. Although answer b can work, the act of using fips to split partitions again can cause more problems. Therefore, answer b is incorrect. Because the fdisk utility won't help you recover from any mistakes that you make with fips, answer c is incorrect.

Question 4

> You just logged in to the root account in Linux and used the **mount /dev/ cdrom mnt/cdrom** command to access the files on your CD-ROM. Assuming that the appropriate directory already exists, what is the absolute path of your CD-ROM files?
>
> ○ a. root/mnt/cdrom
>
> ○ b. /root/mnt/cdrom
>
> ○ c. mnt/cdrom
>
> ○ d. /mnt/cdrom

Answer b is correct. Absolute paths always start with the root directory, which is labeled by a simple forward slash (/). The /root directory is the home directory for the root user. Because root/mnt/cdrom is not an absolute path, answer a is incorrect. Although you could get to your CD-ROM files from your root home directory with the **cd mnt/cdrom** command, mnt/cdrom is still not an absolute path. Therefore, answer c is incorrect. And although /mnt/cdrom is the standard installation directory in most Linux distributions, it does not correspond to the command in the question. Therefore, answer d is incorrect.

Question 5

> Your friend plans to install Linux as a networked system for a dozen users in her small business. She might extend this system to run the business Web site, which would involve increasingly large log files to track users' buying habits. Little growth in personnel is expected, and she wants to limit the space dedicated to her users' personal files. She also plans to upgrade Linux fairly frequently and does not want to have to reload key applications, such as Star Office. Which of the following procedures is best for her situation? Hint: When you evaluate these answers, don't forget the needs of the swap disk. And each computer includes only one physical hard drive.
>
> ○ a. Divide the hard disk into a combination of primary partitions and logical drives. Make sure that the /opt, /var, /home, and / directories are mounted on different volumes.
>
> ○ b. Divide the hard disk into volumes composed of several primary partitions. Make sure that the /opt, /var, /home, and / directories are mounted on different volumes.
>
> ○ c. Divide the hard disk into several separate volumes. Make sure that the /bin, /usr/bin, and /boot directories are each mounted on individual volumes.
>
> ○ d. None of the above.

Answer a is correct. You need the /opt directory on a separate volume to save your applications when you upgrade Linux. You need the /var directory on a separate volume so log files from the Web site don't overwhelm your computer. You need the /home directory on a separate volume if you want to limit the amount of space taken by each user's personal files. Any directory not part of a separate volume is automatically installed in the root directory's (/) volume. With the swap disk, this option requires five different volumes. Because you can't have more than four primary partitions, answer b is incorrect. And because the directories listed in answer c don't meet any of the requirements listed in the question, it is also incorrect.

Question 6

> Which of the following drivers is definitely not associated with a CD-ROM drive?
>
> O a. /dev/sdd
>
> O b. /dev/sbpcd
>
> O c. /dev/hdb
>
> O d. /dev/hda3

Answer d is correct. It is actually the third primary partition on the first regular hard disk. CD-ROMs are generally not split into separate volumes. The /dev/sdd driver is for the fourth SCSI drive. Because it does not list a volume number, it may be a CD-ROM drive. Therefore, answer a is incorrect. The /dev/sbpcd driver is the CD-ROM attachment to an older Sound Blaster card; therefore, answer b is incorrect. Because the /dev/hdb drive is a common device for a CD-ROM on a computer that also has a regular hard disk, answer c is incorrect.

Question 7

> Which of the following file systems is not "real"?
>
> O a. /bin
>
> O b. /opt
>
> O c. /root
>
> O d. /proc

Answer d is correct. The /proc file system does not list any actual files. Instead, it lists currently running programs and kernel routines. The /bin file system includes many standard Linux utilities, so answer a is incorrect. The /opt file system is where many applications are installed, so answer b is incorrect. Because the /root file system is the home directory for the root user, answer c is incorrect.

Question 8

Which of the following programs can you use to manage the configuration of your monitor and video card on most any Linux distribution?

○ a. XF86config

○ b. XF86Setup

○ c. xf86setup

○ d. XConfigurator

Answer b is correct. The XF86Setup tool is the product of the XFree86 group, which can help you configure your monitor and video card. Although there is an xf86config tool, you can't access it from the command line by typing "XF86config". Because Linux commands are case sensitive, answer a is incorrect. For similar reasons, there is no xf86setup tool. Therefore, answer c is incorrect. The XConfigurator tool is currently available only in Red Hat Linux, so answer d is incorrect.

Question 9

Which of the following answers affect memory requirements when you configure your video card in Linux? [Check all correct answers]

❑ a. Horizontal frequency

❑ b. Resolution

❑ c. Number of colors

❑ d. Monitor size

Answers b and c are correct. The resolution is an expression of the number of pixels that your video card can show on your screen. Each color that you add requires additional data. It takes more data to fill more pixels and colors. Although the horizontal frequency tends to increase with a higher graphic mode and number of colors, it is not a reason that your video card needs more memory. Therefore, answer a is incorrect. Although the size of your monitor is normally associated with more pixels, some larger monitors simply have larger pixels. Therefore, the monitor does not change the graphic mode that you set for your video card, and answer d is incorrect.

Question 10

> If you're not careful when you set up your video card and monitor, you could easily break the monitor. Which of the following answers describe the factors that you need to consider to avoid trouble? [Check all correct answers]
>
> ❑ a. Make sure your graphics requirements don't exceed the memory available in your monitor.
>
> ❑ b. Make sure you don't exceed the horizontal frequency limits of your monitor.
>
> ❑ c. Make sure your graphics requirements don't exceed the available memory in your video card.
>
> ❑ d. Make sure you don't exceed the vertical frequency limits of your video card.

Answer b is correct. If you exceed the frequency limits of some monitors, your settings could break the circuitry inside your monitor. Monitors have no memory, so answer a is incorrect. Because tools like XF86Setup don't allow you to set graphic modes or frequencies that exceed the capabilities of your video card, answers c and d are incorrect.

Need to Know More?

 Check out the fips Web page at **www.igd.fhg.de/~aschaefe/fips** for a good guide to using fips. If you want to split your disk partition to accommodate Linux without destroying your current data, this is the tool to use. Read the instructions carefully before using fips.

 Explore the Web site for the Linux Documentation Project at **www.linuxdoc.org**, which is the central repository for Linux manuals, HOWTOs, and a number of other book-length documents. Important HOWTOs for this chapter include the "DOS-Win-to-Linux-HOWTO," the "CD-ROM-HOWTO," and the "XFree86-Video-Timings-HOWTO."

 Investigate the Web page of the Filesystem Hierarchy Standard (FHS) at **www.pathname.com**. It is a simple Web site that contains the current standard for Linux directories. Linux developers and distributors are encouraged to follow FHS to minimize the customization that developers need to do when they set up their programs for different Linux distributions.

 Check out the WINE project Web page at **www.winehq.com**. With this application, you can run some Microsoft Windows-based programs inside Linux. For a list of Windows programs that you can run through WINE, refer to this Web site.

Installation Options

Terms you'll need to understand:

✓ Local device installation

✓ Network installation

✓ Linux Loader (LILO)

✓ **rawrite**

Techniques you'll need to master:

✓ Listing different local Linux installation options including dual-boot systems

✓ Describing different network Linux installation options

✓ Comparing basic characteristics of different Linux distributions

✓ Describing installation procedures common to Linux distributions

The Sair exams are distribution neutral, so this chapter covers basic steps common to all distributions. You can install almost all Linux distributions from local sources or through a network.

Each of the major Linux distributions has different strengths and weaknesses. They share general common installation procedures.

Local Device Installation

There are three basic ways to install Linux on a local computer: by using a CD-ROM, from files copied to a hard drive, and through floppy disks. Most current Linux distributions have many files, which require one or more CD-ROMs.

Linux is usually installed directly from a CD-ROM. Alternately, you can copy the files on the CD-ROM to your hard disk and install Linux from there. It is even possible to install some older Linux distributions with a large number of floppy disks.

Installation by CD-ROM

Some Linux distributions include several gigabytes of files. Currently, the only convenient way to distribute this much information is through a CD-ROM. To start a CD-ROM installation, set your computer's Basic Input/Output System (BIOS) to boot from the CD-ROM.

Alternately, you can start your computer with a Linux boot floppy. Once it detects your CD-ROM, you can continue with a CD-ROM installation. Some Linux distributions come with boot floppies, or you can create a boot floppy from files on the installation CD-ROM.

Installation by Partition

You can also copy appropriate files from your installation CD-ROM to your hard disk, and then start the installation program with boot floppies. When prompted, enter the directory for your Linux installation files.

Installation by Floppy

It is possible to install Linux from floppies. With several dozen floppies, it's possible to install a minimal version of Linux. Once installed, you can then connect to other servers to install more packages. Needless to say, this is a time-consuming process.

Network Installation

You can install Linux through three different types of networks: File Transfer Protocol (FTP), Network File System (NFS), or Samba. FTP is a common way to transfer files to and from other networks, such as the Internet. NFS is the standard Linux network file sharing protocol. Samba is a heterogeneous protocol that allows Linux computers to exchange files with Microsoft and IBM operating systems.

Whichever network you use, the first step is to find Linux boot disks that allow you to connect to a network server. These special boot disks usually detect your network card. However, if these disks don't detect your card, you may need to add information like the Linux name for your network driver, its interrupt request (IRQ) and input/output (I/O) channels, and memory addresses.

Note: Most commands in Linux are lowercase. For example, if you're installing a Novell-compatible network card that's set to IRQ 10 with an I/O address of 0x300, you might use the insmod ne i/o=300 irq=10 command to help Linux recognize your card.

Once you've booted your computer, you'll need the host and domain names or IP address for the remote server. You also need to know the remote directory where the installation files are stored.

When installing Linux over a network, the devil is in the details. If you get "little" things wrong, such as the case of a password or a missing slash in your directory, they can prevent a successful installation.

Don't try installing Linux over a telephone modem. If everything goes perfectly, installation takes several days. If you have any "normal" problem with a modem connection, the process may take quite a bit longer.

Seven Major Distributions

As of this writing, there are perhaps two dozen Linux distributions. Fortunately, they all run the same kind of software. Because of the General Public License (GPL), there are few copyright limitations on what is packaged. Some distributions even repackage identical versions of others, perhaps with a few additional tools. They all share the same basic Linux kernel.

Each distribution comes with a version number. Generally, they follow the same model as Red Hat 7, where the first number signifies a major change, and the second number indicates a relatively small revision.

The distributions discussed in the following sections are listed in the Sair Knowledge Matrix. Sair recommends that you install four different distributions in preparation for this exam. When you install each distribution, focus on their commonalities. You don't need to know specific details of each distribution beyond what is discussed in these sections.

A Note on Kernels

The Linux kernel you see with a distribution may be labeled in a way that is similar to 2.4.27. The format refers to *major.minor.patch*. The first number, in this case 2, means that this is the second major release of the Linux kernel. The second number, 4, means that this is the fourth minor release of the kernel. And the final number, 27, means that this is the twenty-seventh patch to the specified minor release of the kernel.

The second number also tells you whether or not the Linux kernel is in beta test or production release. Odd numbers correspond to test kernels and generally should not be used for production servers. Even numbers correspond to production kernels.

In practice, changes to the *minor* number of a kernel are rather significant. For example, new commands for firewalls and new drivers for Universal Serial Bus (USB) equipment were introduced in Linux kernel version 2.4.

Caldera

The Caldera distribution comes in different flavors, known as Open Linux, eDesktop, or eServer. Its self-described focus is "Linux for Business." Caldera has developed a number of graphical- and Web-based tools for installation and administration.

Debian

The Debian GNU/Linux distribution is a popular option for Linux developers. Its self-described focus is on easy upgrades and security. There are over 2,000 software packages available with Debian. It is one of several distributions maintained and distributed by volunteers.

Mandrake

The creators of Linux-Mandrake build their distribution on top of Red Hat Linux. This is legal and encouraged under the conditions of the GPL. They add features such as additional language choices for installation, more drivers, and TrueType fonts.

Red Hat

Red Hat Linux is perhaps the most widely known Linux distribution. Its installation program includes options for setting up workstations and servers as well as upgrades of previous Linux installations.

Slackware

Slackware has two versions of Linux: a regular distribution along with its compact ZipSlack package, which is suitable for the Zip drive. Slackware is affiliated with Walnut Creek CD-ROM and BDSi, which work with a different Unix derivative known as the Berkeley Standard Distribution.

Stampede

The Stampede distribution seems to be under constant development. As of this writing, this nonprofit organization has worked for years and still has not released version 1.0 of its distribution. Stampede's self-described focus is on ease of use and optimization for the newest processor hardware.

S.u.S.E.

As of this writing, S.u.S.E. has the best-selling Linux distribution in Europe. It seems to have a more comprehensive software distribution. Although most Linux distributions are compressed into one or two CDs, S.u.S.E. Linux, depending on the version, includes up to six CDs.

Another Distribution: Corel Linux

Corel Linux was developed after the Sair exams were released. By some measures, Corel Linux is now the second most widely popular distribution. Like Caldera, Corel has developed a number of graphical tools. Its focus is on getting Linux to the desktop.

As Linux-Mandrake does with Red Hat Linux, Corel Linux uses most of the packages in the Debian GNU/Linux distribution.

Getting Linux

There are a number of ways to obtain Linux. You can purchase many of these distributions in computer stores and bookstores. The full versions often include some service commitment from their distributors.

You can download Linux distributions from the Internet in two ways: from the Web sites of the Linux packagers or from special download sites, such as **www.linuxberg.com** or **www.freshmeat.net**. If you have a CD-writer, you can download ISO files to create distribution CDs on your computer.

You can even get Linux distribution CD-ROMs from third-party distributors, such as **www.linuxmall.com** or **www.cheapbytes.com** for approximately $5US.

Common Installation Procedures

The setup program for every Linux distribution is different, but they share common features. There are approximately 10 basic steps required to install Linux, depending on which distribution you use:

1. Boot from a Linux installation CD-ROM.

2. Select basic parameters: language, mouse, and keyboard.

3. Choose single or dual-boot (if you are planning on more than one operating system).

4. Set up Linux partitions.

5. Format Linux partitions.

6. Install actual software.

7. Select default operating system (applicable to dual-boot setups).

8. Input network settings.

9. Configure the X Window.

10. Create rescue disk(s).

Different distributions handle most of these steps in different ways. Some distributions, such as Corel Linux, make a number of decisions for you automatically. Corel has a four-step installation process. Other distributions allow you to customize your configuration in detail.

Booting the Linux Installation CD-ROM

There are two basic ways to access a Linux installation CD-ROM. You can set up your BIOS to boot your computer directly from the CD-ROM, or you can create boot disks with CD-ROM drivers.

Not all computers can boot from their CD-ROM drives. To test your system, you need to go into your BIOS menu. Restart your computer. When your computer restarts, you'll see an option to go into a BIOS or Setup menu by pressing a key such as F2, Del, or Ctrl. When you enter your Setup menu, look for boot options. Find a boot option where your computer looks first to your CD-ROM drive for boot files.

If you can't find an option to boot from your CD-ROM in your BIOS, you'll need to boot from your floppy drive. Some Linux distributions include floppy boot disks. If you don't have a floppy boot disk, you can create one. You should be able to find at least a rawrite.exe program and a boot.img file on your distribution CD-ROM. The rawrite program is an MS-DOS program that allows you to copy the image of a Linux boot floppy onto a formatted 1.44MB floppy.

The boot.img file is also known as a *boot image*. Linux images are archives of a series of files. The files inside boot.img should detect most CD-ROMs. Some distributions also include images that help your computer detect network and PCMCIA cards (also known as PC Cards).

If you have access to other Linux computers, you can create a boot image with the **dd** (device dump) command. If you mounted a CD-ROM on the /mnt/cdrom directory, you can use the following command:

```
dd if=/mnt/cdrom/images/boot.img of=/dev/fd0
```

This command takes the boot.img input file (if) and sends the files within it to an output file (of). However, there is no one specific output file. The **dd** command actually unpacks the input file to the fd0 device, which is usually the first floppy drive on your computer. Although you need to mount your CD-ROM to make this work, you don't need to mount your floppy drive. The actual command you use depends on your actual devices, mount locations, and the location of the boot.img file.

With some distributions, you may have a couple of other options. In some cases, you can boot the CD-ROM directly from Microsoft Windows. In other cases, you either have to boot your computer to MS-DOS, or shut down Windows and restart in MS-DOS mode.

Basic Input Parameters

Each Linux distribution has to set up basic input parameters for language, keyboards, and mice. Some Linux distributions include instructions in over a dozen languages. Linux setup programs can accommodate input from several different kinds of U.S. keyboards as well as keyboards common in other countries. And those Linux setup programs based on a graphical user interface are also designed to accommodate major pointing devices, such as mice.

Single or Dual-Boot

When you run a Linux setup program, you can choose to have a single or dual-boot. You can dedicate your whole hard disk to Linux, or you can set up partitions to accommodate multiple operating systems.

Each Linux setup program has a partitioning program like fips, fdisk, or Partition Magic that you can use at this time. If you have already set up the volumes you need, continue on to the following section on Linux partitions.

Setting Up Linux Partitions

You can use the Linux setup tools to create volumes for your swap partition and Linux directories of your choice.

Linux setup programs can also work with any partitions or volumes that you have previously created. You need at least two volumes: one for your files and one for your swap partition. You can also assign different volumes to directories such as root (/), /boot, /var, and /opt. Remember, your swap partition should be approximately twice the size of your RAM, up to about 100MB.

 The order of Linux partitions is relatively unimportant. If you can, configure the swap partition first.

Formatting Linux Partitions

Once you create a Linux partition, you need to format it. Linux setup programs use second-level disk format commands on each Linux volume that you create.

You can create multiple swap partitions. In fact, this may help performance if you're installing Linux on multiple hard disks.

 Linux installation programs use the mke2fs program to format regular Linux volumes. This program formats the specified partition to the second extended file system (ext2fs). Linux installation programs also use the **mkswap** command to format a Linux swap partition. Although not generally recommended, you can also configure a Linux swap file with the **swapon** command after Linux is installed.

Installing the Actual Software

In most Linux setup programs, you get to choose the software that you install. Sometimes the choices are general. For example, you can choose between a minimum and a server type installation.

Sometimes the choices are specific. In some Linux setup programs, you get to choose every package that the Linux setup program installs on your computer. Once the choices are made, the Linux setup program unpacks software and copies configuration files onto your system.

Configuring the Boot Sequence

Linux manages multiple operating systems through the Linux Loader (LILO). When your computer runs LILO, you get to choose the operating system that you want to boot.

In this part of the Linux setup, you choose one of three locations for LILO. Each location is suitable for different purposes, as shown in Table 5.1.

Network Settings

Some Linux setup programs allow you to configure network settings before starting the installation process. After all, if you have to access installation files from a different computer, you do need to tell Linux where to find those files.

Even if you're just installing Linux from a CD-ROM, you can use the Linux setup program to make sure your computer gets connected to the network as soon as the Linux installation is complete.

Linux setup programs assume you're connecting your computer to a TCP/IP network. Although other network protocol stacks are available, Linux is built on TCP/IP. If you plan on setting up Linux on another network, you should leave the network settings section blank. You can review an example of this configuration through the Caldera Linux setup program, as shown in Figure 5.1.

To set up Linux for TCP/IP, you may need to know the following:

➤ *Network device*—For example, if your computer has one Ethernet card, your network device is eth0.

➤ *Driver*—Linux setup programs should recognize most network cards. If you know your card is going to be "difficult," you can enter a driver along with any special IRQ or I/O ports.

Table 5.1 LILO installation options.	
Location	**Purpose**
Master Boot Record (MBR)	When you want to use LILO to choose between operating systems.
First sector of primary partition	When you have another boot loader, such as System Commander or Partition Magic, that allows you to choose between operating systems.
Floppy disk	When you don't want to change your MBR or the first sector of a primary partition. Alternately, if you can't install Linux below hard drive cylinder 1024 (see Chapter 4), this is a viable option for setting up Linux.

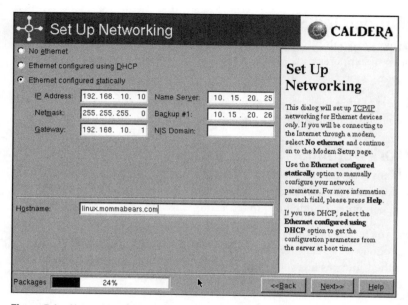

Figure 5.1 Network configuration example based on Caldera Linux setup.

➤ *IP address*—If you have a static IP address, you also need to know the network mask. If your computer will get its IP address from a Dynamic Host Configuration Protocol (DHCP) server, just choose the appropriate option. A DHCP server temporarily assigns IP addresses to different computers on a network.

➤ *Network mask*—If you specified an IP address, you need a network mask. A network mask, such as 255.255.255.0, limits the range of possible IP addresses on your local network. Network masks are sometimes called *subnet masks*.

➤ *Nameserver*—A nameserver includes a database of names, like mommabears.com, and the corresponding IP address of each, such as 192.168.10.10. You need the IP address for your nameserver and any secondary nameservers for your network. Nameservers are also known as Domain Name Servers (DNS) or as the Berkeley Internet Name Daemon (BIND) servers.

➤ *Gateway*—If your network is connected to any other network, you need the IP address of the computer that serves as the junction between the networks. In the example shown in Figure 5.1, the address is 192.168.10.1

➤ *Hostname*—You need a name for your computer, and it needs to be different from any other computer on your network. In the example shown in Figure 5.1, the hostname is linux.

➤ *Domain*—You also need a network name. In the example shown in Figure 5.1, the domain name is mommabears.com. (The fully qualified domain name of the computer is linux.mommabears.com.)

In some ways, these network settings may not seem complete. If you don't use a DNS server on your networks, you can also set up a file (/etc/hosts) with the IP address of each computer on your network. The information in this section does connect you to a local network. The gateway address also allows you to connect to external networks, such as the Internet.

X Window Settings

Current Linux distributions allow you to configure your video card and monitor during installation. As discussed in Chapter 4, this involves configuring your video RAM, resolution, number of colors, monitor size, and frequency settings for both your video card and your monitor.

Make sure that your video card settings do not exceed the capability of your monitor.

Creating Rescue Disks

Once you've configured the setup process, most Linux distributions prompt you to create a rescue disk. Although you may be able to restore some configurations with a generic rescue disk or even the installation CD-ROM, a rescue disk makes this job much easier. Linux uses the **dd** command to unpack the files for a custom rescue image to a 1.44MB floppy.

If you ever need to make a rescue, you'll probably need both your rescue disk and your boot disk.

After Installation

If you're upgrading Linux from one version to another on a production computer, you generally should set up the new version of Linux on a different hard drive. Once installed, you can then copy configuration files from the original version of Linux, and then test and revise the result as required.

You can also reconfigure any settings made during a Linux installation. A number of the tools that help you do this are addressed in the following chapters.

Practice Installations

One of the listed requirements of the Sair Linux/GNU exam is that you install four Linux distributions. Even though installing four different Linux distributions helps most people, this is an arbitrary figure. Install as many different Linux distributions as you need to understand the process discussed in this chapter.

The actual distributions that you choose should not matter. Most Linux distribution setup programs include expert or custom configuration modes. Choose these modes during your installations. When you experiment with the embedded options, you'll learn more about the Linux installation and configuration process.

Practice Questions

Question 1

> You can install Linux from which of the following? [Check all correct answers]
>
> ❑ a. CD-ROM
>
> ❑ b. Floppy disks
>
> ❑ c. Network File System connection
>
> ❑ d. FTP connection

Answers a, b, c, and d are correct. You can install Linux from just about any media or through any network connection that you can configure through a Linux boot disk.

Question 2

> Which of the following is the Linux way to manage your choice between two or more operating systems on your computer?
>
> ○ a. Linux Commander
>
> ○ b. Partition Magic
>
> ○ c. Linux Loader
>
> ○ d. Linux Manager

Answer c is correct. The Linux Loader is more commonly known as LILO, which is the boot manager that you can install on your hard or floppy disk to give you a choice of operating systems. Linux Commander and Linux Manager do not exist; therefore, answers a and d are incorrect. Although you can use Partition Magic to set up a choice between operating systems, it is a commercial product that you install through MS-DOS or Microsoft Windows. Therefore, answer b is incorrect.

Question 3

> How do you set up the installation of Linux over a network?
>
> O a. Use your telephone modem to connect to your Internet Service Provider (ISP). Connect to a network with Linux installation files.
>
> O b. Use the rawrite program to set up network boot floppy disk(s). Use these boot disks to start the Linux setup program. Connect to the appropriate network server after the setup program boots.
>
> O c. Download the appropriate network boot floppy disk(s). Use these boot disks when prompted by your Linux CD-ROM-based setup program. Connect to the appropriate network server after the setup program boots.
>
> O d. Boot your computer from the Linux installation CD. When prompted, enter the IP address of the network server with your Linux installation files.

Answer b is correct. The rawrite program is an MS-DOS-based program used to copy disk images to floppies. These images allow you to boot a Linux system and install appropriate network files. After you use these boot disks, you should be able to connect to the appropriate network server. Installing Linux through a telephone modem is not practical; therefore, answer a is incorrect. Linux CD-ROM-based setup programs generally do not allow you to connect to a network to download installation files; they are already available on CD-ROM. Therefore, answers c and d are incorrect.

Question 4

> Which of the following statements is a characteristic of Linux distributions?
>
> O a. Every Linux distribution can be installed in an MS-DOS partition.
>
> O b. Some Linux distributions use Red Hat kernels.
>
> O c. Some Linux distributions are based on other distributions.
>
> O d. Every Linux distribution can be installed in a Linux swap partition.

Answer c is correct. Under the provisions of the GPL, anyone can repackage anyone else's GNU/Linux distribution. Because Linux generally can't be installed in an MS-DOS partition, answer a is incorrect. There is no kernel exclusive to Red Hat; therefore, answer b is incorrect. Although Linux distributions use swap partitions, their files are installed under various directories. Therefore, answer d is incorrect.

Question 5

> Which of the following commands can you use to copy a boot image to a
> formatted 1.44MB floppy disk? The name of the file is boot.img.
>
> ○ a. **rawrite boot.img a:**
>
> ○ b. **rawrite**
>
> ○ c. **dd if=/mnt/cdrom/images/boot.img a:**
>
> ○ d. **copy boot.img a:**

Answer b is correct. When you run this command in MS-DOS mode, you are
prompted for the image that you want to copy and the location of the floppy
drive. Because the command in answer a does not work, it is not correct. For
more information on the **rawrite** syntax, type the **rawrite -h** command. The **dd**
command is a Linux command. Although you can create boot disks in Linux,
there is no a: drive in a Linux computer; therefore answer c is incorrect. An image
file is an archive of several different files. You can't just copy the image; you need
a command like **rawrite** to unpack the files to your floppy. Therefore, answer d
is incorrect.

Question 6

> Which of the following commands can you use to format or activate a Linux
> swap file?
>
> ○ a. **mkswap**
>
> ○ b. **mke2fs**
>
> ○ c. **ext2fs**
>
> ○ d. **swapon**

Answer d is correct. You can activate a Linux swap file with the **swapon** command.
The **mkswap** command formats Linux swap partitions (not files); therefore, answer a is incorrect. Because the **mke2fs** command formats regular Linux volumes
(not swap partitions), answer b is incorrect. The second extended file system is
sometimes known as ext2fs, but it is not a command, so answer c is incorrect.

Question 7

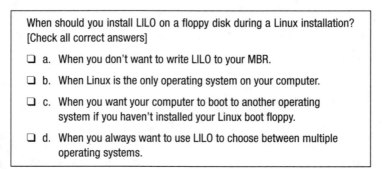

When should you install LILO on a floppy disk during a Linux installation? [Check all correct answers]

❏ a. When you don't want to write LILO to your MBR.

❏ b. When Linux is the only operating system on your computer.

❏ c. When you want your computer to boot to another operating system if you haven't installed your Linux boot floppy.

❏ d. When you always want to use LILO to choose between multiple operating systems.

Answers a and c are correct. Installing LILO on a floppy disk is a viable alternative to installing LILO on your MBR. If you don't insert the boot floppy, your computer boots your original operating system. If Linux is the only operating system on your computer, you want your computer to boot Linux whenever you turn it on. If you set up LILO only on a floppy, your computer won't always boot Linux whenever you turn it on. Therefore, answer b is incorrect. If you don't have your Linux boot floppy, your other operating system(s) will boot from the MBR. Therefore, answer d is incorrect.

Question 8

You're installing Linux on a computer in a TCP/IP network. Which of the following items will you need to set up networking when you install Linux? Hints: Your network is connected to others, and you don't have a DHCP server. [Check all correct answers]

❏ a. IP address for your computer

❏ b. IP address for the gateway computer

❏ c. IP address for a DHCP server

❏ d. IP address for a nameserver

❏ e. IP address for all other computers on your network

Answers a, b, and d are correct. Because your computer isn't getting its address from a DHCP server, you need to designate an IP address for your computer. You need the IP address of the gateway computer to access other connected networks. You need the IP address of at least one nameserver to translate names like coriolis.com to IP addresses. Because you already need an IP address for your computer, a DHCP server won't help you. Therefore, answer c is incorrect. Although it's useful to have the IP addresses for all other computers on your network, you don't need to supply this information during the installation process to connect your computer to the network. Therefore, answer e is incorrect.

Question 9

Where should you configure different Linux partitions during installation?

○ a. You should place more frequently accessed information, such as a swap partition, as close to the center of the hard disk as possible.

○ b. The position of partitions on your hard disk is fairly unimportant.

○ c. You should place more frequently accessed information, such as a swap partition, as close to the edges of the hard disk as possible.

○ d. You should place more frequently accessed information, such as the /root directory, as close to the center of the hard disk as possible.

Answer b is correct. With the speed of current hard disks, the location of any specific partition is not very important. Locating the swap partition closer to the center of a hard disk does help; however, the gain in speed is insignificant. Therefore, answer a is incorrect. Putting a swap partition at the edge of the hard disk would slow down data transfer. Even though the difference is not significant, answer c is incorrect. Because logins as the root user should be rare, access to the root user's home directory, /root, should be infrequent. Any /root directory can be far from the center of a hard disk. Even though the difference is not significant, answer d is incorrect.

Question 10

You've installed Linux on a production server. It's also the server that manages your Web page. You get hundreds of hits each day to your Web page. You've heard about a new Linux kernel, version 2.5.45. You understand that it will help you manage your traffic and log files more efficiently. Should you upgrade your computer with this kernel? Which of the following explanations makes the most sense?

- ○ a. No. Because the last number is odd, you know this kernel is not suitable for production. You should wait for kernel version 2.5.46.

- ○ b. Yes. Because the last number is odd, you know this kernel is completely tested and reliable for your purposes.

- ○ c. No. Because the middle number is odd, you know this kernel is not suitable for production. You should wait for kernel version 2.6.

- ○ d. Yes. Because the middle number is odd, you know this kernel is completely tested and reliable for your purposes.

Answer c is correct. The last number is the patch number and does not determine whether or not a kernel is suitable for production. Although higher patch numbers indicate a kernel that is more developed, answers a and b are still incorrect. When the middle number of a kernel version is odd, it is a developmental kernel not suitable for production. Therefore, answer d is incorrect.

Need to Know More?

 Visit **www.caldera.com,** the Web site for Caldera Systems, with a self-described focus on Linux for business. The Caldera Web site provides hardware compatibility lists (HCLs) and a knowledge base as well as downloads of Caldera's latest version of Linux.

 Check out the Web site for the Corel Linux Community at **http:// linux.corel.com.** Corel Linux focuses on the desktop market, and it has taken an active role in the Windows Is Not an Emulator (WINE) project. A download of its latest version of Linux is also available from this Web site. The Corel Linux version of Linux is openly built upon the Debian distribution.

 Explore the Web site for Debian GNU/Linux at **www.debian.com.** This may be the most popular Linux distribution for Linux developers. Creators of Debian are primarily volunteers. You can also download Debian GNU/Linux from this site.

 Investigate the Web site for the Linux Documentation Project at **www.linuxdoc.org,** which is the central repository for Linux manuals, HOWTOs, and a number of other book-length documents. The relevant HOWTO for this chapter is the "Linux Installation-HOWTO."

 Visit **www.linux-mandrake.com,** the Web site for Linux-Mandrake, created by MandrakeSoft. Its version of Linux builds on Red Hat Linux with a number of additional graphical and other installation tools. You can download its version of Linux from this Web site.

 Visit **www.redhat.com,** the Web site for Red Hat, Inc. Its version of Linux is the current market leader. Red Hat's Web site offers HCLs and a knowledge base as well as downloads of its latest version of Linux.

 Browse the Web site for the Slackware Linux Project at **www.slackware.com.** Slackware's following is similar to that of Debian GNU/Linux. Its standard version of Linux along with its compact ZipSlack packages are available on this Web site. Slackware is affiliated with Walnut Creek CD-ROM and BDSi, which work with a different Unix derivative known as the Berkeley Software Distribution.

Check out the Web site for Stampede GNU/Linux at **www.stampede.org,** a nonprofit organization that is, as of this writing, still developing its distribution. Its focus is on ease of use and optimization for the newest processor hardware. You can download its version of Linux from this site.

 Visit **www.suse.com,** the Web site for S.u.S.E. GmBH, the best-selling Linux distribution in Europe. The S.u.S.E. Web site offers HCLs and a knowledge base as well as downloads of its latest version of Linux.

 Explore the Web site for Turbo Linux at **www.turbolinux.com,** the best selling Linux distribution in Asia. The Turbo Linux Web site allows you to install its distribution by downloading its files to a hard drive or through the use of boot disks to start a Linux connection to its FTP server.

6

Startup and Shutdown

. . . .

Terms you'll need to understand:

✓ Linux Loader (LILO)

✓ vmlinuz

✓ **boot.b**

✓ **map**

✓ **append**

✓ /etc/fstab

✓ rc.d

✓ init.d

✓ /etc/inittab

✓ Shells

✓ **shutdown**

Techniques you'll need to master:

✓ Managing the Linux Loader (LILO)

✓ Editing mounted file systems (/etc/fstab)

✓ Analyzing initialization scripts

✓ Analyzing run level resource control scripts

✓ Explaining initialization commands (/etc/inittab)

✓ Understanding logins

✓ Editing shutdown options

This chapter explains what happens when Linux starts, and what you can do to customize your start process. The Linux Loader (LILO) manages multiple operating systems. LILO launches when you start your computer. If you choose Linux from the LILO menu, it loads the Linux kernel. The kernel loads your hardware and protocols, and then passes the rest of the process to init. The init program mounts your drives as specified in the /etc/fstab file and starts other programs at various run levels with the help of resource control (rc) files. Then it sets up shells and login screens as defined by the /etc/inittab/ initialization file. This file also defines who can shut down your computer and the commands that can be used to shut it down.

Linux Loading Details

LILO is a versatile tool. You can set it up to load Linux directly from your hard drive, and it can also work with other boot managers. You can even set it up to load from a floppy disk. LILO tells Linux special details about your hardware configuration as you boot. Once you choose to load Linux, it starts your Linux kernel.

The Linux kernel is sometimes known by its basic file name, vmlinuz.

When LILO loads on your computer, you see the following prompt, usually for just a few seconds:

```
LILO boot:
```

If you press the Shift key, LILO should stop and wait for your input. If you press the Tab key, LILO lists the available operating systems. For example, if you've set up Linux and Microsoft Windows on your computer, you might see the following:

```
linux    dos
boot:
```

In this case, you have two choices. You can type "linux" or "dos". Even if your other operating system is Microsoft Windows, typing "windows" won't work.

There is no limit to the number of operating systems that you can select through LILO. The only limits are based on the size of your hard drive.

Common LILO Tasks

Whatever your configuration, you'll see at least the following commands in your lilo.conf file:

```
boot=/dev/hda
install=/boot/boot.b
```

The **boot** command specifies the location of your lilo.conf file. The command shown assumes that you installed LILO in the Master Boot Record (MBR) of the first hard disk on your computer. If you installed LILO on the first partition of that drive, you'd see the **boot=/dev/hda1** command. Alternatively, if you installed LILO on a floppy disk, you'd see the **boot=/dev/fd0** command.

LILO then runs the secondary boot loader, the boot.b file. If you have LILO on a floppy disk, this command would read **install=/mnt/boot.b**, because floppy disks are typically mounted on the /mnt directory before Linux loads.

Some Linux distributions configure the following commands in LILO too:

```
message=/boot/messagefile
map=/boot/map
```

When used, the **message** command specifies a message file that you'd see before the LILO **boot:** prompt. The **map** command specifies the location of your boot partitions. By default, the **map** command is located in the /boot/map file.

The following commands govern how long you wait before your default operating system automatically boots:

```
prompt
timeout=100
```

The **prompt** command supersedes any timeout if you press the Shift or Tab key. The **timeout** command specifies how long LILO waits, in tenths of a second, before booting your default operating system. The time shown is equal to 10 seconds. Some versions of Linux substitute the **delay** command for **timeout**; they are, for our purposes here, identical commands.

Multiple Operating Systems

If you do not make a selection at the LILO **boot:** prompt, the operating system that appears depends on the **default** command. On the other hand, if this command is missing, the default operating system is the first one you see in the lilo.conf file.

LILO typically defines a Linux operating system with four commands as in the following:

```
image=/boot/vmlinuz
label=redhat
root=/dev/hda3
read-only
```

The **image** command specifies the location of your Linux kernel. The **label** is what you see when you press the Tab key at the LILO **boot:** prompt, as well as what you need to type to select that operating system. The **root** is the location of the root directory (/). And **read-only** means that the root directory should be mounted in read-only mode. The **read-only** command is usually superseded when the root directory is mounted on its assigned volume. Of course, if any of the preceding files have different names or are in different locations on your system, substitute accordingly.

LILO typically defines other operating systems, such as Microsoft Windows or IBM's OS/2, with three commands as in the following:

```
other=/dev/hda2
label=dos
table=/dev/hda
```

The **other** command specifies the volume with the boot files for the non-Linux operating system. The **label** command is the same as in the Linux section. The **table** command specifies the drive with partition information.

 There are two IDE hard disk controllers on a standard personal computer. You can connect each controller to a "master" and a "slave." The master on the first controller is known as *hda;* the slave on the first controller is known as *hdb.* The master on the second controller is known as *hdc;* the slave on the second controller is known as *hdd.* If you have one hard disk and a CD-ROM drive, the hard disk is most commonly located on hda, whereas the CD-ROM drive is most commonly located on hdb.

Custom LILO Commands

You can customize LILO with the **append** command, which passes messages to your Linux kernel. If you just installed your first Ethernet network card and you know that its IRQ (interrupt request) is set to 12 and its I/O (input/output) address is set to 0x300, you can add the following command to your lilo.conf file:

```
append="ether=12,0x300,eth0"
```

The format for an Ethernet card is **ether=*IRQ, I/O, device***. Because this is your first Ethernet card, the device is eth0. Your second Ethernet card would be eth1.

Alternately, if you have an older Linux kernel, prior to version 2.2.1, you can use the **mem** command to help Linux recognize your RAM above 64MB. For example, the following command tells Linux to recognize your RAM up to 192MB:

```
append="mem=192M"
```

Linux kernels starting with version 2.2.1 should recognize all of the RAM on your computer.

If you edit LILO in any way, use a text editor. Make sure you have a rescue disk ready with your old LILO, and then run the **/sbin/lilo** command to load your new lilo.conf file.

 You can enter **append** commands directly at the LILO **boot:** prompt, but without typing "append". For example, if you wanted to boot Linux and help it recognize your RAM up to 192MB, you would use the **linux mem=192M** command.

Troubleshooting LILO

The LILO prompt can help you troubleshoot boot problems. For example, you know you have a problem when you only see part of the LILO **boot:** prompt, as shown here:

```
LI
```

When you see only this part of the prompt, there are two possible causes. You may have moved or deleted the secondary boot loader file, normally /boot/boot.b. Alternately, your BIOS (Basic Input/Output System) may have trouble reading your hard disk. These are also potential causes if all you see is **L.**, **LIL?**, or **LIL-**.

Alternately, if you don't see any letters when you expect to see the LILO **boot:** prompt, it means that your computer is having trouble finding your lilo.conf file. It may even be missing from your MBR.

If your secondary boot loader (boot.b) file is still present, check the configuration of your hard disk against the specifications listed in your BIOS menu. You may also have the problem described in Chapter 4, where the Linux /boot directory is mounted on a volume that ends above cylinder 1023.

On an older hard drive, cylinder 1023 may be as low as 512MB.

If you're removing Linux from your computer, you can remove LILO from your MBR with the MS-DOS **fdisk /MBR** command. If you really want to do this, load the **fdisk** command on a bootable floppy disk first.

Mounts (/etc/fstab/)

The volumes that you configured when you installed Linux, plus a few more, are included in the /etc/fstab/ file. The volumes shown in Figure 6.1 are mounted when Linux boots on your computer.

Mount File Format

The key information is shown in the first three columns of the /etc/fstab/ file. The other columns are included for reference:

➤ *Volume*—The first column indicates the subject volume. For example, the volume in the first line of Figure 6.1 corresponds to the first logical drive on the first hard disk on your computer.

➤ *Mount point*—The second column corresponds to the directory mounted on the specified volume. For example, the second line of Figure 6.1 shows the /boot directory mounted on the first partition on the first hard drive.

➤ *Format*—The third column corresponds to the way each volume is mounted. For example, ext2 corresponds to the second extended file system.

➤ *Mount option*—The fourth column specifies the types of users that can mount, whether they can read or write, and what can be run from the mounted directory.

```
* <volume>          <mount point>      <format> <mount option> <dump>   <mount order>
/dev/hda5           /                  ext2     defaults       1        1
/dev/hda1           /boot              ext2     defaults       1        2
/dev/cdrom          /mnt/cdrom         iso9660  noauto,owner,ro 0       0
/dev/fd0            /mnt/floppy        auto     noauto,owner   0        0
none                /proc              proc     defaults       0        0
none                /dev/pts           devpts   gid=5,mode=620 0        0
/dev/hda6           swap          ▮    swap     defaults       0        0
~
~
~
~
~
~
~
```

Figure 6.1 A sample /etc/fstab file.

➤ *Dump*—The fifth column specifies whether to dump changes to the memory cache or directly to the mounted volume. If this value is 0, data is written directly to the file system. If the value is 1, data is stored in the cache.

➤ *Mount order*—The sixth column determines when the volume is mounted. If this value is 0, the volume is normally mounted by users after they log in. If this value is 1, the volume is mounted when you start Linux. Mount order is commonly associated with the root (/) directory. If this value is 2, Linux mounts another directory after the root directory.

Mount File Flexibility

The /etc/fstab file is flexible. You can mount additional volumes through this file, but you should test this function before you add volumes. For example, if you've installed both Microsoft Windows and Linux on the same computer, you might be able to mount your Windows C: drive with the following command:

```
mount -t vfat /dev/hda2 /disks/c
```

This command mounts a volume that is formatted to VFAT (Virtual File Allocation Table), which is Microsoft's virtual file system that works with long file names (-**t** corresponds to type). The volume is the second primary partition (/dev/hda2). The mount point is the /disks/c directory.

If you have a VFAT volume mounted on /dev/hda2, this command should work. If it does, you can verify it with the **ls /disks/c** command. You can then make sure Linux mounts this volume whenever you boot by entering the following line in your /etc/fstab file:

```
/dev/hda2      /disks/c      vfat    defaults      0      2
```

The **defaults** option allows any user to mount, read, and write to the given directory. The **0** means that files transferred to and from this directory are cached. The **2** refers to directories that are mounted after the root directory.

If you need to add additional Linux volumes, you can use tools like fdisk or fips to create them. You can then format them with the **mke2fs** command to set up the Linux second extended file system (ext2fs) or the **mkswap** command to set up another swap partition. Once formatted, you can mount a directory on a new volume by adding its entry into the /etc/fstab file.

Loading Sequence

To see how Linux loads on your computer, analyze the /etc/inittab file in detail. In essence, when Linux starts up, it loads scripts in a three-stage process. First, it loads system initialization scripts from an rc.sysint file. Second, it loads scripts associated with different run levels in various rc.d directories. Third, it loads custom scripts in an rc.local file.

When these steps are complete, Linux then sets up your system in a specific run level, as defined by the initdefault variable. Whatever you do, don't set initdefault to 0 or 6. If you do, your system will shut down or reboot whenever you try to start Linux.

Initialization Scripts (rc.sysinit)

The first resource control file to run when you boot Linux is the rc.sysinit file. It starts several programs. It also mounts volumes as defined in the /etc/mtab file as well as some basic network programs.

> The /etc/mtab file lists the volumes from /etc/fstab that are mounted when Linux starts on your computer.

The rc.sysinit script also sets up your PATH variable, which defines where Linux looks for different commands. To check your current path settings, type the command "**echo $PATH**". You might get the following result:

```
/usr/local/bin:/bin:/usr/bin:/usr/X11R6/bin:/home/mj/bin
```

When you type in a command such as **who,** Linux looks through the directories listed in the PATH variable for this command. If you don't include the current directory in PATH, this can be inconvenient. For example, let's assume you created a script named goodidea in your home directory. If you were in your home directory, you'd have to type the **./goodidea** command to run the script. This would not be necessary if your PATH variable included the dot (.).

> There are advantages and disadvantages to including a dot (.) in your PATH variable. For security reasons, this is generally discouraged; *crackers* (malicious users) could place destructive programs with familiar names in users' local directories. For example, if a cracker inserted a program named *who* in your home directory, and you had the dot in your PATH variable, you'd run whatever the cracker wanted you to run when you typed the **who** command. These types of programs are sometimes known as *Trojan horses.* This is not a problem, of course, if you're running a standalone Linux computer.

Run Level Scripts (rc#.d)

The /etc/inittab file runs daemons and scripts at each run level. If you want to see what is run at each level, list the files in the applicable directory. For example, if you want to see what programs are started and shut down when you halt (run level 0), type the following command:

```
ls /etc/rc.d/rc0.d
```

The commands typically start with *S* (for start) or *K* (for kill). For example, if you see the **K23nfsd** command, you know that Linux kills the Network File System (NFS) daemon at the applicable run level. You can see a typical list of daemons and other commands used by your run level scripts in Figure 6.2.

The scripts in each rc.d run level link to files in the init.d directory. Depending on your distribution, you may find the /init.d directory under /etc or /etc/rc.d. The /init.d directory includes scripts that you can use to start or stop daemons after Linux boots on your system. Two example daemons in this directory are Apache (httpd) and the Network File System (nfsd).

The Local Run Level Script (rc.local)

If you have your own scripts that you want run whenever you start Linux, add them to the rc.local shell script. They are run after Linux sets up in the initdefault run level.

Common Run Levels

You learned about run levels in Chapter 3. The following is a list of run levels used by all distributions:

➤ *Shutdown*—All distributions use run level 0 for shutdowns. This level ends all programs and daemons. This level is also known as *halt*. The root or superuser can start this run level with the **init 0** command.

```
[mj@linuxtester mj]$ ls /etc/rc.d/init.d/
anacron     dualconf       identd      killall     network   random    xfs
apmd        dualconf.old.1 ipchains    kudzu       nfs       rwhod     ypbind
arpwatch    functions      irda        linuxconf   nfslock   sendmail
atd         gpm            kdcrotate   lpd         pcmcia    single
crond       halt           keytable    netfs       portmap   syslog
[mj@linuxtester mj]$
```

Figure 6.2   Sample list of daemons.

➤ *Reboot*—All distributions use run level 6 to reboot. This is a two-step process. It first moves Linux to run level 0. When Linux reboots, it moves to a standard multiuser level, usually 2 or 3, depending on your Linux distribution. The root or superuser can start this run level with the **init 6** command.

➤ *Single User*—All distributions have a single-user mode. It is standard when you use a rescue disk to boot your Linux computer. You can also start single-user mode when you don't want anyone else using your Linux computer for administrative reasons. Generally, single-user mode is configured at run level 1 or S.

➤ *Multiuser*—All distributions have some form of multiuser run levels. Sometimes it's available with or without networking. It is generally at run level 2 or 3.

➤ *X Window*—Linux distributions use different graphical user interface (GUI) setups at run levels 3, 4, and/or 5.

You can change your default run level by changing the number associated with the initdefault variable in your /etc/inittab file. For example, you can change your default boot from the X Window to the command-line interface by entering the appropriate multiuser run level.

Only the root or superuser can run the **init** command. The superuser mode is sometimes also known as *sudo*.

Logins

If you've ever used Unix or Linux at the command line, you should be familiar with the following lines of code:

```
login:
Password:
```

Any successful login at the command line starts a command-line shell. The shell that it starts depends on the control files in your home directory.

Shells

A shell is in part a command-line interface for controlling various parts of your computer through the Linux kernel. In essence, it is set up to protect the kernel. If the kernel fails, you need to restart your computer. If your shell fails, you don't have to restart. Instead, you can kill the shell and log in to Linux again.

The shell you get depends on the option that is shown in the Linux password file, known as /etc/passwd. An example from this file for user mj is:

```
mj:x:501:501:michael jang:/home/mj:/bin/bash
```

The most common Linux shell is known as *bash*, which stands for the Bourne Again SHell. When you log in, bash starts to the requirements of its resource control file, known as .bashrc, which is located in your home directory. If you change your shell, you need to change the .profile file in your home directory and create a resource control file for your new shell. For example, if you wanted to use the shell known as *ash*, you'd need a resource control file named .ashrc.

 The dot in front of a file makes it hidden. You can list all files, hidden and otherwise, with the **ls -a** command.

A Note on Passwords

When you look at your /etc/passwd file, you might think your passwords are well hidden. However, if a cracker finds this file, he/she can easily determine your password, especially if you use dictionary words.

The most secure way to create a password is based on a combination of letters and numbers. For example, popular password cracking programs might find a dictionary-based password like *pepper* in a matter of minutes. In contrast, it would probably take the same program weeks to crack a password like *Ie29fteW* (which might stand for "I eat 29 fish tacos every Wednesday").

 In the Linux world, malicious users are known as *crackers*. Linux hackers are people who just want to make, or hack, better software. Crackers, on the other hand, try to crack into your passwords and software for destructive reasons.

Logouts, Cache, and Shutdowns

If you just turn off your Linux computer, you can easily lose data that you thought you saved. For example, when you save data to a floppy drive, Linux may not write to the drive until you unmount it.

It turns out that most of your available memory (RAM + swap partition) is dedicated to programs and cache. As you open more programs, the information in the cache is "flushed" to make room for additional incoming data.

Before you shut down Linux, be sure that you have closed all programs that might have data in your cache. There are several different commands that shut down your Linux system:

➤ *shutdown*—This command is the secure way to shut down your computer. Messages are sent to all of your users advising them of the coming shutdown. If you just want to send the warning, use the **shutdown -k** command. The **shutdown -t 100** command should give your users 100 seconds between the warning message and the time Linux starts shutting down. The **shutdown -c** command cancels any impending shutdown.

➤ *halt*—This command is equivalent to **shutdown -h now**, or **init 0**. If others are logged on to the Linux computer, they won't have any time to save their work.

➤ *reboot*—This command is equivalent to **shutdown -r now**, or **init 6**. Reboot goes to level 0, and then when Linux restarts, proceeds to your standard multiuser level, usually 2 or 3. If others are logged on to the Linux computer, they won't have any time to save their work.

➤ *Ctrl+Alt+Del*—This command is equivalent to the **reboot** command. It is not a normal Linux command, but is often added to the /etc/inittab file. Unfortunately, this command may be available to all users, not just the root or superuser. For this reason, you should probably delete this entry from your /etc/inittab file. Because Ctrl+Alt+Del is commonly used in Microsoft operating systems, the frustration of one user may affect all other users on your system.

➤ *Power failure signal*—Some distributions include power failure signals in their /etc/inittab file. When an uninterruptible power supply (UPS) starts sending power signals to your computer, you have just a few minutes to save your work before you completely lose power. The power failure signal sends messages similar to the **shutdown** command.

On some versions of Linux, regular users may be able to use some of these commands with or without their passwords. You may need to change the permissions for commands like **halt** and **shutdown** to keep your users from shutting down Linux.

 You can log out of a command-line interface shell with three different commands: **logout**, **exit**, and Ctrl+D.

Practice Questions

Question 1

> You have a dual-boot system with Microsoft Windows and Caldera Linux, and their labels in the lilo.conf file are dos and openlinux, respectively. Which of the following commands can you use at the LILO **boot:** prompt? [Check all correct answers]
>
> ❏ a. **linux**
>
> ❏ b. **dos**
>
> ❏ c. **linux ether=10,0x330,eth1**
>
> ❏ d. **openlinux**

Answers b, c, and d are correct. Your options for operating systems are based on their labels as specified in the lilo.conf file, which are specified in this example as dos and openlinux. You can also enter appropriate **append**-type commands at the LILO **boot:** prompt. Because linux is not a label in the lilo.conf file, answer a is not correct.

Question 2

> While in Linux, you accidentally delete your lilo.conf file from your /etc directory, as well as your MBR. You want to restore your MBR so that you can boot into Linux again in the future. You have a printout of your original lilo.conf file. Which of the following should you do?
>
> ○ a. Create a new lilo.conf file that conforms to the requirements of the operating systems on your computer. Run the **lilo** command to write the result to your MBR.
>
> ○ b. Create a new lilo.conf file that conforms to the requirements of the operating systems on your computer. Run the **fdisk /MBR** command to write the result to your MBR.
>
> ○ c. Reboot your computer. When you see the LILO **boot:** prompt, enter the parameters of your lilo.conf file.
>
> ○ d. Run the Linuxconf utility to rebuild your lilo.conf file. Use the **lilo** command to write the result to your MBR.

Answer a is correct. You have a printout of your lilo.conf file, so all you need to do is to enter the information in a text editor and save it to your Master Boot Record with the **lilo** command. Because the **fdisk /MBR** command writes an MS-DOS boot record to your MBR, answer b is incorrect. If you reboot your computer without a lilo.conf file, you won't see a LILO **boot:** prompt. Therefore, answer c is incorrect. Although the Linuxconf utility can be used to rebuild the lilo.conf file, Linuxconf is a utility typically available only on Red Hat Linux. Therefore, answer d is incorrect.

Question 3

You're running a distribution with Linux kernel 2.0.36. You just installed 128MB of RAM for a total of 256MB. You also installed a second Ethernet network card. You set the IRQ of this card to 11 and the I/O memory address to 0x320. Which of the following commands should you set at the LILO **boot:** prompt?

○ a. **linux ether=0x320,11,eth0 mem=128M**

○ b. **linux ether=0x320,11,eth0 mem=256M**

○ c. **linux ether=11,0x320,eth1 mem=128M**

○ d. **linux ether=11,0x320,eth1 mem=256M**

Answer d is correct. These commands add information to your lilo.conf file. The format for the Ethernet card is **ether=*IRQ, I/O, device***. Because this is your second Ethernet card, it corresponds to the eth1 device. The memory that you append is the total RAM on your computer, not just the RAM you recently added. All of the information in answer a does not meet the requirements; therefore, it is incorrect. Answer b has the correct memory level, but is still incorrect. Answer c has the wrong memory level, so it is also incorrect.

Question 4

> You've installed Windows 2000 and S.u.S.E. Linux 7.0 on the same computer. Your computer has three regular IDE hard disks and one regular ATAPI CD-ROM drive. The CD-ROM is in the slave position of the secondary controller. Windows 2000 is installed on the first partition of the first hard disk of the primary controller. S.u.S.E. Linux 7.0 is installed on the first partition of the first hard disk of the secondary controller. Which of the following groups of commands would properly represent these operating systems in a lilo.conf file? Assume the first command represents Windows 2000, and the second command represents S.u.S.E. 7.0.
>
> ○ a. **other=/dev/hda1: root=/dev/hdd1**
>
> ○ b. **root=/dev/hda1: root=/dev/hdc1**
>
> ○ c. **other=/dev/hda1: root=/dev/hdc1**
>
> ○ d. **other=/dev/hda1: root=/dev/hda2**

Answer c is correct. The **other** label represents a non-Linux operating system (Windows 2000), and the **root** command tells LILO the mount location of the root directory for S.u.S.E. Linux 7.0. The first partition of the first hard disk on the first controller is hda1, whereas hdc1 is the first partition of the first hard disk of the second controller (i.e., third in line). Because hdd1 represents the first partition of the second drive on the second controller, answer a is incorrect. The **root** command looks for Linux boot files, so answer b is incorrect. Because hda2 is the second partition of the first hard disk, answer d is incorrect.

Question 5

> You boot your computer, and instead of the standard LILO **boot:** prompt, all you see is **LI**. Which of the following should you check?
>
> ○ a. Make sure you didn't accidentally delete your vmlinuz file.
>
> ○ b. Make sure that the BIOS settings for your hard disk are still correct.
>
> ○ c. Make sure you didn't accidentally delete your lilo.conf file.
>
> ○ d. Make sure that you didn't accidentally delete your /etc/inittab file.

Answer b is correct. Seeing only part of the LILO **boot:** prompt could also indicate a problem with your /boot/boot.b bootloader file. The LILO file starts your Linux kernel, so a deletion of the vmlinuz file wouldn't affect you until you chose

Linux at the LILO **boot:** prompt. Therefore, answer a is incorrect. If you deleted your lilo.conf file, you wouldn't see any part of the LILO **boot:** prompt; therefore, answer c is incorrect. Because the /etc/inittab file is run after the Linux kernel, which is started by LILO, you won't see a problem until after the Linux kernel loads. Therefore, answer d is incorrect.

Question 6

You're looking at your /etc/fstab file. What does the following line tell you? Hint: There is no CD-ROM drive on this computer, and only one disk controller is used.

```
/dev/hdb2    /big    vfat    defaults    0    0
```

○ a. The /big directory can be mounted on the second primary partition of the first hard disk. It is formatted to the Linux virtual file system. It isn't automatically mounted when you boot Linux. Files copied to this directory are cached before they're written to this volume.

○ b. The /big directory can be mounted on the second primary partition of the second hard disk. It is formatted to the Linux virtual file system. It isn't automatically mounted when you boot Linux. Files copied to this directory are cached before they're written to this volume.

○ c. The /big directory can be mounted on the second primary partition of the third hard disk. It is formatted to the MS-DOS VFAT system. It is automatically mounted when you boot Linux. Files copied to this directory are cached before they're written to this volume.

○ d. The /big directory can be mounted on the second primary partition of the second hard disk. It is formatted to the MS-DOS VFAT system. It isn't automatically mounted when you boot Linux. Files copied to this directory are cached before they're written to this volume.

Answer d is correct. The /dev/hdb2 device refers to the second primary partition of the second hard disk. The file system format is MS-DOS's VFAT. Because the last two numbers are 0, file transfers are cached, but the directory isn't automatically mounted when you boot Linux. Because this isn't the first hard disk, and there is no Linux virtual file system, answers a and b are incorrect. By definition, hdb2 is the second primary partition on the second hard disk; therefore, answer c is incorrect.

Question 7

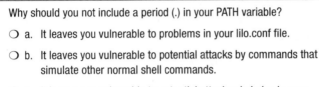

Why should you not include a period (.) in your PATH variable?

- ○ a. It leaves you vulnerable to problems in your lilo.conf file.
- ○ b. It leaves you vulnerable to potential attacks by commands that simulate other normal shell commands.
- ○ c. It leaves you vulnerable to potential attacks via holes in your firewall.
- ○ d. It leaves you vulnerable to potential attacks through cookies.

Answer b is correct. The dot in the PATH variable leaves you vulnerable to potential Trojan horses that masquerade as standard shell commands. Because the PATH variable is not started until after your Linux kernel is started, it has no affect on your lilo.conf file. Therefore, answer a is incorrect. Although a dot in the PATH variable leaves you vulnerable to other attacks, the dot itself does not breach a Linux firewall; therefore, answer c is incorrect. The dot is not related to whether you receive cookies from Web sites; therefore, answer d is incorrect.

Question 8

There are a number of directories and scripts under the rc.d and init.d directories. Which of the following statements best describes their function?

- ○ a. The rc.d resource control scripts are all divided by run levels as defined in the /etc/inittab file. They link to scripts in the init.d directory. You can run the init.d scripts independently after Linux boots on your computer.
- ○ b. The rc.d resource control scripts are all initialized at different run levels as defined in the /etc/inittab file. You can use the init.d scripts to control which run level you use.
- ○ c. The init.d resource control scripts are all initialized at different run levels as defined in the /etc/inittab file. All daemons in these scripts are started at different run levels. You can use the rc.d scripts to control which run level you use.
- ○ d. The init.d resource control scripts are all divided by run levels as defined in the /etc/inittab file. They link to scripts in the rc.d directory. You can run the rc.d scripts independently after Linux boots on your computer.

Answer a is correct. What Linux executes at different run levels is defined in the various numbered resource control directories under the rc.d directory. They link to scripts in the init.d directory, which you can run independently after Linux boots on your computer. Although you can use the **init** command to start different run levels in Linux, the init.d directory just holds scripts. Therefore, answer b is incorrect. Because there are no resource control scripts in the init.d directory, answers c and d are incorrect.

Question 9

> You like the looks of the shell named cash. You're currently using the shell named bash. If you wanted to change the shell that you get when you log in to your computer, which of the following should you do?
>
> ○ a. Delete the .bashrc resource control file in your home directory.
>
> ○ b. Delete the .profile configuration file in your home directory.
>
> ○ c. Change the shell as defined for the root user in the /etc/passwd file.
>
> ○ d. Change the shell as defined for your username in the /etc/passwd file.

Answer d is correct. The /etc/passwd file defines the shell that starts when you log in to a Linux computer. Deleting the .bashrc file is unrelated to making the shell named cash work for you; therefore, answer a is incorrect. Although you should revise the .profile file in your home directory, deleting it won't help customize your configuration for the shell named cash. Therefore, answer b is incorrect. Unless you're the root user, answer c is incorrect.

Question 10

> Which of the following commands actually reboots your computer?
>
> ○ a. **shutdown -h now**
>
> ○ b. **shutdown -c**
>
> ○ c. **halt**
>
> ○ d. **init 6**

Answer d is correct. If you run the **init 6** command as root or superuser, this command moves to run level 0 (halt), and then reboots. The **shutdown -h now** command shuts down your computer without delay. Therefore, answer a is incorrect. Because the **shutdown -c** command just cancels a current shutdown sequence, answer b is incorrect. The **halt** command is equivalent to **shutdown -h now**. Therefore, answer c is incorrect.

Need to Know More?

 Johnson, Dwight, ed. *SuSE Linux 6.0 Installation, Configuration and First Steps.* SuSE GmbH, Nürnberg, Germany, 1998. This book includes several excellent breakdowns of the workings of the LILO configuration file.

 Welsh, Matt, Lar Kaufman, and Matthias Kalle Dalheimer. *Running Linux.* O'Reilly & Associates, Sebastapol, CA, 1999. ISBN 1-56592-469-X. Possibly the key resource book on the Linux operating system. Although much of the information in this book is based on older versions of Linux, the basic data is concise, well written, and applicable today.

 Check out the Web site for the Linux Documentation Project at **www.linuxdoc.org**, which is the central repository for Linux manuals, HOWTOs, and a number of other book-length documents. Important HOWTOs for this chapter include the "Linux From Scratch-HOWTO," with detailed descriptions of run level scripts, and the "LILO mini-HOWTO" for information on the Linux Loader.

Commanding the Shell

- -

Terms you'll need to understand:

✓ Command-line interpreter

✓ Interactivity

✓ Command completion

✓ Environment variables

✓ Shell variables

✓ stdin, stdout, stderr

✓ Pipe

✓ **stty**

✓ **alias**

✓ **cd, ls**

✓ r, w, x, **chmod, umask**

Techniques you'll need to master:

✓ Understanding the command-line interpreter

✓ Explaining interactivity and command completion

✓ Describing user and systemwide shell configuration files

✓ Using and redirecting standard input, standard output, and standard error

✓ Running programs in the background

✓ Managing special shell characters including quotes and backslashes

✓ Setting up aliases

✓ Navigating Linux directories

✓ Understanding permissions

This chapter covers the basics of the shell, which is the Linux command-line interpreter for managing your computer. Although there are several shells available for Linux, today's standard default is the Bourne Again SHell, also known as *bash*. There are a number of files and commands that you can use to customize bash. This shell includes a number of useful features that help you as you work from the command line. And yes, bash also includes a number of key commands.

This chapter is closely related to Chapter 8. In this chapter, you learn the mechanics of the shell, and in Chapter 8, you learn about various commands to use with bash.

Managing the Shell

The Bourne Again SHell (bash) is a user interface to the Linux operating system. You use bash commands to run programs, manage your files, and interact with your hardware through the Linux kernel. You can configure bash with a number of local and systemwide files and variables.

The bash shell is sometimes known as a command-line interpreter, which is a user interface that responds to specific commands, such as **ls**, **cd**, or **cp**. It also responds to programs or scripts that you create.

As you move around the command line, keep in mind that Linux is case sensitive. In other words, the **ls** command lists the files in your current directory, whereas the **LS**, **Ls**, or **lS** commands are meaningless in any current Linux shell.

 Two advantages of the bash shell are its capability of retaining a history of previous commands and the ease with which you can complete a longer command. These characteristics are known as *interactivity* and *command completion*.

Interactivity

You can interact with a history of Linux commands. Open a command-line interface and type the **history** command. If you've previously used the command-line interface, you'll see a result similar to the one shown in Figure 7.1.

By default, you can repeat previous commands in several ways: The easiest way is to use the up and down arrow keys on your keyboard. Go to your command-line interface. When you press the up arrow key, you'll see the previous commands that you used, in order. The list may even include commands that you used during previous sessions. You can reverse the process with the down arrow key.

Alternately, if you remember the first letter of a command that you recently used, you can use an exclamation point (!) to recall that earlier command. For example, if you type "!l", Linux recalls the last time you used a command that started with

```
407  cd figures/
408  ls fig0[67]*
409  ls fig0[467]*
410  ls -i
411  cd ..
412  ls -i *.txt
413  ls
414  cd figures/
415  ls
416  ls fig[04-07]*
417  touch fig10 fig11
418  touch fig12 fig13 fig14
419  ls fig[10-14]
420  ls -r
421  ls -ltr
422  cd ..
423  ls -ltr
424  ls -lr
425  ls -lFr
426  ls -lFri
427  ls -lt
428  ls -itr
429  ls -dir
430  history
[mj@linuxtester mj]$
```

Figure 7.1   Output from the **history** command.

the letter *l* and runs that command. If you used more than one command that started with *l* you can type more letters to distinguish between commands.

Command Completion

Linux shells allow you to use the Tab key to complete commands. With bash, you only need to type part of a command. For example, if you wanted to use the **uncompress** command on a compressed file, type the following letters:

unc

When you press the Tab key, bash completes the command for you. If there is more than one command in your shell that starts with *unc*, press the Tab key again, and you'll see a list of these commands.

Configuring the Shell

There are two sets of configuration files for any shell. Some are systemwide; in other words, they affect all users on your Linux computer. Others are user specific and are stored in a user's home directory. Chapter 6 covered the user-specific configuration files known as .bashrc and .profile.

Depending on your distribution, there are up to four systemwide configuration files for bash: /etc/environment, /etc/profile, /etc/login, and /etc/bashrc. Within these files are two different kinds of variables: *environment variables*, which stay with you even if you change shells, and *shell variables*, which remain constant only as you navigate within a specific shell.

You can create your own shell variable; for example, you can assign the **ls** command to the name *test*, as follows:

```
test=ls
```

You can then run the **ls** command with the following command (note the back quotes around `` `$test` ``):

```
echo `$test`
```

An example of an environment variable is HISTORY. The value determines the number of previous commands that are saved. For example, if you were to run the following command, your shell would remember the last 400 commands that you used:

```
HISTORY=400
```

As an environment variable, HISTORY stays with you from shell to shell.

 Environment variables are generally in uppercase letters. Shell variables may have a combination of uppercase and lowercase letters as well as numbers.

You can move to a different shell at any time. If you've installed the Korn, C, or Bourne shell on your Linux computer, you can start it with the **ksh**, **csh**, or **sh** command, respectively.

 You can export a shell variable. For example, if you have a shell variable named test, you can export it for use with other shells with the **export test** command.

Making the Shell Work for You

There are a number of techniques that you can use with your shell. You can direct the output of one command to a file or even another command. You can set up aliases to define the commands of your choice. You can also move a running program to a background, which saves you the trouble of opening up another virtual terminal or console.

You have flexibility in the commands that you use. There are two different kinds of "wildcard" characters that help you represent more than one file. Linux allows you to use three different kinds of quote characters to manage the input to a command.

Standard Input, Standard Output, and Standard Error

Linux consists of three data streams: data goes in, data comes out, and errors go out a different direction. These concepts are also known as standard input, standard output, and standard error.

 There are three input/output (I/O) channels: *standard input* (stdin), *standard output* (stdout), and *standard error* (stderr).

Standard input (stdin) comes from the keyboard to a command. For example, with the **ls c*** command the *c** is standard input to the **ls** command.

Standard output (stdout) is the result of a command. For example, the files that you see after typing the **ls** command are standard output, which is normally directed to your monitor.

If there is no stdout, there may be a standard error (stderr) message. This is also normally directed to your monitor.

There are two basic ways to redirect stdin, stdout, and stderr. You can pipe one of these data streams to another command, or you can redirect one of these streams to or from a file.

Redirecting Input and Output

One example of redirecting stdin is running a file full of data through a program. Let's assume you have a program called majorprogram, and your program data is typed into the program_data file. To combine these components, you would use the following command:

```
./majorprogram < program_data
```

This command directs each file name in the program_data file to majorprogram.

 The left arrow can work as well with regular commands; for example, the **less < /etc/passwd** command is equivalent to the **less /etc/passwd** command.

Similarly, you can redirect stdout. If you want to save your current list of files in a text file named currentfiles, you can use the following command:

```
ls > currentfiles
```

Alternately, if you want to save the error messages from your script named majorprogram in a file named errorlog, you can redirect the output from your script with the following command:

```
./majorprogram 2> errorlog
```

The **2>** redirects stderr output. The only problem with this redirection is that every time you have a new error, it overwrites your old error in the file named errorlog. So, if you want a full list of errors, use the following command:

```
./majorprogram 2>> errorlog
```

The double arrow writes output to the end of the noted file. You can use double arrows for stdout as well. For example, every time you run the following command, your current files are added to the end of the currentfiles text file:

```
ls >> currentfiles
```

Input and Output Pipes

As you can redirect stdin, stdout, and stderr to and from specific files, you can also pipe these data streams to other commands. If you want to review permissions on a large number of files, you might use two different commands:

```
ls -l > tempfiles
more tempfiles
```

The first command takes your current file listing and stores the result in a file named tempfiles. The second command allows you to read the tempfiles file, one screen at a time. Because your file list probably changes frequently, you should delete the tempfiles file as it becomes out of date.

Piping is convenient because it allows you to combine commands. For example, the following command does the work of the previous two:

```
ls -l | more
```

The pipe (|) takes the stdout from the **ls -l** command and sends the results as stdin to the **more** command. You don't need to create or delete any files, like tempfiles.

Running in the Background

Linux is a multitasking system. When you don't have additional terminals or virtual consoles available, you can still run multiple programs from a single command line. If you are running a program that takes 10 minutes to finish, you don't have to wait to run other programs.

There are two ways to make your program run in the background. For example, let's assume you have a script named test in your current directory. This script starts an alarm in an hour. You want to run test, but you want to keep working while you wait. To do this, you can run the following command:

```
./test &
```

The ampersand (&) sends program execution to the background, which returns you to the command-line interface.

Alternately, if you're running a program to calculate the value of pi to a large number of digits, such a program might take a while to complete. If you forget to use the ampersand (&), you will need another way to send the program to the background. You can use the following commands to do this:

```
<Ctrl>Z
bg
```

When you press Ctrl+Z, you suspend the program that's currently running in your shell. The **bg** command then sends the program to the background.

 There are other ways to get to another command-line interface. You can open additional virtual consoles as discussed in Chapter 3. If you're in a graphical user interface window, you can also open as many shell windows as your RAM can handle.

Special Shell Characters

Special shell characters regulate standard output (stdout). You may already have some special characters assigned to you in your shell. To check, run the **stty -a** command. An example based on the author's Corel Linux setup is shown in Figure 7.2.

As you can see in the figure, echo is one of the special characters. When it's on, whatever you type is shown on your screen. You can turn it off with the **stty -echo** command. Once the command executes, you may feel like you're typing blindly. You can turn echo back on with the **stty echo** command. Note the difference in the two commands: The dash turns the option off.

```
laptop:~# stty -a
speed 38400 baud; rows 32; columns 86; line = 0;
intr = ^C; quit = ^\; erase = ^?; kill = ^U; eof = ^D; eol = <undef>; eol2 = <undef>;
start = ^Q; stop = ^S; susp = ^Z; rprnt = ^R; werase = ^W; lnext = ^V; flush = ^O;
min = 1; time = 0;
-parenb -parodd cs8 -hupcl -cstopb cread -clocal -crtscts
-ignbrk -brkint -ignpar -parmrk -inpck -istrip -inlcr -igncr icrnl ixon -ixoff -iuclc
-ixany -imaxbel
opost -olcuc -ocrnl onlcr -onocr -onlret -ofill -ofdel nl0 cr0 tab0 bs0 vt0 ff0
isig icanon iexten echo echoe echok -echonl -noflsh -xcase -tostop -echoprt echoctl
echoke
laptop:~# stty -echo
laptop:~# Desktop        fig04-01.bmp  figures
laptop:~# laptop:~# ls
Desktop         fig04-01.bmp  figures
laptop:~# ▮
```

Figure 7.2   Typical setup for special shell characters.

Note: The **stty** *-echo option is a relic of computer input from teletype machines.*

You can assign different sets of special characters with the **stty** command. For example, if you want to suspend a program with Ctrl+X (instead of Ctrl+Z), run the following command:

```
stty susp ^X
```

The carat (^) is used to represent the Ctrl key on the keyboard. You can also change other settings that you see in the output to the **stty** -a command. For a full list of settings that you can set or suspend, refer to the man page for **stty**.

Note: The carat (^) is above the number 6 on a standard U.S. keyboard.

Wildcards

There are two other special characters in Linux commands, which are variations on the Microsoft concept of "wildcards." The characters are the asterisk (*) and the question mark (?). The asterisk represents any number of numbers or letters. Each question mark represents one alphanumeric character. For example, if you were to run the following command, you'd get a list of all files that start with the letter *a*:

```
ls a*
```

If you have a file named a, it would be part of this list. In contrast, if you were to run the following command, you'd get a list of all files with two alphanumeric characters starting with *a*:

```
ls a?
```

If you have a file named a, it would not be a part of this list. You can also perform more complex file searches with commands like the following:

```
ls ?at?
```

This command returns files with names like cate, kata, mate, and so on. It would not return files like Catherine, matador, or cat.

 You can use wildcards to apply a command to a number of files. For example, if you were to use the **cat b*** command, you would see the contents of all files in your directory that start with the letter *b*. If the text consists of too much data for you to read on your monitor, you can direct the data to a file; the **cat b* >> b-files** command directs the text of each file that starts with the letter *b* to the file named b-files. The double arrow (>>) ensures that each file that starts with *b* gets appended to the end of the b-files file.

You can even define special characters in more detail with brackets ([]). For example, if you want to see all files in your directory between fig07-01.tif and fig07-06.tif, you can run the following command:

```
ls fig07-0[1-6].tif
```

Alternately, the following command serves the same purpose:

```
ls fig07-0[123456].tif
```

The characters in brackets define the range that you're searching for. This method works just as well with upper- or lowercase letters. For example, if you're searching for all files between fig07-01a.tif and fig07-01g.tif, you can run the following command:

```
ls fig07-01[a-g].tif
```

You can also use multiple search terms; for example, the following command searches for all file names between fig07-01a.tif and fig07-06g.tif:

```
ls fig07-0[1-6][a-g].tif
```

Quotes in the Shell

There are three types of quote characters on your keyboard: the single quote ('), the double quote ("), and the back quote (`). When applied to standard input (stdin), they perform different functions.

Note: You can find the back quote key above the Tab key on a standard U.S. keyboard.

The difference between these characters is in how they affect variables, such as $NAME, and shell commands, such as **date**. With any pair of quotes, the shell sends everything inside the quotes to the command. In the following example, the command **echo** is used. In detail, the difference is as follows:

➤ *Single quotes*—The shell does not process any variables or commands within the quotes.

➤ *Double quotes*—The shell processes variables, such as $NAME, but does not process any commands within the quotes.

➤ *Back quotes*—The shell tries to process every word in quotes as a command. If there are variables, they are evaluated first, and then processed as a command. Thus, if $NAME were in back quotes, it would be processed, and then the result (Michael) would be evaluated as a command.

You can see how this works in the following examples. Assume $NAME=Michael. Remember, **date** is a command that returns the current date and time:

```
echo Welcome $NAME, the date is date
echo 'Welcome $NAME, the date is date'
echo "Welcome $NAME, the date is date"
echo "Welcome $NAME, the date is `date`"
```

The first command has no quotes. The second command is surrounded by single quotes. The third command is surrounded by double quotes. The final command has double quotes as well as back quotes around the command **date**. These commands return the following results:

```
Welcome Michael, the date is date
Welcome $NAME, the date is date
Welcome Michael, the date is date
Welcome Michael, the date is Sat Sep 9 11:16:33 PDT 2000
```

Without quotes, the shell interprets the $NAME variable, but does not run the **date** command. With single quotes, the shell doesn't interpret variables or commands. With double quotes, the result is similar to the result without quotes. If a command is in back quotes, the shell interprets the command.

You can take advantage of back quotes. For example, if you want to run a program on several data files that happen to end in .dat, you can run a command like **./majorprogram `cat *.dat`**.

Backslashes

A backslash (\) tells the shell to ignore spaces (or other special characters). You can use it to manage a directory like the My Documents directory on a Microsoft Windows partition. For example, if you mounted your Windows C: drive on the /dos directory, you could list the contents of the My Documents directory with the **ls /dos/My\ Documents** command. With the backslash, the shell ignores the space and sends the request as stdin to the **ls** command. Without the backslash, the shell would look for the contents of the /dos/My directory.

You can also use the backslash for special characters, like the question mark (?) or asterisk (*).

 When you use the backslash, you are "escaping" the functionality of the next space or character.

Aliases

An example of a shell variable is alias. This variable lists the commands that you can substitute for others. One common alias is:

```
alias dir="ls -l"
```

There is no **dir** command native to Linux. But when you set this alias, you can run the **dir** command instead of **ls -l**. However, because any alias is a shell variable, the alias that you set does not apply if you change shells.

You can delete an alias with the **unalias** command. For example, if you set up **dir** as an alias for **ls -l**, the **unalias dir** command removes this link.

Some Linux distributions set up several aliases by default on your shell. To check your currently active aliases, type the **alias** command.

Navigational Commands

There are two basic navigational commands for getting around the shell. The **cd** command lets you navigate between directories. The **ls** command lets you know what's in a directory (including other directories).

cd

The change directory command is known as **cd**. Those of you familiar with MS-DOS may find a number of similarities between MS-DOS and Linux **cd** commands. Typical **cd** commands are shown in Table 7.1.

A command associated with **cd** is **pwd**. The **pwd** (present working directory) command allows you to check your current directory. You may find it useful to check which directory you are in before you change directories.

 If you want to change to your home directory, use the **cd ~** command. If you're in root or superuser mode, this command brings you to the root user's home directory, /root.

ls

The **ls** command is versatile. Not only does it allow you to list the files and directories in your current directory, but with the proper switches, you can also find the permissions and size of a file. It allows you to check ownership, differentiate between file types, and sort the result in several ways. You can review some examples of this command in Table 7.2.

Perhaps the most important command in this series is **ls -l**, which lists all files in the current directory including size, owner, and permissions. View an example of the result of this command in Figure 7.3.

 The **ls** command is important. Know the switches that can be used with **ls**, especially **-a**, **-F**, **-i**, and **-r**. These switches can be used in any combination. A common combination is **ls -ltr**, which lists your files, with permissions, from oldest to newest. Also, each file output from the **ls** command has its own line, which can be made to work with the **wc** command discussed in Chapter 8.

Table 7.1	cd commands.
Command	**Result**
cd ..	Moves up one directory level. For example, if you're currently in the /home/mj directory, this moves you to the /home directory.
cd ../..	Moves up two directory levels. For example, if you're currently in the /etc/rc.d/rc0.d directory, this moves you to the /etc directory.
cd /home/mj	Changes to the home directory of user mj.
cd ~	Changes to your home directory.

Table 7.2	ls commands.*
Command	**Result**
ls	Lists all nonhidden files in the current directory in alphabetical order.
ls -a	Lists all files in the current directory including hidden files.
ls -r	Lists all nonhidden files in the current directory in reverse alphabetical order.
ls -F	Lists all files by type. The character at the end of each file indicates the file type. For example, a forward slash (/) represents a directory, an asterisk (*) is associated with an executable file, and an "at" (@) represents a linked file.
ls -i	Lists files with *inode* numbers. An inode number represents the location of a file on a volume. Two or more files with the same inode number are two different names for the *identical* file.
ls -l	Lists all the files in the current directory including the current directory (.) and the parent directory (..). Also lists the size, owner, and permissions associated with each file in what is known as *long listing* format.
ls -t	Lists files by the last time they were changed; most recent files are listed first.
ls -u	Lists files by the last time they were accessed; most recent files are listed first.

*Directories are included in all file lists. In Linux, a directory is just a special kind of file. A file is accessed anytime it is read, written to, or executed.

```
[mj@linuxtester mj]$ ls -l
total 192
drwxr-xr-x   5 mj        mj          4096 Aug 20 19:25 Desktop
drwxr-xr-x   2 mj        mj          4096 Sep 11 14:17 figures
drwx------   2 mj        mj          4096 Aug 30 13:11 nsmail
-rw-r--r--   1 mj        mj         76890 Sep 11 12:20 q
-rw-rw-r--   2 mj        mj          7324 Sep 11 12:21 shutdown.txt
drwxrwxr-x   2 mj        mj          4096 Sep 10 16:31 test
-rw-rw-r--   1 root      root           0 Sep 11 14:17 tests
-rwxrwxrwx   1 jm        jm         76890 Sep 11 12:43 ttaatt
-rw-rw-r--   2 mj        mj          7324 Sep 11 12:21 ttt
lrwxrwxrwx   1 mj        mj            12 Sep 11 12:20 vvv -> shutdown.txt
[mj@linuxtester mj]$ _
```

Figure 7.3 A long listing (**ls -l**) in the current directory.

Permissions

As you can see in Figure 7.3, each file is associated with owners, groups, and a series of permissions. The permissions associated with a file are assigned to owners, groups, and everyone else on your Linux computer. Take a look at the following entry, which is a long listing for the batterup file:

```
-rwxrw-r--  1  mj  users  7326  Jan  12  09:09  batterup
```

Permissions are based on the characters on the left of the listing. The 10 characters determine what different users can do with this file. If the first character is not a dash (-), it's not a regular file. It could be a directory (d) or a file linked (l) to another.

The remaining characters can be grouped in threes. The subsequent three characters shown after the dash are *rwx*. In other words, the owner of the file named batterup can read (r), write (w), and execute (x) this file.

The next three characters shown are *rw-*. Users in the same group as the file owner can read this file (r) or edit and write to this file (w). These users cannot execute the file.

The final three characters are *r--*. Users who don't belong to the same group as the file owner can read this file. They can't write to it, nor can they execute it if it's a script.

You can set up these permissions using the following command:

```
chmod 764 batterup
```

Permissions are set with a three-number code. In the preceding command, the first number (7) sets permissions for the owner, the second (6) for the other users in the owners group, and the third (4) for everyone else. Each number represents all permissions given to the owner, group, or everyone else, as described in Table 7.3.

Table 7.3	Numeric permissions.*	
Permission	**Number**	**Comment**
r	4	= r(4)
w	2	= w(2)
x	1	= x(1)
rx	5	= r(4) + x(1)
rw	6	= r(4) + w(2)
wx	3	= w(2) + x(1)
rwx	7	= r(4) + w(2) + x(1)

*Observe how the number is based on the combined values of permissions; for example, the number associated with rx is 4 (the value of r) + 1 (the value of x).

Look at the permissions associated with the batterup file again. Because the first number is 7, the owner of this file has read (r), write (w), and execute (x) permission to this file. Because the second number is 6, other users in the owner's group have read (r) and write (w) permissions on this file. Because the third number is 4, everyone else has just read (r) permissions on this file.

Note: A number of commands in this chapter can only be executed by the root or super-user. If you want to experiment with one of these commands, type "su" and enter the root password when prompted.

umask

When you create a new file or directory, the permissions you get depend on the value of what is known as the *umask*. Open a command-line interface, and type the **umask** command. You may get an output like the following:

```
023
```

Before you interpret this number, you need a clear idea of the numeric value of permissions.

For example, if you gave everyone permissions to your files and directories, you would have read, write, and execute permissions for all users. As discussed in the previous section, these permissions correspond to the number 7 (r+w+x = 4+2+1). When applied to all users, they correspond to 777. You could set up the same permissions for all users on the batterup file with the following command:

```
chmod 777 batterup
```

However, the files and directories that you create generally don't have 777 permissions. The permissions that you get depend on the umask value. Type the **umask** command to find its current value, and then subtract the umask number from 777. If umask=023, then 777-023=754. Consequently, permissions equal 754. When you review the last section and Table 7.3, you can see that 754 corresponds to read, write, and execute permissions for the owner, read and execute permissions for members of the owner's group, and read permissions for all other users.

Practice Questions

Question 1

Which of the following are results of the interactivity and command completion characteristics of the Linux command line? (Note: You may want to reuse the **ls -ltr** command in this question. It is the most recent command that you used starting with the letter *l*.)

○ a. You can interact with your commands with the Tab key; the **stty** command sets up various control and function keys that complete certain commands.

○ b. You can interact with your previous commands using the up and down arrow keys; the Tab key allows you to select or complete a number of commands based on their first few letters.

○ c. You can type "!!" to recall your previous command; the right and left arrow keys allow you to complete a number of commands based on their first few letters.

○ d. You can type "!!" to recall your previous command; the **alias** command sets up various two-letter combinations that take the place of longer commands.

Answer b is correct. The history of a Linux shell allows you to use the up and down arrow keys to recall previously used commands. Although the **stty** command does allow you to set up various control key combinations for certain commands, it is unrelated to Linux command completion. Therefore, answer a is incorrect. Although you can use the !l command with your history to recall the previous command, you can't use the left and right arrow keys to complete previous commands. Therefore, answer c is incorrect. You cannot interact with previous commands using the Tab key. Although you can set up the **alias** command to set up any combination of letters to simulate longer commands, it is not related to command completion. Therefore, answer d is incorrect.

Question 2

> Which of the following statements most accurately describe the character-
> istics of environment and shell variables?
>
> ○ a. An environment variable applies to all users. A shell variable
> remains constant as you move from shell to shell.
>
> ○ b. An environment variable applies to all shells. A shell variable may
> change, or may not even exist, as you move from shell to shell.
>
> ○ c. An environment variable applies to all users. A shell variable may
> change, or may not even exist, as you move from shell to shell.
>
> ○ d. An environment variable applies to all shells. A shell variable
> remains constant as you move from shell to shell.

Answer b is correct. Although environment variables apply to all shells, a shell
variable changes from shell to shell (unless you export that variable). Because
environment variables may not apply to all users, answers a and c are incorrect.
Shell variables are not normally constant from shell to shell; therefore, answer d
is incorrect.

Question 3

> You have a large number of files in your home directory including the
> figures that you need for your seventh presentation. These figures are in
> binary format. Based on your company policy, you've organized your fig-
> ures in the following format: fig07-*xx*, where *xx* is the figure number. You
> want to see if you have figures 10 through 19. You don't want to see any
> other figures in the list. Which of the following commands will list just the
> figures that you want?
>
> ○ a. **ls -ltr fig07-***
>
> ○ b. **ls -ltr fig07-[10-19]**
>
> ○ c. **ls -ltr fig07-1?**
>
> ○ d. **ls -ltr fig07-1***

Answer c is correct. The question mark is a wildcard for the one character position. Because the asterisk is a wildcard for any number of characters, answer a is
incorrect. The bracketed search terms only work for one character at a time; you
would need **ls -ltr fig07-1[0-9]** for this to work. Therefore, answer b is incorrect.
Because the asterisk includes any number of characters, answer d could include
fig07-1, fig07-1000, and so on. Therefore, answer d is also incorrect.

Question 4

> You started a program in a command-line interface, and because you're not in a graphical user interface, you can't just click a button to start another shell. The program seems like it's going to run for a long time. You want it to keep running, but you need to check your email. What can you do? [Check all correct answers]
>
> ❏ a. Press Ctrl+C, and when you see the command-line interface, type the **bg** command to move the process into the background.
>
> ❏ b. Press Ctrl+Z, and when you see the command-line interface, type the **bg** command to move the process into the background.
>
> ❏ c. Press Ctrl+Alt+F2, and when you see the login screen, log in again. Your program will keep running in another virtual console. If F2 doesn't work, try F1, F3, or F4.
>
> ❏ d. Press Ctrl+Z, and when you see the command-line interface, restart the program using an ampersand (&) at the end. This resumes the process in the background. You will then see a command-line interface where you can run another program.

Answers b and c are correct. The Ctrl+Z command suspends a running process, and the **bg** command restarts the process in the background. You can use the Ctrl+Alt+Fx (x is a number from 1 to 6) command to start another virtual console. The program continues to run in your original console. Because the Ctrl+C command stops a running program, answer a is incorrect. Because your program is still running, you do not need to start it again. Although you could use an ampersand (&) if you hadn't already started your program, using it at this time means you would have to start your program again. Therefore, answer d is incorrect.

. . . .

Question 5

You've created a program called filemanager, which uses the files listed in the current directory. You just want to use file names, and you don't want to use any hidden file names. Which of the following commands is the most efficient way to feed data to the filemanager program?

○ a. **ls -l | filemanager**

○ b. **ls -a | filemanager**

○ c. **ls > filemanager**

○ d. **ls | filemanager**

Answer d is correct. The plain **ls** command outputs just the file names in the current directory. With the pipe (|), this information becomes standard input (stdin) for the filemanager program. The **ls -l** command outputs permissions, owners, and so on. Therefore, answer a is incorrect. The **ls -a** command outputs hidden files. Therefore, answer b is incorrect. Because answer c would overwrite your filemanager program with your current file list, answer c is incorrect.

Question 6

There are three different standard I/O channels. Which of the following methods is an allowable way to redirect these channels?

○ a. Stdin can be redirected from a file. If you have a number of input terms in the text file crabgrass and a script named runner, you can execute the **runner << crabgrass** command.

○ b. Stdout can be redirected to a file. If you have a number of input terms in the text file crabgrass and a script named runner, you can direct the output to a third file with the **runner crabgrass 2> otherfile** command.

○ c. Stderr can be redirected to a file. If you have a number of input terms in the text file crabgrass and a script named runner, you can direct the error to a third file with the **runner crabgrass >> logfile** command.

○ d. Stdin can be redirected from a file. Stdout can also be redirected to another file. If you have a number of input terms in the text file crabgrass and a script named runner, you can execute the **runner < crabgrass > otherfile** command.

Answer d is correct. You can direct standard input (stdin) from a file with the left arrow (<) switch. You can direct standard output (stdout) to a file with the right arrow (>) switch. You cannot redirect with a double left arrow (<<); therefore, answer a is incorrect. Because stdout cannot be redirected with the error redirect arrow (2>), answer b is incorrect. If you're redirecting standard error (stderr), you need to use 2>>, and not the double right arrow (>>). Therefore, answer c is incorrect.

Question 7

A user wants to open a text file from an MS-DOS directory named big memo.txt. Whenever he tries to open the file, he sees the following message:

```
big: No such file or directory
```

This user needs your help. Which of the following commands do you tell this user to run? This file is part of the /disks/c/data directory.

○ a. **vi /disks/c/data/big memo.txt**

○ b. **vi /disks/c/data/big\ memo.txt**

○ c. **vi /disks/c/data/big/ memo.txt /**

○ d. **vi /disks/c/data/big\memo.txt**

Answer b is correct. The backslash (\) keeps the shell from interpreting characters such as the question mark (?), asterisk (*), and space. The backslash in answer b allows the vi editor to see these characters for what they are, instead of interpreting them as wildcards or new files. Because there is no backslash that "escapes" the space in answers a and c, these answers are both incorrect. Because there is no space after the backslash, answer d opens the bigmemo.txt file; therefore, this answer is incorrect.

Question 8

Which of the following commands lists the files in your directory with inode numbers? The output should allow you to differentiate between regular files, directories, and executable files. It should also list the most newly revised file last.

- ○ a. **ls -ltr**
- ○ b. **ls -itr**
- ○ c. **ls -iFr**
- ○ d. **ls -dir**

Answer c is correct. The switches in this command give you inode numbers (**-i**), help you differentiate between regular files, directories, and executable files (**-F**), and set up the order so that the oldest file is first and the newest file is last (**-r**). A long listing does not give you inode numbers; therefore, answer a is incorrect. Nothing in answer b allows you to differentiate between files and directories, so it is also incorrect. Because answer d only gives you the inode number of the current directory, it is also incorrect.

Question 9

Which of the following values of umask corresponds to read and execute permissions for the file owner, write and execute permissions for other members of the owner's group, and execute permissions for other users on a Linux computer?

- ○ a. 531
- ○ b. 731
- ○ c. 246
- ○ d. 642

Answer c is correct. The umask is the value that you subtract from full read (r), write (w), and execute (x) permissions for each type of user. Read and execute permissions (4 +1) correspond to the number 5, so the first number of umask is (7-5=) 2. Write and execute permissions (2 +1) correspond to the number 3, so the second number of umask is (7-3=) 4. Execute permissions correspond to the number 1, so the third number of umask is (7-1=) 6.

Question 10

> What should you do before running the **chmod** command on a file?
>
> ○ a. Login as the owner of the **chmod** file.
>
> ○ b. Type the **su** command, and then type the root password when prompted.
>
> ○ c. Make sure the file is not hidden.
>
> ○ d. Ask the Linux administrator for help.

Answer b is correct. The **chmod** command requires root or superuser permissions; otherwise, anyone can change the permissions on the files in your home directory. The owner of the **chmod** file is the root user. You can make this command work by logging in as the root user; however, this practice is strongly discouraged. Therefore, answer a is incorrect. The hidden characteristics of a file do not affect the ability to run the **chmod** command on that file. Therefore, answer c is incorrect. Although a knowledgeable Linux administrator can help you with this problem, as a Certified Linux Professional, you should know how to use the **chmod** command. Therefore, answer d is incorrect.

Need to Know More?

Muster, John. *Unix Made Easy.* Osborne/McGraw-Hill, Berkeley, CA, 1996. ISBN 0-07882-173-8. A solid textbook for the command-line interface. Although this is a book on Unix, it is often used as a teaching text in conjunction with various Linux distributions.

The Web site at **http://linux.ctyme.com** is Mark Perkel's index to Linux **man** pages. If you don't have immediate access to a Linux command line or its **man** pages, this Web site includes a searchable online reference.

The Web site for the Linux Newbie Administrator Guide at **http://sunsite.auc.dk/linux-newbie/index.htm** is a good general reference for installing and configuring Linux. Section 5 of this online document includes Linux shortcuts and commands, with a focus on the command-line interface.

Using the Shell

Terms you'll need to understand:

- ✓ cp, mv, rm, ln
- ✓ mkdir, rmdir
- ✓ file
- ✓ cat
- ✓ head, tail
- ✓ more, less
- ✓ wc
- ✓ find, locate
- ✓ grep
- ✓ mdir, mmove, mcopy
- ✓ tar, gzip, gunzip
- ✓ du, df

Techniques you'll need to master:

- ✓ Creating, deleting, and linking files and directories
- ✓ Reading and paging through files from the top or the bottom
- ✓ Manipulating and finding files
- ✓ Using MS-DOS file tools
- ✓ Archiving and compressing multiple files (and vice versa)
- ✓ Finding the amount of space taken by files and directories, and on volumes

This chapter covers the execution of a number of different commands. The interpretation of these commands is based on the Bourne Again SHell (bash), discussed in Chapter 7. Some basic commands help you create and delete files and directories. Others help you read files in different ways. Some commands allow you to use the characteristics of a file. The bash shell even includes commands that allow you to copy to an MS-DOS floppy without mounting.

Using these commands, you can manipulate a group of files for backups and compressed storage as well as find the amount of space taken by each file and volume.

Creating and Deleting Files and Directories

A Linux directory is just a special file. Yet, the bash shell has special commands for creating and deleting directories. It's easy to create a file. You can copy from an existing file or save to the file name of your choice from an editor or another application. It's also easy to delete a file; so easy that some commands for deleting files can be dangerous.

 When you use the **cp**, **mv**, or **rm** command, the **-i** switch prompts for confirmation before overwriting a file. Alternately, each of these commands has a **-f** switch that overwrites existing files without prompting. The **cp** and **rm** commands also have a **-r** switch, which recursively copies or deletes subdirectories. When used in combination, the **-rf** switches can be quite dangerous, especially for the root or superuser.

cp

The simplest version of the copy command is **cp file1 file2**. The contents of file1 are copied and placed in destination file2. The destination file has a new creation date and inode number. Other copy commands can overwrite destination files under various circumstances. You can even use a switch for the **cp** command to copy the contents of one or more subdirectories. Examples of how the **cp** command works are shown in Table 8.1.

mv

If you want to rename a file in Linux, you move it. The **mv** command changes the name of a file. Unless you're moving a file to a different volume, everything about the file, including the inode number, stays the same. Examples of **mv** commands are shown in Table 8.2.

Table 8.1   cp commands.

Command	Result
cp file1 file2	Copies the contents of source file1 to destination file2. The destination file has a new creation date and inode number.
cp file* Dir1	Copies multiple files (with names starting with file) to a directory.
cp -f file1 file2	If you already have a file named file2, this command overwrites its contents without prompting.
cp -i file1 file2	If you already have a file named file2, this command prompts you for confirmation before overwriting this file.
cp -p file1 file2	Copies the contents of source file1 to destination file2. The destination file has the same inode number and creation date as the source file.
cp -r Dir1 Dir2	Copies the contents of the directory named Dir1, including sub-directories, to Dir2. The effect is recursive; in other words, if there are subdirectories under Dir1's subdirectories, their files and directories are also copied.
cp -u file1 file2	If you already have a file named file2, and file1 is newer, this command overwrites file2's contents without prompting.

Identical files have the same inode number, and normally, the **cp -p** command results in two files with the same inode number. But you can't have the same inode number on different volumes. The **cp -p** command doesn't work as intended if you're copying a file from one volume to another.

rm

You can use **rm** to remove files and directories. One of the reasons that administrators are advised to run Linux in root or superuser mode only when necessary is that small mistakes in this command can easily delete all of your Linux files. For

Table 8.2   mv commands.

Command	Result
mv file1 file2	Changes the name of a file from file1 to file2. If the source and destination files are located on the same volume, the files retain the same inode number.
mv file* Dir1	Moves multiple files to a directory.
mv -f file1 file2	If you already have a file named file2, this command overwrites its contents without prompting.
mv -i file1 file2	If you already have a file named file2, this command prompts you for confirmation before overwriting this file.

example, suppose you want to remove a group of temporary directories in your root directory: a.tmp, b.tmp, and c.tmp. You want to use the **rm -r *.tmp** command, but instead you type the following:

```
rm -r * .tmp
```

Because there is a space between the asterisk and **.tmp**, the shell assumes that you want to recursively delete all directories, and then delete the file named .tmp. The result would not be good.

 Even if you're the Linux administrator with root user privileges, don't log in as the root user. Small mistakes can lead to the deletion of all of the files on your Linux computer.

For this reason, it can be useful to enter the following **alias** command:

```
alias rm="rm -i"
```

This command makes sure that whenever you use the **rm** command, the shell prompts you for confirmation before you delete any file. Some Linux distributions set up this alias as a shell variable for root users. The key **rm** commands are shown in Table 8.3.

In

Instead of just copying or moving a file, you can link it. Links are common, especially for those programs that start at various run levels. When you link a file, you're creating another path to a currently existing file. For example, if both you and a colleague are working on a file named project, you can create a linked file in your home directory. Assume the project file is in the /home/jm

Table 8.3	rm commands.
Command	**Result**
rm file1	Deletes file1 without prompting for confirmation.
rm -d Dir1	Deletes Dir1 without prompting for confirmation
rm -i file1	Deletes file1 after prompting for confirmation from the user.
rm -f file2	If you already have a file named file2, this command overwrites its contents without prompting.
rm -r *	Removes files recursively; if there are any subdirectories in the current directory, this command deletes them (and all of their files) as well.

directory. To create a link to a file in mj's home directory, you would use the following command:

```
ln /home/jm/project /home/mj/project
```

When you work on either file, the change and results are visible and accessible to those who access both directories. This is sometimes known as a *hard link*. With a hard link, because both files retain the same inode number, both files are identical. If the original file is deleted, the hard-linked file remains in place with the original inode number.

 The **ln file1 file2** command leads to the same result as the **cp -p file1 file2** command.

One useful option for links is *symbolic mode*, which allows you to see the linked file. For example, suppose you were to run the following command:

```
ln -s /home/jm/project /home/mj/project
```

You would see the linked file when you run a long listing (**ls -l**) of that file. This is known as a *soft link*. The linked file has a different inode number. If the original file is deleted, the soft-linked file is also deleted.

mkdir

You can create directories with the **mkdir** command. The directory that you create does not have to be based in your current directory. You can make several levels of directories if you choose. You can also assign the permissions of your choice to the directory that you create. The key **mkdir** commands are shown in Table 8.4.

Table 8.4 mkdir commands.	
Command	**Result**
mkdir -p dir1/dir2	Creates a directory named dir2. If dir1 does not exist, the **-p** switch makes sure to create that directory as well. Both are created as subdirectories of the current directory.
mkdir -m 755/home/mj/dir3	Creates a directory named dir3 as a subdirectory in mj's home directory. The permissions (755) are rwx for the owner and r-x for other members of the group and everyone else.

rmdir

You can delete empty directories with the **rmdir** command. The directory that you remove does have to be based in your current directory. You can delete several levels of directories if the directory that you delete empties others. For example, with the following command, you can delete the directories named dir1 and dir3:

```
rmdir -p dir1/dir3
```

This command deletes directory dir3 if it is empty. If the only "file" in directory dir1 is dir3, this command also deletes directory dir1.

File Management Commands

The bash shell includes a number of commands to help you read files in different ways. You can verify different types of files, and you can read files from the top or from the bottom. This read can be limited to a few lines or it can set you up to page through the entire file. You can also count the lines, words, and alphanumeric characters within a file. Furthermore, you can search through a file with the search term of your choice.

Because it is difficult to define words or lines in binary files, most of these commands work best with text files.

file

Although some distributions differentiate between file types by color, there are no standard extensions in Linux. Executable files don't normally end in .exe, and document files may not end in .doc. The **file** command allows you view the type of each file. You can review how this works in Figure 8.1.

```
[mj@linuxtester log]$ file *
boot.log:          English text
boot.log.1:        English text
cron:              can't read `cron' (Permission denied).
cron.1:            can't read `cron.1' (Permission denied).
dmesg:             ASCII text
htmlaccess.log:    empty
lastlog:           data
maillog:           can't read `maillog' (Permission denied).
maillog.1:         can't read `maillog.1' (Permission denied).
messages:          can't read `messages' (Permission denied).
messages.1:        can't read `messages.1' (Permission denied).
netconf.log:       empty
netconf.log.1:     English text
secure:            can't read `secure' (Permission denied).
secure.1:          can't read `secure.1' (Permission denied).
sendmail.st:       empty
spooler:           empty
spooler.1:         empty
uucp:              directory
wtmp:              data
wtmp.1:            data
xdm-error.log:     English text
[mj@linuxtester log]$ 
```

Figure 8.1   Reviewing different file types.

As you can see in Figure 8.1, you are not able to see the file type if you don't have the proper permissions.

cat

The concatenate (**cat**) command sends the text of a file to standard output. You can use the **cat** command on any file. The following command sends the text of the file to your screen:

```
cat file
```

head and tail

The **head** and **tail** commands are like two sides of a coin. The **head** command provides you with a view of the first few lines of a file. The **tail** command provides you with a view of the last few lines of that same file. You can regulate the amount of the file that you see with switches. For example, if you were to use the following command, you'd see the first 15 lines of the bully.txt file.

```
head -n15 bully.txt
```

If you substitute **tail** for **head**, you'll see the last 15 lines of this file. Table 8.5 lists more switches for use with these commands.

more and less

The **more** and **less** commands aren't opposites like **head** and **tail**. They both start at the beginning of a text file. When you run these commands on a text file, you review the contents of the file one page at a time. The **less** command is more versatile; unlike **more**, it allows you to scroll up and down any large text file with the Page Up and Page Down buttons on your keyboard.

Because they can read text a little bit at a time, these commands can open a file more quickly than a text editor like vi. The **less** command also has some of the advantages of the vi editor, because you can use some vi commands to search through a file.

Table 8.5	head and tail commands.
Command	**Result**
head 400b bully.txt	You see the first 400 bytes of the file known as bully.txt.
tail 4k bully.txt	You see the final 4KB of the file known as bully.txt.
head 3m bully.txt	You see the first 3MB of the file known as bully.txt.
tail -n22 bully.txt	You see the final 22 lines of the file known as bully.txt.

Table 8.6 Commands that can be used after less is run on a text file.	
Command	Result
space	Pressing the spacebar on your keyboard scrolls forward one page in your screen.
Page Up	Scrolls back one page on your screen.
Page Down	Scrolls forward one page on your screen.
#z	# represents a number. The command **8z** scrolls forward eight lines in the file. If you do not use a number, this command is equivalent to the space command.
/abc	Searches through the file for the text string *abc*. This command is also used in the Linux vi text editor.

There are two sets of options with each command. A command like the following sets up the file named bigfile with line numbers:

```
less -N bigfile
```

Once the text file is open, you can run other commands as described in Table 8.6.

The **more** and **less** commands are also known as *pagers* because they allow you to review text files one page at a time.

File Manipulation Commands

There are several commands that allow you to learn about and search for and through different files. The **wc** command allows you to get a count of the number of lines, words, and characters in a file. The **find** and **locate** commands search for specific files. The **grep** command lets you search through a file for a text string without opening it.

wc

The **wc** command is fairly straightforward. With any text file, you have a certain number of lines, words, and characters. With the **wc** command, you can find all three characteristics. For example, suppose you were to check the showoff text file as follows:

```
wc showoff
```

You would get something like the following:

```
1914    9298    76066
```

Table 8.7	Examples of the wc command.*
Command	**Result**
wc -l showoff	Number of lines in the file showoff.
wc -w showoff	Number of words in the file showoff.
wc -c showoff	Number of characters in the file showoff.

You can use the -l, -w, and -c switches in any combination.

These numbers correspond to the number of lines, words, and characters in this file, respectively. You can get any individual figure based on the commands shown in Table 8.7.

find

The **find** command looks through directories and subdirectories for the file(s) of your choice. For example, if you want to find a file named fig07-02.tif, you could use the following command:

```
find / -name fig07-02.tif
```

This command searches in the root directory and all subdirectories for the fig07-02.tif file. This search can take quite some time. If you have more information, you may want to substitute a lower-level directory for the root (/).

With the **find** command, you can also use wildcards like the asterisk (*) and question mark (?) in your search term.

locate

An alternative to **find** is the **locate** command. This command searches through a database of your files. By default, if you keep Linux running on your computer, the database associated with the **locate** command is created overnight. If you're searching for a file that wasn't created since the last database update, the **locate** command finds files much more quickly than **find**.

The **locate** command is also more flexible; if you use the following command, it returns all files that include the text string *fig0*.

```
locate fig0
```

The **locate** command works as if asterisks are assumed before and after the search term.

The **locate** command works like **grep** on a database of your files. In some distributions, the **slocate** command is used for this purpose.

grep

The **grep** command is a handy way to search through a file. As a system administrator, you may have long lists of users. If you want to search through your /etc/passwd file for a user named "michael jang," you could try the following command:

```
grep "michael jang" /etc/passwd
```

If the user named "michael jang" exists, you would see a line similar to the following:

```
mj:x:500:500:michael jang:/home/mj:/bin/bash
```

This preceding line tells you the home directory and default shell for that user. If the search string exists in more than one line, you'll see those lines as well. You can even use **grep** to search through a series of files with commands like the following:

```
grep mj *
grep -c bash /etc/passwd
```

The first command looks for the string *mj* in all files in the current directory. The second command counts (**-c**) the number of lines that include the word *bash*.

To use the asterisk (*) and other wildcards as search terms (rather than as wildcards), use a backslash. For example, if you wanted to search for asterisks in the /etc/passwd file, use the **grep */etc/passwd** command.

Multiple Commands

It's a common practice to use more than one Linux command in a line. For example, if you're using the **find** command and you know that the result will have a large number of files, you can use a command like **grep** to search through the result. Specifically, let's say you want to find your Netscape cache file. You might start with the following command:

```
find / -name netscape
```

However, you might get discouraged when you see hundreds of files flashing past you on your terminal screen. An alternative is to combine commands like this:

```
find / -name netscape | grep cache
```

This command searches through the results of the **find** command for the text string *cache*. Only those files with both strings are output to the screen. Other possible command combinations include the following:

```
who | grep mj
ps aux | grep netscape
```

The first command, **who**, lists all users currently logged on to your Linux system. When you pipe (|) the result to the **grep mj** command, you'll find the number of times that user mj is currently logged on to your system.

The letter **w** is also a bash command. Both **w** and **who** show users who are currently logged on.

The second command, **ps**, lists the processes currently running on your Linux system. The three switches, **aux** (a dash is not required for **ps** command switches), lead to a very long list of processes: all processes run by all users (**a**) each associated with the user name (**u**) independent of the virtual terminal (**x**). You need a tool like **grep** to search through these processes. This combined command returns all processes with the word *netscape*.

Commands like **who** and **ps** are discussed in detail in Chapter 11.

MS-DOS File Tools

Linux includes tools that you can use to view an MS-DOS directory. Yes, you can use regular Linux commands such as **ls** and **cd** to review a mounted MS-DOS directory. But with MS-DOS tools, you don't have to mount the MS-DOS directory. Instead you can run familiar looking commands like the following:

```
mdir a:
mmove fig07-01.tif a:
mcopy a:rh1.txt
```

The first command lists the current files in your a: drive. The second command moves the fig07-01.tif file from your current directory to the a: drive. The third command copies the file rh1.txt from your a: drive to your current directory. These commands do *not* work if you've already mounted your floppy drive.

Managing Multiple Files

There are two basic commands that are used as common Linux ways to manage multiple files: **gzip** and **tar**. For those of you familiar with Microsoft Windows-based "zip" utilities, these two commands break the zip process down into two parts. The **tar** command collects a series of files into an archive, and the **gzip** command compresses a file.

Archiving by tar

The **tar** command is known as the tape archive command for historical reasons: Backups used to be primarily made to tape drives. Although tape drives are now less common, **tar** is the main Linux backup utility. It is designed to copy a series of files into a single large file. If you want to back up the files in your current directory, you might run the following command:

```
tar cvzf goodbackup.tar *
```

This command creates (c) a backup, listing every file name in the archive (v=verbose) in compressed format (z=zip) in the file (f) named goodbackup.tar. Files in subdirectories are also saved to this archive. You can then save this archived file to a backup area such as another volume or a tape drive.

 When setting up an archive, it's good practice to save to a file with the .tar extension. Many Linux downloads are archived in .tar format.

You can just as easily unarchive files with the following command:

```
tar tkvzf goodbackup.tar
```

This command lists (t) the files in your archive. When it restores, it does not over-write your current files (k=keep old files). In verbose (v) mode, you see everything that happens. If you stored files in a zipped format, you need to restore from the zipped (z) format. Finally, the command is restoring from the backup file (f) named goodbackup.tar. You can review some of the available **tar** switches in Table 8.8. Note that the first switch in the **tar** command should start with **c, t,** or **x**.

Table 8.8	Command switches for tar.
Switch	**Purpose**
c	Create an archive
t	List files in a current archive
x	Extract files from an archive
d	Compare files between an archive and a current directory
f	Use the following file name for the archive
k	Do not overwrite existing files
v	Verbose option; list all files going in or coming out of an archive
r	Add files to the end of an archive
z	Zip; compress files to or from an archive

There are a number of **tar** commands that you can use to create and extract archives. Some typical commands include the following. Read them over, referring to the descriptions in Table 8.8:

```
tar xvf download.tar
tar cvf backup.tar
```

gzip and gunzip

You can compress a file with the **gzip** command. You can also further compress a **tar** file that's already been compressed with the **z** option. The syntax of this command is fairly simple:

```
gzip goodarchive.tar
```

The **gzip** command compresses the target file and adds a .gz extension to the end of the file name. The **gunzip** command reverses the process as follows:

```
gunzip goodarchive.tar.gz
```

 When you download a new Linux program from the Internet, it often has a .tar.gz extension at the end of the file. You can use the **gunzip** and **tar** commands to extract the files that you need from this type of download.

Disk Management Commands

There are two very similar disk management commands available in Linux: **du** and **df**. The directory usage (**du**) command lists the amount of space used by each file in and below your current directory. The free disk space (**df**) command lists

```
144      ./.kde
4        ./.gimp/brushes
4        ./.gimp/gradients
168      ./.gimp/palettes
4        ./.gimp/patterns
4        ./.gimp/plug-ins
4        ./.gimp/gfig
4        ./.gimp/tmp
4        ./.gimp/scripts
4        ./.gimp/gflares
380      ./.gimp
2696     ./figures
4        ./.xauth/refcount/root/linuxtester
8        ./.xauth/refcount/root
12       ./.xauth/refcount
16       ./.xauth
4        ./.netscape/cache
4        ./.netscape/archive
4        ./.netscape/xover-cache/host-news
8        ./.netscape/xover-cache
280      ./.netscape
4        ./nsmail
4        ./test
3824
[mj@linuxtester mj]$ _
```

Figure 8.2   Output from the **du** command.

the amount of space available on each hard disk volume. Figure 8.2 shows the output you get if you run the **du** command in a Linux user's home directory.

The number you see on the left is the size of the file, in kilobytes, which is the default from both the **df** and **du** commands. The applicable file is shown on the right. For example, you may see the following:

```
1941    ./.gimp/tmp
```

The first dot (.) means that you start in your current directory. The slash (/) navigates to a subdirectory, in this case .gimp. In other words, this line means there are 1941 kilobytes of disk space dedicated to the .gimp/tmp subdirectory.

The **df** command shows how full each file system is on your computer. As you can see in Figure 8.3, the **df** command assesses each file system and displays the results in bytes. It includes any other file systems, such as your floppy or CD-ROM drives, that are currently mounted.

The **-m** switch gives you results in megabytes, and the **-k** switch gives you results in kilobytes.

```
[root@linuxtester mj]# df
Filesystem      1k-blocks       Used Available Use% Mounted on
/dev/hda5        1930708      720580   1112052  39% /
/dev/hda1          17534        2483     14146  15% /boot
/dev/fd0            1423         584       839  41% /mnt/floppy
/dev/hdc          658364      658364         0 100% /mnt/cdrom
[root@linuxtester mj]# _
```

Figure 8.3   Output from the **df** command shows available disk space on each volume.

Practice Questions

Question 1

> Which of the following commands deletes all of your Linux files without prompting you?
>
> ○ a. **rm -i * **
>
> ○ b. **rmdir -r / home/mj/tmp**
>
> ○ c. **rm -rF / home/mj/tmp**
>
> ○ d. **rm -v * /home/mj/tmp**

Answer c is correct. Remember to read these command options carefully! Because there is a space between the first forward slash (/) and home/mj/tmp, this **rm** command first removes all files and directories in your root (/) directory. The **rm -i** command prompts you before deleting files, so answer a is incorrect. Because there is no -r switch for the **rmdir** command, answer b is incorrect. Although the **rm -v * /home/mj/tmp** command first deletes all files in your current directory before deleting all files in the /home/mj/tmp directory, it does not delete all of your Linux files. Therefore, answer d is incorrect.

Question 2

> What is the purpose of the **w** command?
>
> ○ a. There is no purpose; there are no single-letter bash commands.
>
> ○ b. Lists currently logged on users.
>
> ○ c. Lists currently active programs.
>
> ○ d. Used as a general manual.

Answer b is correct. The **w** command, like **who,** lists all currently logged on users. Because **w** is a command, answer a is incorrect. The **ps** utility lists currently active programs, so answer c is incorrect. Because the **man** command calls out the manual for specific commands, answer d is incorrect.

Question 3

Your user has a number of test files named test1, test2, test3, and so on through test 100. Which of the following commands would delete only files named test10 through test19?

○ a. **rm -i test1***

○ b. **rm test1[09]**

○ c. **rm test1?**

○ d. **rm test10?**

Answer c is correct. The question mark (?) works as a wildcard for one character. Because the **rm -i test1*** command removes the desired files as well as the test1 and test100 files, answer a is incorrect. The **rm test1[09]** command removes the test10 and test19 files, so answer b is incorrect. Because the **rm test10?** command only removes the test100 file, answer d is incorrect.

Question 4

Which of the following commands is the most efficient and accurate way to count the number of files in your current directory? Include all hidden files and directories in your count. (Commands are separated by a semicolon.)

○ a. **ls -l > wc -l**

○ b. **ls -a > tempcount; wc -l tempcount**

○ c. **ls -lar l wc -l**

○ d. **ls -a l wc -l**

Answer d is the best available answer. The **ls -a** command counts the current files and directories including the current directory (.) and the parent directory (..). Because each file is on its own line, when you pipe the result to the **wc -l** command, you get the number of files as a result. If you use the **ls -l > wc -l** command, you'll find output in a file named wc. Therefore, answer a is incorrect. Although answer b works, it is not as efficient as answer d. Therefore, answer b is incorrect. Because answer c has more switches than you need for the **ls** command, it is also incorrect.

Question 5

Which of the following commands creates the /home/mj/project/book directory? Assume /home/mj is your home directory. Your **pwd** is /home/jm, and neither the project nor the book directory currently exists.

- ○ a. **mkdir -p ~/project/book**
- ○ b. **mkdir -rF /home/mj/project/book**
- ○ c. **mkdir -p project/book**
- ○ d. **mkdir -r /home/mj/project/book**

Answer a is correct. The tilde (~) represents your home directory (as discussed in Chapter 7). The -p switch for **mkdir** creates all specified levels of directories. Because there is no -**r** or -**F** switch for the **mkdir** command, answers b and d are incorrect. Because you're currently in the /home/jm directory, answer c is incorrect.

Question 6

You've set up your own shell named kash. You want to know the number of users who set up kash as their default shell. There are no other words in any of the noted files that include the string *kash*. Which of the following commands would give you this number?

- ○ a. **grep kash I wc -l /etc/passwd**
- ○ b. **wc -l /etc/passwd I grep kash**
- ○ c. **grep /etc/passwd kash I wc -l**
- ○ d. **grep kash /etc/passwd I wc -l**

Answer d is correct. The first term after the **grep** command is the search term that is used to search through standard input—in this case, the /etc/passwd file. This returns each line that includes the string *kash*. The output is sent to the **wc** -**l** command, which counts the number of lines. There is no search file in answer a, so it is incorrect. The number of lines in the /etc/passwd file is unrelated to the number of users with the *kash* shell, so answer b is incorrect. Because /etc/passwd is not a search term, answer c is incorrect.

Question 7

Which of the following commands do the same thing? Assume that file1 and file2 are both on the same Linux volume.

○ a. **ln -s file1 file2; cp -p file1 file2**

○ b. **ln file1 file2; cp -r file1 file2**

○ c. **ln file1 file2; cp -p file1 file2**

○ d. **ln -s file1 file2; cp file1 file2**

Answer c is correct. The key to this question is inode numbers. A hard link (**ln**) and a **cp -p** command both retain the same inode number for the source and destination files. This doesn't work only if you're copying a file from one volume to another. The **ln -s** command does not preserve inode numbers, so answers a and d are incorrect. Because the **cp -r** command does not preserve inode numbers, answer b is incorrect.

Question 8

You've downloaded a new Linux application from the Internet. The installation files are archived together in a file named newapp.tar.gz. You've downloaded it to your /tmp directory. What commands are required to reveal the installation files? Make sure you have the commands in the correct order.

○ a. **tar xvf newapp.tar.gz; gunzip newapp.gz**

○ b. **gzip newapp.tar.gz; tar xvf newapp.tar**

○ c. **gunzip newapp.tar; tar xvf newapp.gz**

○ d. **gunzip newapp.tar.gz; tar xvf newapp.tar**

Answer d is correct. You need the **gunzip** command to uncompress a file with a .gz extension. Then you can unarchive the files with the **tar xvf** command. The **tar xvf** command doesn't uncompress files, so answer a is incorrect. The **gzip** command compresses files, so answer b is incorrect. Because you've downloaded the newapp.tar.gz file, you need to apply the **gunzip** command to this file first before you get to the newapp.tar file. Therefore, answer c is incorrect.

Question 9

Which of the following commands copies files to or from an unmounted MS-DOS floppy disk on your Linux computer? This Linux floppy is normally mounted on the /mnt/floppy directory. The device name is fd0.

○ a. **mount /dev/fd0 /mnt/floppy**

○ b. **mcopy *.txt a:**

○ c. **cp *.txt /mnt/floppy**

○ d. **cp *.txt a:**

Answer b is correct. Linux includes a set of MS-DOS tools, or mtools, that allow you to interface directly with an unmounted floppy drive. These tools include commands such as **mcopy, mdir,** and **mmove.** You don't need to mount the floppy to use mtools, so answer a is incorrect. You can't use a Linux command to copy files to an unmounted floppy drive, so answer c is incorrect. Because you can't use a Linux command to copy files to an unmounted MS-DOS drive, answer d is incorrect.

Question 10

How would you find the number of kilobytes that are free on each of your hard disk volumes? You shouldn't have to translate from bytes or megabytes.

○ a. **df**

○ b. **df -m**

○ c. **df -b**

○ d. **du -k**

Answer a is correct. By default, the **df** command gives you the free space on each of your hard disk volumes, in kilobytes. Although the **-k** switch also serves this purpose, it is not required. The **df -m** command gives you a result in megabytes, so answer b is incorrect. The **df -b** switch does not exist, so answer c is also incorrect. Although the **du -k** command gives you the space occupied by each file and directory in kilobytes, it does not tell you about the space available in your Linux volumes. Therefore, answer d is incorrect.

Need to Know More?

 Hughes, Phil. *Linux for Dummies Quick Reference.* IDG Books World-wide, Inc., Foster City, CA, 1998. ISBN 0-76450-302-2. A quick reference book that can be handy for basic Linux options at the command-line interface.

 Muster, John. *Unix Made Easy.* Osborne/McGraw-Hill, Berkeley, CA, 1996. ISBN 0-07882-173-8. A solid textbook for the command-line interface. Although this is a book on Unix, it is often used as a teaching text in conjunction with various Linux distributions.

 The **http://linux.ctyme.com** Web site is Mark Perkel's index to Linux man pages. If you don't have immediate access to a Linux command line or its man pages, this Web site includes a searchable online reference.

9

Managing Printers

. . . .

Terms you'll need to understand:

✓ Printer configuration utility

✓ Line printer daemon

✓ **lpr**, **lpq**, **lprm**, **lpc**

✓ Print filters: nenscript, magic

✓ /etc/printcap

✓ sd, af, if, of, lf, tr

✓ **rp**, **rm**

Techniques you'll need to master:

✓ Setting up a printer with a printer configuration utility

✓ Explaining various line printer commands

✓ Describing different print filters

✓ Decoding entries in the /etc/printcap file

In this chapter, you learn about configuring printers on Linux. A number of distributions have their own graphical printer configuration utilities that manage the printer configuration file, known as */etc/printcap*. There are several Linux commands associated with the Linux line printer daemon (**lpd**). Some printers need data translated through a print filter. Once you learn these basics, you'll be able to deconstruct the components of the /etc/printcap file.

Printer Configuration Utilities

As mentioned previously, several Linux distributions include their own graphical printer configuration utility. Some examples include Red Hat Linux's printtool, Caldera's COAS, S.u.S.E.'s YaST2, and Corel's Control Center. Each of these utilities prompts you for parameters for the /etc/printcap file, which determines how Linux communicates with your printer. Although you're not tested on distribution-specific printer utilities, these tools can help familiarize you with the parameters in the /etc/printcap file. Figure 9.1 shows Red Hat's printtool utility, and Figure 9.2 shows the printer menu of the Caldera COAS utility.

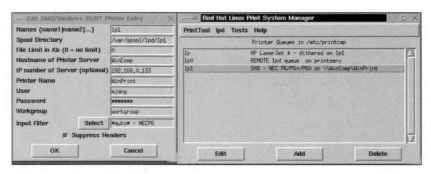

Figure 9.1   Red Hat Linux printtool utility.

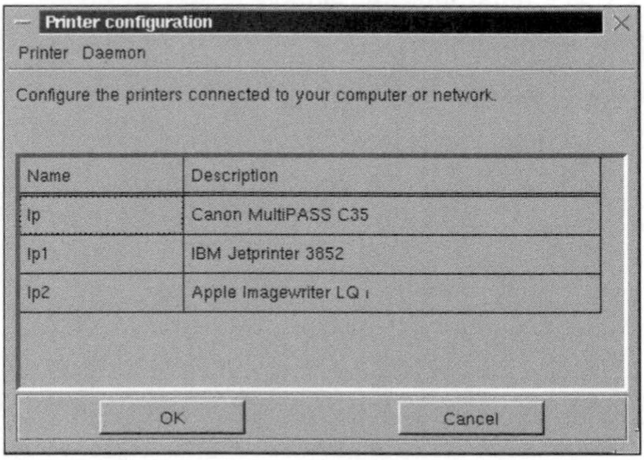

Figure 9.2   Caldera Linux COAS printer configuration utility.

The lp Commands

Once you've set up one or more printers, you can manage them with the commands associated with the line printer daemon (**lpd**). These commands include the line printer request (**lpr**), the line printer query (**lpq**), the line printer remove (**lprm**), and the line printer control program (**lpc**).

 The line printer daemon (**lpd**) is normally started when you boot Linux. Once you start a print job, the **lpd** looks for these jobs in your print spool directory, and then sends them to your printer.

lpr

When you use the **cat** command on a file, the shell sends the result to standard output (stdout), which normally means that you see the result on your screen. In contrast, when you use **lpr**, the shell sends the result to a spool file on the local computer, then on to a print server computer, and finally to the printer. The **lpr** is a client. When it produces a spool file, the result is processed by a server, the **lpd**. The **lpd** print server can be local or remote on a network. So when you run the following command, your shell sends the result to the default printer as defined in /etc/printcap:

```
lpr file1
```

You can send this print job to another printer with the following command:

```
lpr -P colorprinter file1
```

Assuming you have a printer named colorprinter in your /etc/printcap file, this command sends the job to that printer instead. Other important switches for the **lpr** command are shown in Table 9.1.

Table 9.1	lpr commands.
Command	**Result**
lpr -h file1	Prints file1 without a job control page, which normally contains the user account and host name of the source computer. The job control page is also known as the burst page.
lpr -P other file1	Prints file1 to the printer named other, as defined in the /etc/printcap file.
lpr -s file1	Creates a symbolic link to file1, which avoids creating a spool file. This was required for larger (>1MB) files on the Berkeley Standard Distribution version of **lpr**. Current Linux distributions use the LPRng program, which makes this unnecessary.

lpq

The line printer query (**lpq**) command gives you the current print queue. Examples of this command are shown in Table 9.2. This command also includes a list of job numbers, which you might need for the **lprm** command.

lprm

If a print job isn't already in your printer's memory, the line printer remove (**lprm**) command can delete print jobs currently in your queue. With **lprm**, you can remove a print job in one of three ways: by print job number, by user, or by printer. Examples of this command are shown in Table 9.3.

Users can use **lprm** to remove their own print jobs. The root or superuser can use this command to remove anyone's print job.

lpc

The line printer control (**lpc**) command allows you to control a number of characteristics of each printer. As shown in Table 9.4, this command lets you check printer status, kill active print jobs, or even redirect jobs to a different printer.

Printer Languages

When you want to print a file, Linux translates the file into a format that your printer can use. Printers have their own fonts embedded in their memory. If you're just printing text, Linux can send ASCII codes to your printer, which are translated into your printer's fonts. This is commonly known as *text-mode printing*.

Table 9.2	lpq commands.
Command	Result
lpq	Returns the current print queue for the default printer, as defined in your /etc/printcap file.
lpq -P print1	Returns the print queue for the print1 printer. Substitute a printer name based on the name shown in your /etc/printcap file.

Table 9.3	lprm commands.
Command	Result
lprm 188	Removes print job 188, as defined in the output to the **lpq** command.
lprm -P hp2 mj	Removes print jobs of user mj from the printer labeled hp2 in your /etc/printcap file.

Table 9.4 lpc commands.	
Command	**Result**
lpc -P canon1 status	Displays the status of the printer named canon1. In other words, the output tells you whether you can send print jobs to a queue, the number of jobs in the queue, whether the printer will accept jobs, and communication status with the printer.
lpc disable	Disables sending jobs (*spooling*) to a print queue for the default printer. Opposite of **lpc enable**.
lpc stop	Stops communication between the print queue and your printer. The **lpc start** command restarts transfers from the print queue.

On the other hand, if you're printing graphics, you probably don't want to use your printer's fonts. Your printer needs instructions on what to do with every dot or pixel. Linux has print filters to translate the file into standard printer graphic formats, such as PostScript or PCL (Printer Control Language).

Text versus Graphic

The only true text documents are those that are printed with your printer's fonts. If you print a file from an editor like vi or emacs, without using any typesetting commands, you're printing a text document. Text documents require the least amount of data be sent to your printer; all that is needed is one ASCII bit per letter, instead of dozens or hundreds of bits for the dots that create each letter.

Documents that use markup languages, such as TeX and HTML, are written in text. They use commands to convert different lines of text to different fonts. These fonts are then translated, pixel-by-pixel, to your printer.

Just about all other documents printed today require a graphical interface. Documents that use the WYSIWYG (what you see is what you get) system are completely graphical; every letter is converted, pixel-by-pixel, on your screen and then sent to the printer.

But neither markup languages nor WYSIWYG graphics correspond to actual printer languages. You still need filters to convert graphic formats to a format that a printer can use. It is the converted file that is stored in your spool directory.

*Note: Some printers convert WYSIWYG graphics after they receive print jobs. If you have one of these types of printers, be sure to set **rp=raw** in the /etc/printcap file, as explained later in this chapter.*

Filters

Filters translate what you want to print from your applications and editors to the various languages that a printer can understand. The two major printer graphic languages are Hewlett Packard's PCL and Adobe's PostScript. These languages fall into different categories; some applications use PostScript to translate your files to PCL. There are three major types of graphic filters that work with these languages: nenscript, ghostscript, and magic. You need to set up the filter that you'll use in your /etc/printcap file.

 Most Linux applications work with PostScript files. Linux drivers for PostScript printers are more common as a result.

Nenscript is a GNU clone of the commercially available enscript printer filter. Like its GNU cousin, a2ps, it converts text into PostScript format. Both nenscript and a2ps are more flexible than other PostScript filters because they allow you to print two pages of text on a single sheet.

Ghostscript is a PostScript interpreter, which allows Linux to display PostScript files in graphical user interfaces, as well as a translator, which sends PostScript data to many printers.

Magic filters aren't really filters at all. They are scripts that automatically detect the type of data inside a file, and then call up the appropriate filter to convert the data for your printer. In a way, this works like the **file** command from Chapter 8. Magic filters convert from modes like DVI or PostScript to Hewlett Packard's PCL.

Note: DVI files are the processed data from LaTeX or TeX input files.

There is also one major filter, known as lpf. This is a filter for text files. The lpf filter reformats ASCII text to avoid "stair-stepping," when printers add an extra line after every word.

Spool Directories

Print spools are generally located in the /var/spool/lpd directory. Each job gets its own file. On older Linux systems that use the BSD (Berkeley Standard Distribution) version of the line printer daemon, Linux can't handle spool files larger than 1MB, which is the reason for the **lpr -s** command. If you have trouble managing your spool with commands like **lprm** and **lpc**, you may be able to kill print jobs directly by deleting files in your spool directory.

Print spools, like log files, are normally stored in the /var directory or one of its subdirectories.

The /etc/printcap File

All of the settings for different printers are stored in the /etc/printcap file. In this section, you'll analyze a typical /etc/printcap file, with a view towards making it work for you. An example of the /etc/printcap file from the Corel Linux distribution is shown in Figure 9.3.

This file can be rather confusing at first glance, so let's start by reviewing some of the codes available for this file. You'll then be able to interpret this file or the one currently in your Linux distribution.

/etc/printcap codes

The codes in the /etc/printcap file can be divided into the following categories: printer names, filters, spools, log files, and special printer codes. There is also a format for separate entries in this file. For example, the first section shown in Figure 9.3 may be shown as three long code lines:

```
lp|Generic dot-matrix printer entry:lp=/dev/lp0:\
sd=var/spool/lpd/lp:af=/var/log/lp-acct:\
lf=/var/log/lp-errs:\pl#66:pw#80:pc#150:mx#0:sh
```

```
# /etc/printcap: printer capability database. See printcap(5).
# You can use the filter entries df, tf, cf, gf etc. for
# your own filters. See /etc/filter.ps, /etc/filter.pcl and
# the printcap(5) manual page for further details.

lp|Generic dot-matrix printer entry:\
        :lp=/dev/lp0:\
        :sd=/var/spool/lpd/lp:\
        :af=/var/log/lp-acct:\
        :lf=/var/log/lp-errs:\|
        :pl#66:\
        :pw#80:\
        :pc#150:\
        :mx#0:\
        :sh:

# rlp|Remote printer entry:\
#       :lp=:\
#       :rm=remotehost:\
#       :rp=remoteprinter:\
#       :sd=/var/spool/lpd/remote:\
#       :mx#0:\
#       :sh:
```

Figure 9.3 A typical /etc/printcap printer configuration file.

Unfortunately, this type of code management can make life more difficult for all but the most knowledgeable of Linux administrators. The way you set up and present code in this file or any other program helps communicate your intent to other administrators. There are three punctuation marks that help you manage /etc/printcap code.

➤ *Colon* (:)—Colons divide code lines. If you see a colon, even inside a line, it starts a new command.

Note: The first line in a /etc/printcap paragraph usually defines a printer. You can see that the line shown previously starts with lp, which is the code for the default printer.

➤ *Backslash* (\)—If a line ends with a backslash, it means that the code continues onto the next line. Recall from Chapter 7 that the backslash tells the shell to ignore characters like empty spaces, carriage returns, and so on.

➤ *Pipe* (|)—Lines after a pipe in the /etc/printcap file are comments. As you can see, the ones shown in the preceding code lines and in the figure describe some type of printer. But these comments are significant because you can use them to specify a particular printer.

Printer names are based on the drivers installed and available in your /dev/ directory. Typical printer names include lp, lp1, lp2, sp1, and lj1.

The default printer has the lp label in the /etc/printcap file. If there is no printer with this label, the first printer in this file becomes the default.

The print filters discussed earlier can be assigned as input filters (if) or output filters (of). If you have multiple print jobs on a single printer, only the input filter is used on every print job. The output filter is applied only to the first of a series of print jobs.

The spool directory (sd) is where the filtered print jobs are stored before they're sent to the printer. Linux needs a place to store these print jobs because printers aren't always available. For example, your printer could be disconnected or busy with another print job. Also, it can take time for Linux to contact printers on remote computers.

When you print, Linux can keep track of print costs and print errors. The log files dedicated to these functions are the accounting filter (**af**) and the line filter (**lf**). The accounting filter is self-explanatory. The line filter collects errors.

There are also a number of other codes. Some of the more important codes are documented in Table 9.5.

Table 9.5	Special codes for the /etc/printcap file.
Code	Function
rm	Remote machine: Set this equal to the hostname or IP address of the remote print server (for example, the **rm=192.168.0.66** command tells the line printer daemon [**lpd**] that your remote printer's IP address is 192.168.0.66).
rp	Remote printer: If you're printing a PostScript file and your printer cannot detect this type of file, set this value equal to **raw** (**rp=raw**).
mx	Maximum file size: Helps you work with the older BSD line printer daemon (**lpd**). If you do not want a maximum file size, set this value to 0 (**mx=0**).
pw	Page width, in characters: The standard page width on U.S. letter size paper is 80 (**pw#80**).
pl	Page length, in number of lines: The standard page length on U.S. letter size paper is 66 (**pl#66**).
sh	Suppress header: When you see this command, your printer won't print a page with the job and user name.

Note: Much more information on the syntax inside the /etc/printcap file is available on its man page.

A Typical /etc/printcap File

Once you know the basic syntax, you can read most typical /etc/printcap files. Return to Figure 9.3. You know that lp is the name of the default printer, and its device is located in the device file /dev/lp0. Files that you send to this printer are first spooled in the directory defined by sd, which is /var/spool/lpd/lp:.

In a similar vein, the output from the accounting filter is stored in the /var/log/lp-acct file. Errors are taken by the line filter and sent to the /var/log/lp-errs file. The page length (**pl**) is 66 lines. The page width (**pw**) is 80 characters. The price code (**pc**) is 1.5 cents per page. There is no limit on the size of the printer spool file (**mx#0**). The suppress header (**sh**) command keeps the printer from printing a page with your user name and print job number.

You'll look at other examples in the practice questions.

Practice Questions

Question 1

> Which of the following commands is normally used when you start or reboot Linux?
>
> ○ a. **lpr**
>
> ○ b. **lpd**
>
> ○ c. **lprm**
>
> ○ d. **lpc**

Answer b is correct. The line printer daemon (**lpd**) is automatically started at one or more of your run levels, depending on your Linux distribution. Because the **lpr** (line print request) command prints files, it is not normally used when you start or reboot Linux. Therefore, answer a is incorrect. The **lprm** (line printer remove) command is used to remove print jobs. If you're starting or rebooting Linux, you shouldn't have any print jobs (although it is possible); therefore, answer c is incorrect. The **lpc** (line print control program) command helps you control current print jobs. For the same reason that **lprm** is incorrect, answer d is also incorrect.

Question 2

> There are several utilities related to the **lpd**. Which of the following statements most closely matches the utility with its purpose?
>
> ○ a. The **lpd** takes jobs from your applications and manages them through your spool directory all the way to your printer.
>
> ○ b. The **lpq** command allows you to manage the operation of the Linux print system.
>
> ○ c. The **lprm** command allows you to remove print jobs from your application directories.
>
> ○ d. The **lpc** command allows the root or superuser to manage and reprioritize different print jobs.

Answer d is correct. The line printer control (**lpc**) command does allow a root or superuser to cancel or delay specific print jobs. Because the line printer daemon (**lpd**) doesn't take jobs from your applications, answer a is incorrect. The line printer query (**lpq**) only allows you to see the print jobs currently in the queue, so answer b is incorrect. Although the line printer remove (**lprm**) command does allow you to remove print jobs, these are stored in the print spool, which is separate from any application directory. Therefore, answer c is incorrect.

Question 3

Which of the following is used to translate print jobs from text or graphical applications to a format that a printer can actually use?

○ a. Input translator

○ b. Printer filter

○ c. Line printer daemon

○ d. Stair-step manager

Answer b is correct. Printer filters, as configured in your /etc/printcap file, allow your applications to send print jobs in a language that your printer can use. Because there is no print-related purpose for an input translator, answer a is incorrect. Although the line printer daemon (**lpd**) uses printer filters, the daemon itself is not a printer filter; therefore, answer c is incorrect. Although stair-stepping is a problem for text, it is not an issue for graphical applications. Therefore, answer d is incorrect.

Question 4

Which of the following steps do you need to take to delete a specific print job? The owner of the print job is named sam, and you don't know the print job number. It's his only current print job. Others also have print jobs in progress. The name of the printer is hp, and it is not your default printer. Select the option that works in the shortest number of steps.

○ a. Use **lpc -P** to find the print job number, and then delete it by number with the **lprm** command.

○ b. Use **lpq -a** to find the print job number, and then delete it by number with the **lprm** command.

○ c. Use **lprm -P hp sam** to delete all of sam's current print jobs.

○ d. Use **lpc -P hp sam** to delete all of sam's current print jobs.

Answer c is correct. The **lprm** command removes print jobs. The -P switch specifies the printer. And you can specify print jobs to remove by user. The **lpc** command helps you if you know the print job number. Because the printer isn't specified in answer a, that answer is incorrect. Because there is no -a switch for the **lpq** command, answer b is incorrect. You can use the **lpc** command to abort all current print jobs; however, there are no options to specify print jobs by user. Therefore, answer d is incorrect.

Question 5

Based on the following entry from the /etc/printcap file, where is your printer filter?

```
lp|laser:lp=dev/lp2:sd=/var/spool/lpd/lp2:\
af=/var/log/lp-acct:lf=/var/log/lp-errs:\
if=/var/spool/lpd/lp2/manager
```

○ a. /var/spool/lpd/lp2

○ b. /var/log/lp-acct

○ c. /var/log/lp-errs

○ d. /var/spool/lpd/lp2/manager

Answer d is correct. Examining the line of code, the input filter (if) signifies the location of your printer filter. Because the letters *sd* represent the spool directory, answer a is incorrect. The letters *af* represent the accounting filter, so answer b is incorrect. The letters *lf* represent the line filter, which is where print errors are sent, so answer c is incorrect.

Question 6

You've brought a portable text printer from the United States to Europe and can only find narrow paper. You want to use the printer's font. Assume that you want to set up your printer to use no more than 70 characters per line. Which of the following commands would help Linux manage your print jobs to accommodate the narrow paper?

○ a. **of=/var/spool/lpd/lp0/pw70**

○ b. **pw#70**

○ c. **pl#70**

○ d. **pw=/var/spool/lpd/lp0/70**

Answer b is correct. This command limits the text printout to 70 characters per line. Because *of* represents the output filter and is not related to output to a text printer, answer a is incorrect. The letters *pl* represent the number of lines on each page, so answer c is incorrect. Because **pw=/var/spool/lpd/lp0/70** is in an incorrect format for this command, answer d is incorrect.

Question 7

Based on the following entry from the /etc/printcap file, where is the remote printer? You are located on the nicenetwork.rgb domain.

```
lp|lr2|Color Laser:rp=text:\
rm=lr2:sd=/var/spool/lpd/lp2:\
af=/var/log/lp-acct:\
lf=/var/log/lp-errs:\
if=/var/spool/lpd/lp2/manager
```

○ a. lp.nicenetwork.rgb

○ b. 192.168.0.13

○ c. lr2.nicenetwork.rgb

○ d. af.nicenetwork.rgb

Answer c is correct. The location of the remote printer is set equal to **rm**. Because **lp** is the print device, it is not related to the remote print location. Therefore, answer a is incorrect. Although 192.168.0.13 could be the IP address for lr2, you have no information that tells you that this is so. Therefore, answer b is incorrect. The letters *af* represent the accounting filter, and it is not related to the location of the remote printer. Therefore, answer d is incorrect.

Question 8

Which of the following print filters converts data from several known formats to Hewlett Packard's PCL?

○ a. PostScript

○ b. Nenscript

○ c. Lpf

○ d. Magic

Answer d is correct. Magic is the only filter on this list that can detect the format of the input file. PostScript itself is a printer language different from PCL, so answer a is incorrect. Because nenscript converts files to the PostScript language, answer b is incorrect. Because lpf is a filter for text printers, answer c is incorrect.

Question 9

> Which of the following files contains the main configuration data for how data is sent to your spool directory and then on to your printer?
>
> ○ a. /var/spool/lp/lp0
>
> ○ b. /etc/printcap
>
> ○ c. /etc/spool/lp/lp0
>
> ○ d. /var/printcap

Answer b is correct. The /etc/printcap file is the main configuration file that contains filters, your spool directory definition, and so on. Although answer a is the spool directory, it does not contain filters. Therefore, answer a is incorrect. Because /etc/spool/lp/lp0 is not a spool directory, answer c is incorrect. Spool directories are kept under the /var directory. Because configuration files are kept under the /etc directory, answer d is incorrect.

Question 10

> Which of the following is graphical printer configuration utility that comes with every Linux distribution?
>
> ○ a. printtool
>
> ○ b. COAS
>
> ○ c. YaST
>
> ○ d. KDE Control Center
>
> ○ e. None of the above

Answer e is correct. There are no graphical printer configuration utilities that come standard with all Linux distributions. The printtool utility comes with Red Hat Linux. Therefore, answer a is incorrect. The COAS utility comes with Caldera Linux. Therefore, answer b is incorrect. The YaST utility comes with S.u.S.E. Linux. Therefore, answer c is incorrect. In general, you can't use the KDE Control Center to configure printers; however, a printer configuration tool is built into the Corel Linux version of this utility. Nevertheless, because this is not available with all distributions, answer d is incorrect.

Need to Know More?

 The Web site at **http://linux.ctyme.com** is Mark Perkel's index to Linux man pages. If you don't have immediate access to a Linux command line or its man pages, this Web site includes a searchable online reference. Important man pages for this chapter include printcap, **lpc**, **lpd**, **lpr**, and **lprm**.

 The Web site for the Linux Documentation Project at **www.linuxdoc.org** is the central repository for Linux manuals, HOWTOs, and a number of other book-length documents. Important HOWTOs for this chapter include the "Printing-HOWTO," which can help you print from just about any format to just about any printer, and the "Printing Usage-HOWTO," which is more focused on the actual commands that you use.

The X Window

Terms you'll need to understand:

✓ **startx**, **xdm**

✓ .xinitrc, Xsession

✓ X11, XF86Config

✓ X Server, Display Manager, Widgets

✓ Window manager, applications

✓ SuperProbe, xf86config, XF86Setup, Xconfigurator, SaX

✓ GNOME, KDE, fvwm, Enlightenment, AfterStep, WindowMaker, Blackbox

✓ Virtual display

Techniques you'll need to master:

✓ Describing how the X Window starts

✓ Understanding the structure of the X Server configuration file

✓ Describing the five major X Window components

✓ Locating different X11 configuration files and programs

✓ Using various X Window configuration utilities

✓ Describing characteristics of several window managers

✓ Managing information inside X Windows

In this chapter, you work with the X Window, which is the Linux graphical user interface (GUI). The Linux X Window system is almost completely modular. It works from several different kinds of configuration files and utilities. The different window managers give you a different "look and feel" on your GUI desktop.

Starting the X Window

You can start the X Window from the command-line interface, or you can set it to start automatically through your /etc/inittab configuration file. Whether you use the X Window start command **startx** or **xdm** (X Display Manager), the X Window start program uses configuration files based on your hardware. It then runs through systemwide and user-specific initialization files.

The X Window is also known as X11.

X Window Start Commands

There are two basic ways to start the X Window. You can log in at the command-line interface and use the **startx** command, or you can run the **xdm** command after login to start an X login window. If you have an init level dedicated to the **xdm**, you can set your /etc/inittab file to make sure that Linux starts at that run level.

Because **startx** is a Linux script, you can look through it (with a text editor) for initialization files. If you've already set up **xdm**, its initialization files take precedence.

In either case, **startx** or **xdm** first checks the user's home directory for configuration files. If none are available, it then checks for systemwide initialization files, which are generally located in a subdirectory of the /etc/X11/xinit directory.

Note: Depending on your distribution, you may also be able to use commands like X to start your X Window.

Configuration Files

The key configuration file is /etc/X11/XF86Config, which sets up your mouse, keyboard, monitor, and video controller. Although Linux can detect the settings of many video controllers and monitors, you can often improve the performance of your system by customizing this file. The sample xf86config.eg file includes a guide to customizing /etc/X11/XF86Config, which can be divided into eight major sections:

➤ *Files*—Includes the file locations for colors and fonts.

➤ *ServerFlags*—Governs the response of your X Window to special commands. For example, you can exit the X Window by using Ctrl+Alt+Backspace. A **DontZap** command in this section disables this option.

Note: In Red Hat Linux, this key combination may have to be pressed twice.

➤ *Keyboard*—Sets up the parameters for your keyboard. Includes settings for special keys as well as keyboard features, such as Num Lock and Auto Repeat.

➤ *Pointer*—Sets up a pointing device, usually a mouse. Mouse options include protocol (Microsoft, PS/2, Logitech, etc.), speed in bits per second (baud), and three-button emulation.

➤ *Monitor*—Sets the allowable horizontal and vertical frequency rates for your monitor. Setting this too high could overload your monitor. Also sets the refresh rate for your monitor.

➤ *Device*—Provides settings for your video controller including allowable horizontal and vertical frequency rates.

➤ *Screen*—Provides allowable and default graphics modes, which specify the number and dimensions of pixels shown on your monitor. Example modes are 640×480, 800×600, and 1024×768.

➤ *Xinput*—Provides settings for other input hardware, such as pens with graphic tablets, game adapters, and even touchscreens.

The preceding list just scratches the surface of possible options. A full list is available in the man page for the XF86Config file.

Note: Three-button emulation allows you to use a two-button mouse where three buttons are required. When it's on, you simulate a middle button by pressing the left and right buttons simultaneously.

Initialization Files

There are two main initialization files. The xinitrc file is associated with **startx**, and the Xsession file is associated with **xdm**. The main initialization files in the /etc/X11/xinit directory are scripts that defer to corresponding files in users' home directories. Once a choice is made, the initialization files call up other scripts that allocate resources, like memory, keyboard settings, window managers, and the XF86Config file.

Note: If you have X Window initialization files in your home directory, they are probably hidden. You can list them with the ls -a command. Hidden files such as .xinitrc have a period in front of them. Keep in mind that the actual location for user and systemwide configuration files will vary.

X Window Architecture

As mentioned previously, the X Window is modular. You can mix and match components from different categories. Whichever components you select, you need five different groups of components to set up the X Window architecture: servers, display managers, widgets, window managers, and applications.

The X Server communicates directly with video hardware. The display manager sets up the X Window environment and sets up a login screen. The basic items that you see in a GUI, such as menu bars, are built with widgets. The actual GUI is a window manager, and all GUI applications should work with any window manager. This system can be set up in a client-server arrangement over a network.

 When you set up the X Window, Linux first starts the X Server, which puts your computer into graphics mode. It can then start a display manger to allow you to log in. Once you log in, Linux starts the window manager of your choice.

Server

Despite its name, the X Server is set up on a client computer. It communicates directly with your video controller. Before Linux can draw a picture on your monitor, the X Server sends the information to your video hardware. Whether the input comes from an application or from your mouse, the X Server processes this data and sends appropriate input/output commands to your video controller.

Display Manager

The display manager that you see is a graphical login screen. Some window managers, such as KDE (K Desktop Environment) and GNOME (GNU Network Object Model Environment), have their own display manger. Others, like **xdm**, are configured at a specific level in the /etc/inittab file. The screen that you see varies by Linux distribution. Whichever display manager is used, a successful login activates the window manager.

Building Blocks (Widgets)

In Linux, a widget is a library program. Developers build the components of a window manager from widgets. These components include menu bars, scroll bars, task bars, and so on. Different window managers may be built from different widget libraries.

Window Manager

The window manager determines how the GUI looks on your monitor. There are several different kinds of window managers available including GNOME, KDE, Afterstep, Window Maker, fvwm, Blackbox, and Enlightenment.

The two most common default window managers are GNOME and KDE. The GNOME window manager is built from the GTK+ widget library. The KDE window manager is built from the Quicktime (Qt) widget library.

Applications

For the most part, GUI applications, such as Netscape Communicator and WordPerfect, work with but are not part of the X Window architecture. Nevertheless, GUI applications also store user-specific configuration files. You may already have some hidden application configuration files in your home directory.

The GNOME and KDE packages include applications such as office suites.

X Window Configuration Utilities

Editing the XF86Config file can be a difficult process for all but the most skilled administrators. There are a number of good tools available to help you configure this file. Although some of these tools are graphical, they do not suffer from the perceived flaws of other Linux GUI utilities. In other words, they are reliable. For the most part, they include all of the features that most administrators need to configure their systems.

Some of these utilities can even help you install or revise settings for your keyboard and mouse.

 Before you start any of these utilities, back up your X Server configuration file, which is normally /etc/X11/XF86Config.

SuperProbe

The SuperProbe utility is a text command that detects key parts of your video controller, including the chipset on the card and the data converter. Most importantly, it identifies an appropriate X Server for you. If you want to try to use this utility, close all currently running programs first because SuperProbe can make Linux "hang" or stop working on your computer.

The X Servers are based on the work of the XFree86 project. The server names reflect their video controllers. For example, you can assign the XF86_SVGA server to an SVGA card, the XF86_P9000 server to the Orchid P9000 card, and so on.

When you run SuperProbe, the utility warns you that it can make your computer hang. Within five seconds, your monitor screen may go blank as the utility probes your video hardware. If it detects the hardware you have, you'll see the results on your screen, as shown in Figure 10.1.

If you're setting up your configuration files without any of the other X Window configuration utilities, your next step is to link (**ln**) the X Server to the **X** command.

xf86config

The xf86config utility is used at the command line to configure your video controller and monitor as well as your keyboard and mouse.

The xf86config utility represents one of the rare cases where graphical utilities are preferred. The lists used by xf86config are long and tedious. However, because it allows you to set your monitor and video controller settings from outside files, it's easier to keep this utility more up to date.

If you want more information on the available options at each step, review the next section on the XF86Setup utility. Although XF86Setup is a GUI utility, the options are nearly identical.

```
laptop:~# SuperProbe

SuperProbe Version 2.20 (17 June 1999)
        (c) Copyright 1993,1994 by David Wexelblat <dwex@xfree86.org>
        (c) Copyright 1994-1998 by The XFree86 Project, Inc

        This work is derived from the 'vgadoc2.zip' and
        'vgadoc3.zip' documentation packages produced by Finn
        Thoegersen, and released with all appropriate permissions
        having been obtained.  Additional information obtained from
        'Programmer's Guide to the EGA and VGA, 2nd ed', by Richard
        Ferraro, and from manufacturer's data books

Bug reports are welcome, and should be sent to XFree86@XFree86.org.
In particular, reports of chipsets that this program fails to
correctly detect are appreciated.

Before submitting a report, please make sure that you have the
latest version of SuperProbe (see http://www.xfree86.org/FAQ).

WARNING - THIS SOFTWARE COULD HANG YOUR MACHINE.
          READ THE SuperProbe.1 MANUAL PAGE BEFORE
          RUNNING THIS PROGRAM.

          INTERRUPT WITHIN FIVE SECONDS TO ABORT!

First video: Super-VGA
        Chipset: Yamaha 6388 VPDC (Port Probed)
        RAMDAC:  Generic 8-bit pseudo-color DAC
                 (with 6-bit wide lookup tables (or in 6-bit mode))
laptop:~# █
```

Figure 10.1 The SuperProbe utility at work.

The Cards database file for xf86config is located in the /usr/X11R6/lib/X11 directory. The Monitor database file is usually located in this directory or in a subdirectory. If you're having trouble finding either of these files (the locations will vary), use the **locate** or **find** command.

XF86Setup

Almost all video cards can be set up with a minimal video server. The XF86Setup utility uses a 16-color VGA server known as XF86_VGA16 to create a GUI. This command works even if you only have a command-line interface. As you can see in Figure 10.2, there are six sections to this utility: Mouse, Keyboard, Card, Monitor, Modeselection, and Other.

If your mouse isn't working, you can use the Tab key to switch between available options. Once your option is highlighted, press the Spacebar to select the option that you want.

Once you've finished your reconfiguration, click the Done button at the bottom of the screen. As you navigate through the available screens, the Done and Abort options can be selected at any time. After you click Done and confirm your changes, XF86Setup overwrites the /etc/X11/XF86Config file.

Note: The version of XF86Setup discussed in this section is based on version 3.3. Although later versions of this utility are available, they were released after the Sair Linux exams were originally created.

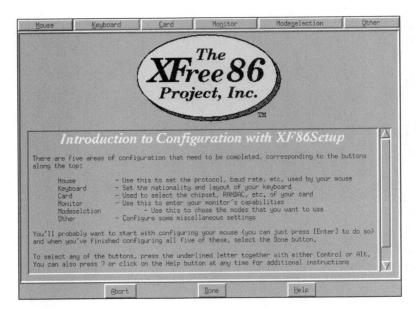

Figure 10.2   The XF86Setup utility.

Mouse

As shown in Figure 10.3, you can customize your mouse in any number of ways. But the key objective is to get a working mouse. All other items shown in Figure 10.3 that are not described in the following list are less important. To get a working mouse, choose from the following options:

➤ *Protocol*—The protocol you choose selects a driver, which determines how your computer communicates with your mouse.

➤ *Device*—The mouse device is based on how your mouse is connected to your computer. Although a PS/2 mouse is set up for the /dev/psaux device, a serial mouse is generally attached to a COM port. If you don't see an option for COM ports, you should see something like /dev/ttyS0 or /dev/cua0, which corresponds to COM1 (/dev/ttyS1 or /dev/cua1 corresponds to COM2, etc.).

➤ *3 Buttons*—If you only have a two-button mouse, you'll want to emulate three buttons. The middle button is used for a number of Linux GUI pop-up menus including copy and paste operations.

Note: You can't configure special devices, such as joysticks and graphic tablets, with XF86Setup. If you want to use one of these devices in a Linux GUI, you'll need to add its settings directly to the /etc/X11/XF86Config file.

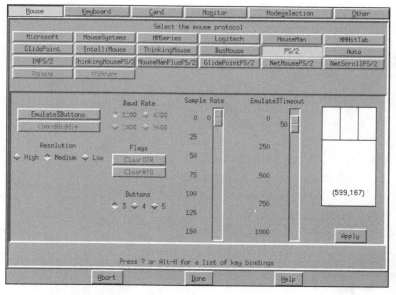

Figure 10.3 XF86Setup mouse configuration options.

Keyboard

If you're working with a keyboard that isn't standard in the United States, you can use the options in this section to select a keyboard model and language that more closely match your hardware. These options also allow you to manage the functionality of some keys.

Card

The X Server is located on the client computer. It communicates directly with your video controller. As you can see in Figure 10.4, there are a wide variety of cards to choose from.

Even if your card is part of this list, XF86Setup may not recognize all of the features of your card. If you click Detailed Setup, you'll see options in the menu that allow you to set the RAM, chipset, clock setting, and video server associated with your video controller card. You can even use this section to set up a generic card.

Monitor

You can select from 10 different types of monitors through the Monitor section of the XF86Setup utility. Each monitor that you select has a different available range of horizontal and vertical frequencies. Check the documentation for your monitor. If you select frequencies that exceed the capabilities of your monitor, you could damage it beyond repair.

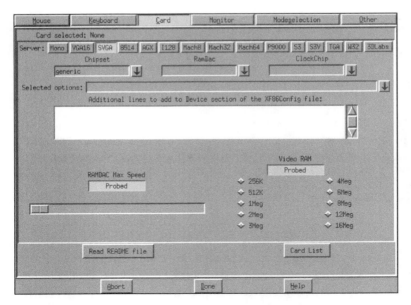

Figure 10.4   XF86Setup video controller card configuration options.

Modeselection

You can select two types of modes: pixel dimensions and color depth. The XF86Setup utility allows you to select pixel dimensions from 320×200 to 1600×1200. It allows you to select color depth in bits: 8, 16, 24, or 32.

If you select more than one graphics mode, you can switch between these modes using the Ctrl+Alt+Num+ and Ctrl+Alt+Num- commands. Num+ and Num- are the plus and minus keys on the numeric keypad. Using this method assumes the Allow Video Mode Switching option is enabled as described in the next section.

Other

The two key options in this section are Allow Server To Be Killed With Hotkey Sequence Ctrl+Alt+Backspace and Allow Video Mode Switching. The first option allows you to exit the X Server by pressing the noted keys. That option returns you to the command-line interface or an X login window, depending on the level set as initdefault in your /etc/inittab configuration file.

Xconfigurator

Red Hat Linux has its own set of graphical configuration utilities including Xconfigurator, mouseconfig, and kbdconfig. Although they're released under the General Public License (GPL), they are generally available only on Red Hat and derived distributions.

You can configure the X Window, or X11, with Xconfigurator nearly as well as with XF86Setup. If your mouse doesn't work, you can use the Tab, Arrow, Page Up, Page Down, and Spacebar keys to navigate Xconfigurator's menus. The database of video controllers and monitors is somewhat limited: You can set up a custom monitor with the same criteria as used on other utilities.

Don't exceed the horizontal or vertical refresh capabilities of your monitor. When prompted, don't probe your video controller. Select the amount of memory available on your video card from the available menu. Also don't select a clock chip; the X Server can set this when you start the X Window.

SaX

S.u.S.E. has its own graphical configuration utility known as SaX. You can start it from a command-line interface or one of the S.u.S.E. menus. SaX is divided into five sections: mouse, keyboard, card, monitor, and desktop. SaX is almost as complete as the X86Setup utility.

Window Managers

Window managers determine what you see in a GUI desktop. As strange as it sounds, a window manager is also an application. Linux window managers don't interface directly with the kernel; you can shut down any window manager without shutting down Linux.

The following sections provide a brief overview of seven different window managers. There are several dozen window managers that you can configure and install on your Linux computer. If you're familiar with Linux, you've probably heard about at least two of these window managers: GNOME and KDE.

Linux window managers can be divided into three categories. The first window managers, such as fvwm, include a minimum of frills, which keeps them simple. They demand little in resources. A second group emphasizes customizability; these window managers include Enlightenment, Afterstep, Window Maker, and Blackbox. The third group's window managers, which include GNOME and KDE, contain their own login screens, applications, icons, menu bars, and so on for a complete desktop package.

GNOME

GNOME is a complete desktop package, which includes utilities such as a package manager, pop-up menus, and other utilities. GNOME applications include an office suite, financial programs, and more. It is based on the GTK+ widget library, which is released under the GPL. As of this writing, GNOME is the default window manager for Red Hat Linux.

 GNOME also includes a display manager, used in place of **xdm**, to manage logins. You can set up the GNOME display manager to log in to a window manager other than GNOME.

KDE

Like GNOME, KDE is a complete package, which includes utilities such as a control panel, package manager, taskbar with icons, and pop-up menus. KDE applications include an office suite, a package manager, and a mail reader. KDE is based on the Qt widget library, which was recently relicensed under the GPL. It is perhaps the window manager that most closely resembles Microsoft Windows in its look and feel. As of this writing, KDE is the default window manager for Corel, S.u.S.E., and Caldera Linux.

KDE also includes a display manager, used in place of **xdm**, to manage logins. You can set up the KDE display manager to log in to a window manager other than KDE.

fvwm

The fvwm window manager was the standard before the development of KDE and GNOME. Because it requires a relatively small amount of memory, it was popular in an age when memory was more expensive. Most of its options are contained in the pop-up menus. Version 2 of fvwm updated the look and feel of this GUI. A later version known as fvwm95 was designed to look something like Microsoft Windows 95.

Enlightenment

As of this writing, the Enlightenment window manager is a work in progress. Other window managers borrow code from each other, whereas Enlightenment is unique. It's designed to be the most configurable of window managers, which makes it more suitable for users who aren't satisfied with any other window manager. It is usually installed on higher-end workstations for users who need the power, not for their window manager, but for their graphical applications.

AfterStep

Although the AfterStep window manager is based on fvwm code, it is designed to look like the GUI for the NeXTStep operating system. Originally designed for the NeXT workstation, NeXTStep was designed to be a more intuitive GUI. NeXT was developed by Apple engineers who wanted to extend the user friendliness of the Macintosh operating system.

AfterStep includes a "wharf" of icons, which allows you to launch programs seemingly like a pictorial version of the Microsoft Windows Start menu.

WindowMaker

The WindowMaker window manager is similar in feel to AfterStep. As an official part of the GNU project, its developers are currently incorporating GNOME features into its GUI.

Blackbox

The Blackbox window manager is designed to run in a minimum of RAM. Images are cached after they're drawn on your screen. Unlike many of the other window managers, Blackbox includes support for KDE, but not for GNOME applications.

Window Manager Commonalities

There are a wide variety of Linux window managers. As discussed in the previous sections, each window manager has a number of special features. Even though this chapter does not review all available Linux window managers, all window managers share some commonalities. They have virtual displays. You can copy and paste text between different windows. In addition, within individual X Windows, you can scroll up and down a file, resize the window, or change the size of the font.

Several window managers make it possible to incorporate features and applications from the GNOME and KDE packages.

Virtual Displays

With most GUIs, what you see on the monitor is all the display room that you get. To get more room in other GUIs, you need another monitor. With the Linux X Window, most window managers actually include several virtual displays. You can switch between displays by clicking on a pager, which moves you from one virtual display to another.

An example of a virtual display pager is shown in Figure 10.5 on the right. The numbers 1, 2, 3, and 4 signify the virtual displays available in this window manager.

Hidden Windows

If you can't find a window that's open or you think your system is "locked," there are a couple of things that you can try before you close your X Window. Your window may only be hidden; pressing the Alt+Tab keys toggles you between available windows. Your window may be in another virtual display; try clicking the other pages of the virtual display pager.

Copy and Paste

As of this writing, Linux window managers don't include a regular clipboard that allows you to copy and paste between applications. But you can copy text

Figure 10.5   Window manager taskbars often include pagers.

between two applications in the X Window. This assumes that you have a three-button mouse or have set up three-button emulation with a tool like XF86Setup. Use the following steps to copy text between two applications:

1. Highlight the text that you want to copy.

2. Move the cursor to the destination window.

3. Click the middle mouse button. If you have only two mouse buttons, and you have set up three-button emulation, click both buttons simultaneously.

Practice Questions

Question 1

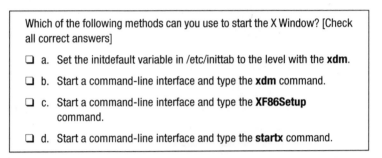

Which of the following methods can you use to start the X Window? [Check all correct answers]

☐ a. Set the initdefault variable in /etc/inittab to the level with the **xdm**.

☐ b. Start a command-line interface and type the **xdm** command.

☐ c. Start a command-line interface and type the **XF86Setup** command.

☐ d. Start a command-line interface and type the **startx** command.

Answers a, b, c, and d are correct. The initdefault variable determines the run level started by Linux after it runs through other startup routines. Although the **xdm** command doesn't start a window manager, it does start an X Window login screen. Although the **XF86Setup** command doesn't start a "normal" GUI, it does start an X Window (XF86_VGA16). The **startx** command starts the X Window, assuming you've already configured it for your system.

Question 2

When Johnny uses the **startx** command to start the X Window, the X Server needs initialization files. Assume initialization files are available in all of the following directories. Which directory's initialization files does **startx** use to set up Johnny's X Window?

○ a. /etc/X11/xinit/

○ b. ~

○ c. /home/johnny/init

○ d. /etc/

Answer b is correct. The initialization files in any user's home directory, as signified by the tilde (~), take precedence. The systemwide initialization files are located in the /etc/X11/xinit directory. Because these files find initialization files in Johnny's home directory, answer a is incorrect. As of this writing, no Linux distribution keeps initialization files in the /home/johnny/init directory; therefore, answer c is incorrect. Although there are a lot of initialization files in the /etc/ directory, none are related to starting the X Window; therefore, answer d is incorrect.

Question 3

You're configuring the X Window in a Red Hat Linux system. Which of the following utilities can you use? [Check all correct answers]

❑ a. Xconfigurator

❑ b. xf86setup

❑ c. XF86Config

❑ d. XF86Setup

Answers a and d are correct. The Xconfigurator is used with the Red Hat Linux distribution. The XFree86 project's XF86Setup utility is generally included in all Linux distributions. Because the case of the **xf86setup** command is not correct (should be **XF86Setup**), this command would not work. Therefore, answer b is incorrect. Although there is an xf86config utility that configures the X Window, you can't start it with the **XF86Config** command. Therefore, answer c is incorrect.

Question 4

Window managers are applications. Assume you have a program that has run out of control. You can't move your mouse, but you can type a command-line command in an xterm window. You're running in superuser mode. Which of the following commands can you use to stop your window manager without stopping or restarting Linux?

○ a. Ctrl+Alt+Del

○ b. **reboot**

○ c. Ctrl+Alt+Backspace

○ d. Ctrl+Alt+Num+

Answer c is correct. The Ctrl+Alt+Backspace keys, when pressed together, force Linux to exit your window manager. Because the Ctrl+Alt+Del and **reboot** commands stop and restart Linux, answers a and b are incorrect. Although the Ctrl+Alt+Num+ command does switch video modes, it does not exit your window manager. Therefore, answer d is incorrect.

Question 5

> Which of the following configuration utilities can help you set up your keyboard and mouse as well as your video hardware?
>
> ○ a. SuperProbe
>
> ○ b. XF86Config
>
> ○ c. XF86Setup
>
> ○ d. Xconfigurator

Answer c is correct. The XF86Setup utility includes sections that help you configure mice or pointing devices and keyboards. And it helps you configure your monitor and video controller. Because the SuperProbe utility just probes for your current video hardware, answer a is incorrect. XF86Config is not a valid configuration utility (it's xf86config); therefore, answer b is incorrect. Because the Xconfigurator only allows you to configure your monitor and video controller, answer d is incorrect.

Question 6

> Why can you shut down a window manager, such as KDE or GNOME, without rebooting Linux?
>
> ○ a. A window manager is just another application.
>
> ○ b. Window managers are set up to respond to the Ctrl+Alt+Backspace command by shutting down.
>
> ○ c. When you shut down a complete window manager like KDE or GNOME, you have no choice. You have to halt or reboot Linux.
>
> ○ d. Window managers include special commands in their menus that allow you to log off.

Answer a is correct. Because window managers are applications, they do not directly affect the kernel. When they lock up, you can shut them down without rebooting Linux. Although you can use the Ctrl+Alt+Backspace keys to shut down window managers, that option does not explain why you don't have to reboot Linux. Therefore, answer b is incorrect. Because you can shut down KDE or GNOME with the Ctrl+Alt+Backspace keys without rebooting, answer c is incorrect. Although window managers do include special commands that allow you to log off, in KDE and GNOME, you still end up in their login screens. And that option does not explain why you don't have to reboot Linux. Therefore, answer d is incorrect.

Question 7

You've set up Linux to start the X Window automatically. Which of the following is a correct sequence of events when Linux starts the GUI?

○ a. Linux starts the X Server, and then continues with the GNOME display manager. When you log in, Linux starts the Blackbox window manager.

○ b. Linux starts the **xdm** display manager. When you log in, Linux starts the X Server, and then continues with the KDE window manager.

○ c. Linux starts the X Server, and then continues on with the **xdm** window manager. When you log in, Linux starts the Enlightenment display manager.

○ d. Linux starts the GNOME display manager. When you log in, Linux starts the X Server, and then continues with the GNOME window manager.

Answer a is correct. Linux has to start the X Server before you see anything graphical on your screen. You then see a display manager for logins. When you log in, you continue on to a window manager. The GNOME display manager can start other window managers. Because you need an X Server before you see a display manager, answers b and d are incorrect. Because **xdm** is a display manager, not a window manager, answer c is incorrect.

Question 8

Which of the following features allows you to move between displays in a window manager?

○ a. Virtual console

○ b. Ctrl+Alt+F2

○ c. Pager

○ d. Unused video memory

Answer c is correct. A pager allows you to move between virtual displays in your window manager. Virtual consoles allow you to move between different text-based login screens; therefore, answer a is incorrect. Because the Ctrl+Alt+F2 command allows you to move to the second virtual console, this is unrelated to virtual displays. Therefore, answer b is incorrect. Although unused video memory allows window mangers to create virtual displays, that feature itself does not allow you to move between virtual displays. Therefore, answer d is incorrect.

Question 9

You have a text editor open in your window manager, and you want to copy some of the commands and output to a terminal window. What steps would you take? Note: You have set up your two-button mouse to emulate three buttons.

○ a. Highlight the desired text in the editor. Right-click it, and choose Copy. Move your cursor to the second window. Press the right mouse button, and choose the Paste option that appears.

○ b. Highlight the desired text in the editor. Left-click it, and choose Copy. Move your cursor to the second window. Press both mouse buttons, and choose the Paste option that appears.

○ c. Highlight the desired text in the editor. Move your cursor to the second window. Press the right mouse button, and choose the Paste option that appears.

○ d. Highlight the desired text in the editor. Move your cursor to the second window. Press both mouse buttons simultaneously.

Answer d is correct. The middle button automatically pastes whatever you have highlighted in another window. Although a right-click opens a pop-up menu containing a Copy option in some applications, this option is not available in all applications. Therefore, answer a is incorrect. Once you highlight some words, a left-click generally deselects those words. Therefore, answer b is incorrect. Although a right-click in the target application sometimes brings up a pop-up menu with a Paste option, this is not always true. Therefore, answer c is incorrect.

Question 10

> You have a very capable video controller and monitor. You've used the XF86Setup utility to configure several graphics modes. Which keys do you press to switch between graphics modes?
>
> ○ a. Ctrl+Alt+Backspace
>
> ○ b. Ctrl+Alt++
>
> ○ c. Ctrl+Alt+Num-
>
> ○ d. Ctrl+Alt+F3

Answer c is correct. The Ctrl+Alt+Num+ and Ctrl+Alt+Num- key combinations allow you to switch between your selected graphics modes. The Ctrl+Alt+Backspace key combination exits the X Window; therefore, answer a is incorrect. The plus key in Ctrl+Alt++ is not on the numeric keypad; therefore, answer b is incorrect. Because Ctrl+Alt+F3 switches to a virtual text console, answer d is incorrect.

Need to Know More?

 The official Web site of the developers of the Blackbox window manager at **http://blackbox.alug.org** includes support for KDE applications. You may note that this is a subdomain of the Amarillo Linux Users Group.

 The official home page for the AfterStep window manager at **www.afterstep.org** is designed with the look and feel of Apple's NeXTStep GUI.

 The official Enlightenment Web site is at **www.enlightenment.org**. Enlightenment is designed to be the most configurable window manager.

 Investigate the home page for the fvwm desktop at **www.fvwm.org**. The fvwm desktop is designed just as a window manager for other applications.

 The home page for the GNOME Project is located at **www.gnome.org**. The GNOME project consists of a group of developers who are, like KDE, working on a window manager and a complete package of applications.

 The **www.kde.org** Web site is the official home page for the KDE, which includes a window manager and other applications such as a fully featured office suite.

 Check out the Web site for the XFree86 project at **www.xfree86.org**. XFree86 is a nonprofit organization dedicated to creating video drivers for Linux, Unix, and related operating systems. Use the database on this site to match an appropriate X Server to your video controller.

System Administration

Terms you'll need to understand:

✓ /etc/passwd

✓ Username, password, group

✓ Home directory

✓ Login shell

✓ **adduser**, **useradd**, **userdel**, **newusers**

✓ Linuxconf, COAS, YaST

✓ **who**, **w**

✓ **ps**, **kill**, **nice**, **renice**

✓ **lsmod**, **insmod**, **rmmod**

✓ **chown**, **chgrp**

Techniques you'll need to master:

✓ Explaining the data inside the /etc/passwd file

✓ Setting up a user account

✓ Describing the command-line commands to create new users

✓ Understanding the GUI utilities to create new users

✓ Using commands to identify logged on users and their processes

✓ Identifying, installing, and removing device drivers through kernel modules

✓ Explaining the commands to change the ownership and group of a file or directory

A system administrator installs, configures, and maintains operating systems, sets up users, manages software, and secures networks. In other words, a system administrator needs to know each topic covered on all four Sair Linux/GNU Certified Administrator exams.

At its core, a system administrator's job is to set up users, maintain software, install hardware, monitor running programs, maintain networks, and create back-ups. This chapter covers basic user setup utilities, hardware installation commands, program management utilities, and backup routines. Although these topics are covered in much more detail on the System Administration exam, they are also subjects you need to know when you configure a Linux computer. When you install and configure Linux, you need to be able to perform some basic system administration tasks, including those described in this chapter.

User Accounts

Everyone who logs on to a Linux system needs a user account. Every user account has some rights and privileges that may differ by directory. Users have usernames, passwords, and home directories. Users are configured through an /etc/passwd file. You can create new users by editing that file in a text editor. You can also create new users with three different command-line commands. And several distributions allow you to create new users through their graphical configuration utilities.

The examples shown in the following sections are based on setting up a new user with the username tr. When you set up users for yourself, substitute appropriately.

The Password File

Every user gets a line in your /etc/passwd file. When you open it, you'll see lines such as the following:

```
mj:b7RHH:503:100:Michael Jang:/home/mj:/bin/bash
```

This line tells Linux just about everything it needs to log in the user named Michael Jang. Every column is divided by a colon (:). The purpose of each column is shown in Table 11.1. The example column is taken from the preceding code line.

Every user gets one of these lines. You can set up new users by creating new lines in your /etc/passwd file that follow the format of the preceding code line.

All Linux utilities that create new users perform three basic functions: First, they add a new line to the /etc/passwd file for the user. Second, they create a home directory, assigning ownership to that user. Third, they copy shell startup configuration files, usually from the /etc/skel directory, to the user's new home directory.

Table 11.1	Setup of the /etc/passwd file.*	
Column	**Example**	**Function**
1	mj	Username
2	b7RHH	Password (see table note)
3	503	User ID (every username is associated with a unique user ID)
4	100	Group number (100 usually corresponds to the group named users)
5	Michael Jang	Information about the user
6	/home/mj	User's home directory
7	/bin/bash	User's login shell

*If you see an x or an asterisk (*) in the second column of your /etc/passwd file, user passwords are encrypted.

The commands discussed in the following section generally require root or superuser privileges to run. To go into superuser mode, type the **su** command. Enter the root password when prompted.

Direct User Setup

You can create a user account directly. Open the /etc/passwd file in a text editor, such as emacs or vi. Follow these steps to set up a user account:

1. Start a new line. Copy the applicable information from another user's /etc/ passwd entry (such as the code line shown earlier).

2. Change the username, user ID, and home directory. For example, if you're setting up a new account for Theodore Roosevelt, you might insert "tr" in the first column (username), the number "504" in the third column (user ID), "Theodore Roosevelt" in the fifth column (information about the user), and "/home/tr" in the sixth column (user's home directory). Make sure that the information you enter is unique relative to other entries in your /etc/ passwd file. Unless you want to assign tr to a different group, you don't have to change the group number.

3. Save the /etc/passwd file. (You can save the file only if you're logged in as the root or superuser.)

4. Set up your new user's home directory. The **mkdir -p /home/tr** command, discussed in Chapter 8, should work for the superuser from any command-line interface.

5. Make sure your new user can access his home directory. Give him ownership with the **chown tr /home/tr** and **chgrp 100 /home/tr** commands. If the username or group number is different, substitute appropriately.

6. Assign a new password with the **passwd tr** command. Once complete, user tr can assign a new password to himself with the same command.

7. Copy basic initialization files, which are normally stored in the /etc/skel directory. These are the files, such as .bashrc and .bash_profile, covered in Chapter 6. Change your identity to the new user with the **su - tr** command. Copy these files with the **cp /etc/skel/.* /home/tr** command.

8. Log out, and tell your new user about his new username and password.

Note: The steps are slightly different if you have encrypted passwords in a /etc/ shadow file. Details of this process are not covered on this Sair Installation and Configuration exam.

adduser

When you're working with a large number of users, you need a method that can help you add users quickly. One way of automating the user creation process is to use the **adduser** command. To use the **adduser** command to set up tr's account, type the following:

```
adduser tr
```

Depending on your distribution, this command may prompt you for other settings, such as group and password. Alternately, it may take settings from the control file /etc/adduser.conf. In some distributions, the **adduser** command works just like the **useradd** command.

useradd

You can also use the **useradd** command to create a new user. To use the **useradd** command to set up tr's account, type the following:

```
useradd tr
```

This command sets up user tr with the defaults shown when you run the **useradd** **-D** command. If you want to change some of these defaults for your new user, execute the **man useradd** command, and use the switches shown to modify the defaults.

userdel

The **userdel** command is also straightforward. If you have a user named Theodore Roosevelt who just left your company, you'll want to deactivate his account. Once you've retrieved any files you need from his home directory, run the following command:

```
userdel -r tr
```

This command deletes tr's information from the /etc/passwd file. The **-r** switch deletes the /home/tr directory including any files and directories that it may contain.

newusers

The **newusers** command is designed to handle a large number of users from a batch file of usernames and passwords, as described on the **newusers** man page. If you create a list of users and passwords in a file named new-batch, you can then set up these users with the following command:

```
newusers new-batch
```

If you save this batch file, make sure it's secure. You might want to hide it, encrypt it, or delete it. A list of usernames and passwords is a very tempting tool for anyone who wants to crack your system.

Linuxconf

Red Hat Linux's graphical user interface (GUI) configuration utility is known as Linuxconf. Because it's licensed under the General Public License (GPL), other Linux companies are free to incorporate it into their distributions. It's an "all-in-one" utility that allows you to configure everything from networking to user accounts. To start Linuxconf from the X Window, open up a command-line shell, go into root or superuser mode, and type the **linuxconf** command. You can set up a new user account in Linuxconf as shown in Figure 11.1.

The input shown in Figure 11.1 sets up the user tr with the noted group, home directory, shell (command interpreter), and user ID. As always, be sure to use unique usernames, user ID numbers, and home directories.

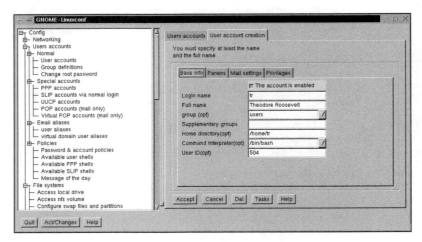

Figure 11.1   Setting up a new user account with Linuxconf.

Note: Figure 11.1 shows the Linuxconf interface in the X Window. The Linuxconf screen that you get from a command line virtual terminal is somewhat different.

COAS

Caldera has several GUI user creation utilities including LISA, COAS, and Webmin. Each of these utilities allows a system administrator to configure everything from networking to user accounts. You can set up a new user account in COAS as shown in Figure 11.2.

The input shown in Figure 11.2 sets up the user tr with the noted user ID, group, shell (command interpreter), and home directory. As always, be sure to use unique usernames, user ID numbers, and home directories.

YaST

S.u.S.E. Linux has its own proprietary all-in-one configuration package known as YaST (Yet another Setup Tool). Like Linuxconf, you can open it in a command-line interface or in the GUI. Once open, navigate to the System Administration menu, and then navigate to User Administration for the menu shown in Figure 11.3.

The input shown in Figure 11.3 sets up the user tr with the noted user ID, group, home directory, and shell (command interpreter). As always, be sure to use unique usernames, user ID numbers, and home directories.

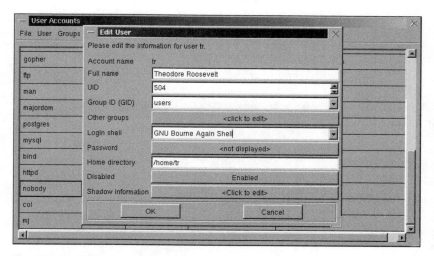

Figure 11.2   Setting up a new user account with COAS.

```
┌─────────────────────────USER ADMINISTRATION──────────────────────────┐
│ In this dialog you can get information about existing users, create new│
│ users, and modify and delete existing users.                          │
│                                                                        │
│  User name                        :tr        :                         │
│                                                                        │
│  Numerical user ID                :504       :                         │
│                                                                        │
│  Group (numeric or by name)       :users     :                         │
│                                                                        │
│  Home directory                   :/home/tr          :                 │
│                                                                        │
│  Login shell                      :/bin/bash         :                 │
│                                                                        │
│  Password                         :*******   :                         │
│  Re-enter password                :*******   :                         │
│                                                                        │
│  Access to modem permitted        [X]                                  │
│                                                                        │
│   Detailed description of the user                                     │
│  :Theodore Roosevelt_                                :                  │
│  F1=Help                  F3=Selection list    F4=Create user          │
│  F5=Delete user           F6=Password times    F10=Leave screen        │
└────────────────────────────────────────────────────────────────────────┘
```

Figure 11.3   Setting up a new user account with YaST.

System Administration Commands

As you start using Linux, you'll want to make sure all parts of the system are running smoothly. There are commands that you can use to monitor currently logged on users, as well as the processes they are running.

If any of your users have a problem with any application, you can use the **kill** command to kill that application. If an important program or procedure is about to run, commands such as **nice** and **renice** can help you raise or lower the priority associated with the program of your choice.

who and w

Although the **who** and **w** commands both tell you which accounts are currently logged on to the Linux system, the **w** command actually goes into more detail. As an administrator, you should check logons regularly; for example, the following output from **who** shows the same person logged on from two different locations:

```
mj       tty1      Sep 22 10:24
tr       ttyp1     Sep 21 21:28     (linux2.mommabears.com)
mj       ttyp0     Sep 21 21:18     (cracker.notnice.cba)
```

Because user mj is logged on from the local computer and remotely from the cracker computer, you should be concerned that someone else is using mj's username and password to break into your system.

Network logins to your Linux computer come into terminals such as ttyp0 or ttyp1. Logins on the local computer don't include the *p*.

The **w** command also tells you about the demand for computer resources. For example, the following output from **w** shows a system with three users that has been up for nearly a full day:

```
10:27am  up 23:38,  3 users,  load average: 0.15, 0.03, 0.01
USER   TTY    FROM         LOGIN@  IDLE    JCPU   PCPU   WHAT
mj     tty1                10:24am 3:02    0.10s  0.10s  -bash
tr     ttyp1  linux2.mo.   Thu 9pm 12:59m  0.11s  0.11s  -bash
mj     ttyp0  cracker.cb   Thu 9pm 12:59m  0.12s  0.12s  find passwd
```

More importantly, it shows the process currently being run by user mj from the remote location. Because that user is running the **find** command to look for password files, you have even more reason for concern.

ps

The **ps** command shows currently running processes or programs. When you type the **ps** command by itself, you see the processes associated with your setup. If you type the **ps aux** command, you can see everything running on your Linux system including daemons. Another useful variation is **ps l**, which returns a "long list" associated with each currently running process. Important categories from this command include:

➤ *PID*—The process identifier. Every process is associated with a number known as a process identifier.

➤ *PPID*—The parent process identifier. Every process has a parent except **init**. If you can't kill a process, you might be able to kill the parent process.

➤ *PRI*—The priority value. Higher priority programs get attention from your CPU more quickly. The highest priority program has a PRI of -20. The lowest priority program has a PRI of 19.

➤ *STAT*—The current status of the process. There are three options: Running (R), Sleeping (S), or Swapped (SW) to the swap partition.

As discussed in the following sections, if you have a program that's running out of control, you need the PID number to kill the problem program. Alternately, if you need to run a program that's stuck waiting for CPU resources, you can use its PID to raise its priority.

You can also use the **top** command to see the processes that are overloading your system. The **top** command lists the processes that are most heavily loading your CPU and RAM memory. But it only lists as many processes as it can show on your screen.

kill

By reputation, Linux doesn't crash. There are reports of users and Web sites powered by Linux running without reboots for months at a time. One reason behind this is that system administrators can manage troublesome programs with the **kill** command.

For example, if a program like Netscape locks up on you while you're browsing the Internet, follow these steps to kill the program:

1. Open a command-line shell. If you can't open a command-line shell inside an X Window, start a new virtual console with the Ctrl+Alt+F*x* command, where *x* is a number between 1 and 6.

2. Run the **ps aux | grep netscape** command. The number after your username is the PID of the process that is currently running Netscape on your computer. Record that number. For purposes of this exercise, assume the number is 1711.

3. Run the **kill 1711** command. If your PID is different, substitute accordingly. If the **kill** command doesn't work, run the **ps auxl | grep netscape** command to find the PPID. You may need to kill the parent process first.

nice and renice

The **nice** and **renice** commands let you run programs at different relative priorities. The priority of any program can range from -20 (highest) to 19 (lowest). The **nice** program starts another process with an adjusted priority. For example, you could set Netscape to start after all others are finished with the **nice -n 20 netscape** command. If you need to focus Linux on one specific program, you need its PID. Once you find the program's PID (assume it's 1711 for this exercise), you can raise its priority with the **renice -10 1711** command.

Note: To understand priorities, keep in mind that everything seems reversed in Linux. If you want to make a program more important, use a negative number.

Kernel Module Management

The Linux kernel translates commands between your applications and your computer hardware. Each piece of hardware, such as a hard disk, modem, CPU, or video controller, has a device driver. In some cases, drivers are integrated within the kernel. In other cases, modules are added to the kernel at runtime or when you start Linux on your computer. In either case, the kernel communicates directly with your hardware.

There are three basic commands used to manage Linux kernel modules: **lsmod**, **insmod**, and **rmmod**.

lsmod

To see the loaded modules that are currently running on your system, run the **/sbin/lsmod** command. Take a look at the following sample output from this command:

```
Module          Size    Used by
sound           56616   0       (autoclean) (unused)
soundcore       2412    3       (autoclean) [sound]
soundlow        252     0       (autoclean) [sound]
3c589_cs        8312    1
ds              6820    2       [3c589_cs serial_cs]
i82365          30260   2
pcmcia_core     45988   0       [3c589_cs serial_cs ds i82365]
nls_iso8859-1   2024    1       (autoclean)
nls_cp437       3548    1       (autoclean)
```

Each loaded module is associated with a device driver. The amount of memory used is listed in bytes. The Used By column shows the number of programs currently using that driver. The modules loaded when you start Linux are taken from the /etc/conf.modules file.

insmod

When you install new hardware, Linux may not detect it. When you install a new kernel, you may need to install new drivers. Linux drivers are associated with a specific kernel. If the version number is *x.y.z*, you can find the drivers in the /lib/modules/x.y.z directory. Some hardware comes with its own Linux modules, which can be downloaded from the Internet or loaded from a floppy disk. For example, if you just installed a Linksys Etherfast PCMCIA card in your computer, run the following command to load the driver:

```
insmod /lib/modules/2.4.8/pcmcia/wavelan_cs.o
```

Linux drivers are generally stored in files with an .o extension. If your driver is in a different directory, substitute appropriately.

Once you've confirmed that your driver works, add it to your /etc/conf.modules file. Then you won't have to use the **insmod** command to install this driver every time you start Linux.

rmmod

You can and should remove unneeded modules, because they take up memory that can be used by your programs. For example, if you're no longer using the wavelan_cs.o module, the following command removes the driver module:

```
rmmod wavelan_cs
```

Note that wavelan_cs is the module name as you would see it in the output from the **lsmod** command.

Permissions and Ownership

What you can do to control and manipulate Linux files depends on the permissions, owners, and groups associated with that file. You set up permissions with commands like **mkdir** and **chmod** in Chapters 7 and 8. But permissions don't do you much good if files and directories are associated with the wrong owners or groups. You can change the owner and group associated with a file or a directory with the **chown** (change ownership) and **chgrp** (change group) commands.

As you read through the following sections, look at these commands in the context of the following output from the **ls -l** command:

```
drwxr-x---  1  tr  users  7326 Jan 12 09:09    /home/tr
```

chown

Earlier, you assigned ownership of a directory to a new user with the **chown tr /home/tr** command. Based on the preceding example, only the owner of a file has read, write, and execute (rwx) permissions on that file, which in this case is a directory.

chgrp

Earlier, you assigned a directory to a group with the **chgrp 100 /home/tr** command. This command assigned the /home/tr directory to the group named users. Every user who is part of the users group has read and execute (rx) permissions on the /home/tr directory.

Practice Questions

Question 1

Based on the output from the **who** command, how can you tell if someone is logged in to Linux through a network connection?

O a. You see something like linux4.mommabears.com at the end of the user's entry.

O b. You see a terminal like tty9 associated with a user.

O c. You see a terminal like ttyp3 associated with a user.

O d. You see a username listed a second time in the output.

Answer c is correct. A terminal name with a *p* is associated with a network logon to Linux. Because answer a does not specify terminal names, you can't tell whether linux4.mommabears.com is the local computer. Therefore, answer a is incorrect. Although tty9 is a higher terminal number than you might normally see on a Linux computer, it is still a local logon. Therefore, answer b is incorrect. Because you can log on locally with virtual terminals more than once, a second instance of a username does not mean that user has also logged on remotely. Therefore, answer d is incorrect.

Question 2

Which of the following commands tells you the drivers that are currently loaded with your Linux kernel?

O a. **insmod**

O b. **lsmod**

O c. **rmmod**

O d. **cat /etc/conf.modules**

Answer b is correct. The **lsmod** command lists currently loaded drivers. The **insmod** command installs but does not list drivers; therefore, answer a is incorrect. Because the **rmmod** command removes but does not list drivers, answer c is incorrect. Although the /etc/conf.modules file lists the drivers loaded into Linux at runtime (when you start), it does not include any drivers that you might have added with the **insmod** command. Therefore, answer d is incorrect.

Question 3

> You've set up a Linux computer with two different network cards. When you
> check status with the **lsmod** command, you only see the driver for one of
> the cards, which is assigned to the **eth0** driver. Which command gets your
> Fast Ethernet card D-Link DFE-650 driver installed? The DFE-650 card works
> with the pcnet_cs driver. The driver can be found in the /lib/modules/2.4.6/
> net directory.
>
> ○ a. **insmod /lib/modules/2.4.6/net/pcnet_cs**
>
> ○ b. **insmod pcnet_cs.o**
>
> ○ c. **insmod dfe_650 pcnet_cs.o**
>
> ○ d. **insmod /lib/modules/2.4.6/net/pcnet_cs.o**

Answer d is correct. Linux drivers have a .o extension. Answer a does not include a
.o extension; therefore, answer a is incorrect. Unless the driver directory is part of
your $PATH variable, you need to call out the full directory location for the
driver. Because answer b does not include the full path to the pcnet_cs.o driver,
answer b is incorrect. Because the driver is not named dfe_650, answer c is incorrect.

Question 4

> Which of the following commands can you use to find the number of pro-
> cesses or programs currently running on your Linux system? This applies to
> all processes, not just those started by any one user.
>
> ○ a. **ps l**
>
> ○ b. **w**
>
> ○ c. **ps aux**
>
> ○ d. **top**

Answer c is correct. The **ps aux** command lists all currently running processes
including daemons and processes started by other users. Although the **ps l** command lists PID numbers, it does not list all processes started by all users. Therefore,
answer a is incorrect. The **w** command lists current users and logon terminals,
which are not closely related to the number of currently running processes. Therefore, answer b is incorrect. The **top** command is more suited to finding the program
that's putting the most load on the system. Therefore, answer d is incorrect.

Question 5

Which of the following commands lists all currently logged on users and their command-line interface shells?

- ○ a. **w**
- ○ b. **who**
- ○ c. **top**
- ○ d. **w l grep bash**

Answer a is correct. The **w** command lists currently logged on users and their shells. The **who** command doesn't include users' shells; therefore, answer b is incorrect. The **top** command may not show processes from all users; therefore, answer c is incorrect. Because answer d would only show those users who use the **bash** shell, answer d is incorrect.

Question 6

Others in your group (users) aren't able to access files in your home directory. Your username is tr. You've assigned read, write, and execute permissions to the group. Based on the following output from the **ls -l /home/tr** command, which of the following commands solves your problem? Note: You don't want to give permissions to your home directory to everyone.

```
drwxrwx---  2 tr   tr   1024   Dec 16 20:45   tr
```

- ○ a. **chown users /home/tr**
- ○ b. **chgrp users /home/tr**
- ○ c. **chmod 777 /home/tr**
- ○ d. **chgrp /home/tr users**

Answer b is correct. You need to change the group associated with the /home/tr directory to users. Answer a uses the **chown** command, which is for usernames. But users is a Linux group. Even if you could use *users* as a username, the **chown users /home/tr** command still wouldn't address the group problem. Therefore, answer a is incorrect. Although **chmod 777 /home/tr** would allow others in your group to access your directory, it would allow everyone with a username on your system permissions to access your directory. Therefore, answer c is incorrect. Because answer d has the directory and group in the wrong order, answer d is also incorrect.

Question 7

There are a variety of tools available to set up a new user. Yet, they essentially perform the same functions on your Linux system. Which one of the following operations is not done when you set up a new user? Assume the new username is tr.

- ○ a. Copy files like .bash_profile from the /etc/skel directory
- ○ b. Add the username and home directory to the /etc/passwd file
- ○ c. Set up the user's shell profile in /home/tr/.bash_profile
- ○ d. Assign ownership of the /home/tr directory to tr
- ○ e. Assign tr to a specific group and set up the /home/tr directory for that group

Answer c is correct. When you set up a new user, you don't need to edit the .bash_profile file. Because files like .bash_profile are copied from /etc/skel to the user's home directory, answer a is incorrect. All usernames and their home directories must be a part of the /etc/passwd file; therefore, answer b is incorrect. The user tr needs to own his/her own home directory to use it; therefore, answer d is incorrect. Because you want the user tr and his/her home directory to be a part of the same group, answer e is incorrect.

Question 8

One of your users calls you and says that his system is locked up in GIMP, an image editing program. Which of the following commands will help you find the process identifier for GIMP? Assume that user is the only one currently using GIMP on your system.

- ○ a. **ps aux l grep gimp**
- ○ b. **ps l gimp**
- ○ c. **ps l grep gimp**
- ○ d. **top**

Answer a is correct. This command lists all currently running processes and sends the output to the **grep gimp** command, which looks for the text string *gimp*. Because the **ps** command alone just lists your own currently running processes, answers b and c are incorrect. Although the **top** command would work if GIMP is using all the CPU or memory resources on your system, that may not be the problem. Therefore, answer d is incorrect.

Question 9

> Which of the following commands is suited to setting up a large number of users and passwords from a batch file?
>
> ○ a. **linuxconf**
>
> ○ b. **newusers**
>
> ○ c. **useradd**
>
> ○ d. **userbatch**

Answer b is correct. The **newusers** command is set up to create users from a batch file of usernames and passwords. Because **linuxconf** only allows you to create users one at a time, answer a is incorrect. Although you can set up **useradd** in a script to take usernames from a batch file, you still need to assign passwords. Therefore, answer c is incorrect. There is no **userbatch** command; therefore, answer d is incorrect.

Question 10

> Netscape seems to have locked up your system. You can't close it in your X Window. You've logged in to a different virtual console and have run the **top** command. You know that the PID for Netscape is 1436. How do you stop Netscape?
>
> ○ a. **stop 1436**
>
> ○ b. **kill 1436**
>
> ○ c. **kill netscape**
>
> ○ d. **stop netscape**

Answer b is correct. This command kills the process with PID 1436, which you've identified as the process for Netscape. There is no **stop** command; therefore, answers a and d are incorrect. Because the **kill** command only recognizes PIDs, answer c is incorrect.

Need to Know More?

 Volkerding, Patrick, Kevin Reichard, and Eric Foster-Johnson. *Linux Configuration and Installation.* M&T Books, Foster City, CA, 1998. ISBN 0-76457-005-6. A step-by-step guide that covers the configuration commands in this chapter and is based on the Slackware distribution.

 The Linux System Administrators' Guide at **www.tml.hut.fi/~viu/linux/ sag** is written for newer administrators. You can also find a copy of this guide through the Linux Documentation Project at **www.linuxdoc.org**.

Network Configuration

Terms you'll need to understand:

✓ LAN, WAN

✓ Domain, hostname

✓ Hardware address

✓ Address classes

✓ Network mask

✓ Gateway

✓ DNS, DHCP

✓ NFS, Samba

✓ Apache, sendmail

✓ Web browsers, FTP clients

✓ Telnet, mail manager

Techniques you'll need to master:

✓ Describing a local area network

✓ Understanding domain names, IP addresses, and hardware addresses

✓ Enumerating the five IP address classes

✓ Using network masks

✓ Understanding gateways and access to other networks

✓ Describing network address services: DNS and DHCP

✓ Detailing other network services: NFS, Samba, sendmail, and Apache

Linux networking is a complex topic, deserving of its own exam. Nevertheless, for this exam, you need to know enough about networking to configure a Linux computer on a local area network (LAN), which is also connected to an outside network, such as the Internet.

You also need to know about some of the available Linux networking services, such as the Network File System (NFS), Apache, or sendmail. However, you do not need to know how to configure these services for the Installation and Configuration exam.

Note: This chapter provides the briefest of introductions to TCP/IP on Linux, which is sufficient for the Sair Linux/GNU Installation and Configuration exam. Other network protocol stacks are not covered. There are a number of "simplifications" in this chapter that allow a less experienced reader to quickly comprehend the fundamentals. If you're setting up a Linux network, consult some of the books in the "Need to Know More?" section at the end of this chapter.

Network Fundamentals

A network consists of two or more computer systems set up to communicate with each other. To some extent, the "media" you use doesn't matter. You can set up a network using parallel cables, telephone modems, Ethernet cards, wireless adapters, or any other media that allows your computers to exchange information. If you can connect these computers directly or through a hub, you can set up a LAN. Each LAN typically has a special IP address known as a *network address*.

A LAN connects computers that are close to each other, such as within an office or a building. An internet consists of two or more connected LANs. Some internets are wide area networks (WAN). A WAN consists of two or more geographically separate networks. The biggest WAN is the Internet.

Note: Two or more LANs that are administered together within a fairly small geographic area are sometimes known as a metropolitan area network (MAN).

Any network or group of networks that are managed by the same group are often known as a *domain*.

When you configure your computer for a network, you assign it an IP address. Before one computer can actually communicate with another, it has to translate this IP address to the hardware address of its network card.

LANs and WANs

Linux LANs are usually configured to a standard known as IEEE 802.3, more popularly known as Ethernet. This type of network is much faster than a telephone modem; Ethernet networks allow computers to communicate at speeds of 10, 100, or even 1,000 megabits per second (Mbps).

Note: Regular Ethernet has a maximum speed of 10Mbps, Fast Ethernet has a maximum speed of 100Mbps, and Gigabit Ethernet has a maximum speed of 1,000Mbps.

But the distance between computers on an Ethernet is limited to a few hundred meters, depending on the type of connection. In essence, the amount of area that LANs can cover is limited, but LANs are fast. In contrast, connections between LANs in a WAN can cover the distance of the Internet, but the speed of the connection is limited. Even "high-speed" WAN connections are typically limited to 1Mbps or less.

 Although you can install Linux over a LAN connection or even through the Internet, it's still generally faster to install Linux from local media, such as a CD-ROM, as discussed in Chapter 5.

The Internet

Even if you've never set up a network, chances are good that you already know something about networking from your experience with the Internet. When connecting to the Internet, most users work through an Internet Service Provider (ISP).

Note: Some larger companies have direct connections to the Internet and act as their own ISPs.

When you connect, your computer becomes a part of that ISP's LAN. You get an IP address, which is a set of four numbers between 0 and 255 divided by periods. For example, the IP address of **www.mommabears.com** is 199.93.70.2.

 If you're currently connected to a network, you can find your IP address with the **/sbin/ifconfig** command.

You connect to the Internet through your ISP's *gateway,* which is a computer that connects that ISP to the rest of the Internet. When you search for a domain name, such as mommabears.com, your computer has to find the mommabears' IP address through your ISP's Domain Name Service (DNS) server. Alternately, you may have the IP address in your /etc/hosts database file.

Domains

When you install Linux, most installation programs ask for your domain name. What the program expects is a name like ilikelinux.now. Unless your computer serves information or otherwise directly connects to the Internet, the name you use does not matter. Just be sure to use the same domain name when you install Linux on each of the computers on your network.

Note: If your computer does connect to the Internet, your ISP may assign you a specific name. This is a common practice with higher speed connections, such as cable modems or digital subscriber lines.

You can divide a domain into a number of subdomains. Each subdomain can represent a different LAN. For example, net1.ilikelinux.now, net2.ilikelinux.now, and net3.ilikelinux.now can represent three different LANs.

Hostname

Every Linux computer on a network needs a hostname. The fully qualified domain name of your computer consists of the hostname and domain name. For example, if your computer has a hostname of bigshot, and your domain name is ilikelinux.now, your fully qualified domain name is bigshot.ilikelinux.now. Every hostname or fully qualified domain name is associated with an IP address.

This works with subdomains as well. For example, if the computer with the hostname of bigshot is on the net1.ilikelinux.now LAN, the fully qualified domain name becomes bigshot.net1.ilikelinux.now.

Note: Your ISP may assign you a fully qualified domain name, which you'll need to set up for any computer that connects directly to the Internet. This is common for higher speed services. You can still assign a second name to that computer, which is consistent with what you set up for your internal network.

If you set up an internal Web server on your LAN, it's easy to get to the home page. Open your Web browser, and type the fully qualified domain name of your Web server in the address or location box.

Hardware Address

Computers call each other by hardware addresses such as 00-60-08-8D-41-93. These are hexadecimal numbers, also known as base 16. Every network card built today is configured with a unique hexadecimal hardware address. When you configure a TCP/IP network, you associate an IP address with a hardware address.

Note: There are 16 digits in hexadecimal notation: 0, 1, 2, 3, 4, 5, 6, 7, 8, 9, A, B, C, D, E, F. If you have a working network card or modem, you can find its hexadecimal hardware address with the /sbin/ifconfig command.

Basic Communication

Now you can put it all together. When you communicate with another computer, you call the hostname or fully qualified domain name of the other computer, such as linux1 or linux1.mommabears.com. TCP/IP uses either the /etc/hosts file or a DNS server to translate this name to an IP address. With a network mask, your computer can figure out whether the destination computer is on your LAN. If the computer is on your LAN, your message searches computer by computer, if necessary, to find the destination.

Once contact is made, each computer identifies its hardware address. Finally, real communication begins. Messages are sent between computers using host and destination addresses that correspond to the appropriate hardware addresses.

IP Addressing

Every computer on a TCP/IP network needs an IP address before it can communicate with others. You or your ISP can assign a permanent address, or IP addresses can be "leased" from what is known as a Dynamic Host Configuration Protocol (DHCP) server.

To set up IP addresses for your network, you need a network address and a network mask. IP addresses that share the same network address and network mask are on the same LAN.

Network addresses fall into one of five different address classes. Network masks define a range of IP addresses that you can assign with a specific network address.

Every network with a connection to other networks needs a gateway IP address for that connection. In Linux, you can limit access to and from your network with the /etc/hosts.allow and /etc/hosts.deny files.

 IP addresses consist of four numbers between 0 and 255. One example of a valid IP address is 254.1.158.33. Each of these numbers is also known as an *octet*. This format of numbers and periods is sometimes known as *dotted-decimal notation* or *dotted-quad format*.

The Sair Linux/GNU exams assume the use of IP version 4 (IPv4), which has been in use since the 1970s. Although the Internet is currently in transition to IP version 6 (IPv6), your IPv4 addresses will still work after the transition is complete.

Address Classes

IP addresses range from 0.0.0.0 to 255.255.255.255. These addresses are divided into five different address classes, A through E. When available, you can assign IP addresses from Class A, B, or C. The range of addresses of each of the five different classes is shown in Table 12.1.

 One special IP address, 127.0.0.1, is known as the *loopback address*. In Linux, this address is also known as *localhost*.

Addresses

If your network is set up to connect to the Internet, you can't just select any IP address. There are a number of *private* IP addresses that you can freely use on your internal network. However, for your connection to the Internet, you need at least one *public* IP address. Each of the computers on your network can access the Internet simultaneously using your public IP address.

Unfortunately, most public IP addresses are taken. Those that are still available are generally assigned by ISPs.

Note: Because public IP addresses are used for communication between computers and networks on the Internet, no two computers on the Internet can share the same public IP address. On the other hand, because private IP addresses are not used for communication on the Internet, you may see the same private IP addresses on different private networks.

To get a public address on the Internet, talk to your ISP. You'll either get a static IP address with a subnet or network mask, or instructions to get your address from a DHCP server. You can then apply that address to the computer on your network that connects to the Internet.

Table 12.1	IP address classes.*	
Class	**Range**	**Comment**
A	1.1.1.1-126.255.255.254	Allows networks of up to 16 million computers
B	128.0.0.1-191.255.255.254	Allows networks of up to 65,000 computers
C	192.0.0.1-223.255.255.254	Allows networks of up to 254 computers
D	224.0.0.1-239.255.255.254	Reserved for multicasts
E	240.0.0.1-255.255.255.254	Experimental use

*Addresses not covered in these ranges are reserved for special uses.

Note: You could, at some expense, get public IP addresses for each computer on your network. However, because they expose every computer on your network to direct access by others, this practice is discouraged.

To set up the computers inside your network with private IP addresses, you need a network address and a network mask. These two parameters define a range of IP addresses. By convention, there are three ranges of private IP addresses, as shown in Table 12.2.

When you choose a network address and network mask, you typically choose a subset of one of the IP address groups shown in Table 12.2. For example, if you have a network address of 10.0.0.0 and a network mask of 255.255.255.0, the range of possible addresses is 10.0.0.0 through 10.0.0.255, which consists of 256 different addresses. But the first address in this subnetwork, 10.0.0.0, is reserved as the network address. And the last address in this subnetwork, 10.0.0.255, is reserved as the broadcast address. You can't assign either address to a specific computer. That leaves 254 addresses on this subnetwork that you can assign to actual computers.

Note: The broadcast address for any network is used to communicate with all computers on that network.

Network Mask

A network mask allows you to determine if a specific IP address is on the same LAN. It also allows you to differentiate network addresses from host addresses. When you put the network address together with the network mask, you can define the range of host addresses that you can assign to your computers.

Note: The rules listed in this section are oversimplifications. You need to know this topic in more detail for the Networking exam. See the "Need to Know More?" section at the end of this chapter for more information on IP addressing.

Several examples of network addresses, host addresses, and network masks are shown in Table 12.3. The Host Address Range column defines the IP addresses that you can assign on your internal network.

Table 12.2 Private IP address ranges.	
Range	**Comment**
10.0.0.1-10.255.255.254	Class A address. Can accommodate about 16 million computers in one domain.
172.168.0.1-172.168.255.254	Class B address. Can accommodate about 65,000 computers in one domain.
192.168.0.1-192.168.255.254	Class C address. Can accommodate up to 254 computers in one domain.

Table 12.3   Example network addresses and network masks.

Network Address	Network Mask	Host Address Range	Number of Usable IP Addresses
10.0.0.0	255.0.0.0	10.0.0.1-10.255.255.254	16,777,214
10.53.0.0	255.255.0.0	10.53.0.1-10.53.255.254	65,534
10.126.13.0	255.255.255.0	10.126.13.1-10.126.13.254	254
172.168.0.0	255.255.0.0	172.168.0.1-172.168.255.254	65,534
172.168.156.0	255.255.255.0	172.168.156.1-172.168.156.254	254
192.168.0.0	255.255.255.0	192.168.0.1-192.168.0.254	254

From Table 12.3, you can derive the following "rules" for IP addressing:

➤ A network IP address is never used for a specific computer. This address precedes the host address range.

➤ The 255s in a network mask correspond to the network address. For example, if your IP address is 10.162.4.23 and your network mask is 255.255.255.0, the network address is 10.162.4.0. The "host" part of the IP address is 23.

➤ The last address in an IP address range is never used. For example, from the last network shown in Table 12.3, the last address is 192.168.0.255, which is reserved as the broadcast address.

➤ For Class A addresses, you can have a network mask of 255.0.0.0, 255.255.0.0, or 255.255.255.0. For Class B addresses, you can have a network mask of 255.255.0.0 or 255.255.255.0. For Class C addresses, you can have a network mask of 255.255.255.0. Although there are other network masks available, understanding all masks is not important to this chapter.

    Be able to use a network mask to break down an IP address into a network address and a host address.

Setting Up a Network

Before you set up a TCP/IP network, you need to select a set of addresses. Based on the previous sections, you can choose a network address and network mask. When you put the two together, you get a range of IP addresses that you can assign within a LAN.

Perhaps the most common network mask is 255.255.255.0. As discussed earlier, this network mask allows you to choose from 254 IP addresses. In other words, if your network address is 192.168.0.0, this network mask allows you to assign 192.168.0.1, 192.168.0.2, 192.168.0.3, and so on through 192.168.0.254 to different computers on your network.

Note: The first address in any network range is the network address. The last address in any network range is the broadcast address. For example, take a network address of 192.168.0.0 and a network mask of 255.255.255.0. The network address is 192.168.0.0, and the broadcast address is 192.168.0.255.

Gateway

The gateway address is the IP address of the computer that's connected to another network, such as the Internet. On a typical LAN, only one computer is directly connected to another network. That computer usually has two network cards: One is connected to the LAN, and the other is connected to the other network. One IP address is assigned to each network card. The gateway address is the IP address of the network card on the LAN.

Take a look at Figure 12.1, which shows a LAN consisting of five computers. The computer that is shown between the hub and the Internet is the gateway computer. The gateway address for all the other computers on this LAN is 192.168.1.3, which is the address that the gateway computer uses on the LAN.

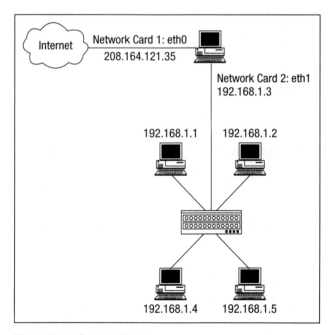

Figure 12.1   Typical LAN with a gateway.

A gateway IP address is in the same range of host IP addresses as other addresses assigned on your network.

Access Controls

On the gateway computer, there are a number of ways to limit access. You can set limits in both directions: to keep unwanted users out, and to keep users on your network from accessing other networks such as the Internet. You can control access by IP address or computer name in the /etc/hosts.allow and /etc/hosts.deny files. At the minimum, you want to deny access to other private IP addresses and any services, such as email or internal Web sites, that you don't want outsiders to use.

Note: The primary way to control access to and from your network is through a firewall utility, such as iptables or ipchains.

Other Network Services

When you're installing Linux, you may need to configure a DNS server, a DHCP server, NFS, and Samba connections.

Among the network services that you can set up on Linux are sendmail and Apache. Sendmail lets you set up a mail server on your Linux computer. Apache lets you set up a Web server on your Linux computer. Although you don't need to know any of these services in detail, it can be helpful to know some basics.

Domain Name Service (DNS)

A DNS server translates names like **www.mommabears.com** to IP addresses like 199.93.70.2. If you're setting up any computer for Internet access, you need access to DNS servers. When you configure Linux for Internet or other network access, you need the IP address of some DNS servers. If you're accessing the Internet through an ISP, ask the ISP for the IP addresses of its DNS servers.

Linux looks for DNS server IP addresses in the /etc/resolv.conf file. If your ISP tells you that the DNS server you should use is 24.1.80.33, add the following line to that file:

```
nameserver 24.1.80.33
```

However, your ISP's main DNS server can't help you with the IP addresses inside your private network. DNS servers on the Internet aren't allowed to carry "private" IP addresses in their databases. You can set up an equivalent service with a database of hostnames and IP addresses in the /etc/hosts file by using a list similar to the following example:

```
192.168.16.1      linux1.mommabears.com      linux1
192.168.16.2      windows1.mommabears.com    windows1
192.168.16.3      laptop1.mommabears.com     laptop1
192.168.16.4      linux2.mommabears.com      linux2
192.168.16.5      examcram.mommabears.com    examcram
```

As you can see, this example lists the hostname and fully qualified domain name associated with each IP address. The drawback is that you need an identical copy of this file on every computer in your network. If you have a large number of computers on your network, this can become difficult to maintain. In that case, it may be easier to set up your own DNS server.

Dynamic Host Configuration Protocol (DHCP)

Computers "lease" IP addresses from a DHCP server for a specified period of time. If a computer is still active when a leased IP address expires, it can renew the lease for an additional period. When a lease from an inactive computer expires, a DHCP server can reassign that address to a different computer.

There are two reasons you might want to use DHCP. If you don't have enough IP addresses for your network, DHCP can help manage what's available. If you have a lot of computers on your network, DHCP can help you avoid the hassle of assigning an IP address to every computer. DHCP requires a server daemon known as **dhcpd**. You can set up this daemon on any Linux computer on your network.

As mentioned earlier, when you connect to the Internet, you need a public IP address. The number of IP addresses available to ISPs is limited. ISPs use DHCP to ration IP addresses among their members. If your ISP uses DHCP to assign an IP address to you, you can set up Linux to receive this address from your ISP's DHCP server through the /etc/dhcpc/config configuration file.

Network File System (NFS)

Once two computers make a connection, they need a common language to share files and printers. The NFS is the main language used to share information between Linux computers. NFS is run by the network file system daemon, **nfsd**. Once set up, you can mount remote directories as easily as you can mount local floppy drives and CD-ROM drives.

The directories that you choose to share are set up in the /etc/exports configuration file. When you're ready, you can set up your /etc/fstab file to mount NFS directories every time you boot Linux.

Samba

Microsoft Windows computers communicate with each other through a language that uses server message blocks (SMB). Linux emulates this language through the Samba system. You need two daemons to run Samba: **smbd** and **nmbd**. The **smb** daemon is the common language; the **nmb** daemon allows Linux to recognize and use Microsoft-based computer names. Once Samba is set up, you can browse Linux computers as easily as any other Microsoft Windows computer in the Windows Network Neighborhood. And you can browse Microsoft Windows systems just as easily from Linux.

The sharing of directories and printers is set up in the /etc/samba/smb.conf or /etc/smb.comf configuration file. You can set up Samba to share in a Microsoft Windows domain governed by Windows NT/2000 servers or workstations, or you can set up Samba to share in Workgroups with Windows 95/98/ME systems.

sendmail

When you set up email for your users, you can assign addresses through your ISP, or you can set up your own email server. If your users have a lot of email, you may want to set up your own mail server. Depending on your distribution, sendmail or smail is the mail server of choice. You can set up sendmail to carry messages through common receipt protocols, such as POP (Post Office Protocol) or IMAP (Internet Message Access Protocol). You can also set up sendmail to transmit messages through other mail protocols such as SMTP (Simple Mail Transfer Protocol).

Note: Mail servers that use POP often use an updated version known as POP3. Similarly, the current version of IMAP is known as IMAP4.

Sendmail is known as a *mail transfer agent*. Sendmail user accounts are based on files in the /var/spool/mail directory.

Apache

The Linux Web server is known as Apache. When you set up Apache on Linux, you install the http daemon, **httpd**. You can configure Apache based on three files in your /etc/httpd/conf directory:

➤ *access.conf*—Sets up directories for use by your browser. The directory that you specify in this file becomes home to your home page file.

➤ *httpd.conf*—Is the main Apache configuration file. You can set up multiple Web sites on one computer (virtual hosting) through this file.

➤ *srm.conf*—Defines directory names that come after the fully qualified domain name.

On some distributions, this configuration information is consolidated in the /etc/httpd/conf/access.conf file. You may also find these configuration files in the /etc/apache directory.

Network Applications

Network daemons, such as NFS and Samba, allow you to share files and printers with other computers on your network. Network applications allow you to use other services, such as Apache and sendmail. Although you can't just access a shared Web page, you can browse it with a network application known as Netscape Communicator. And although you can't just access a share of a mail server, you can access individual messages with applications such as Netscape Messenger. With FTP (File Transfer Protocol), you can share files on remote servers. With Telnet, you can log on and administer remote Linux computers.

Web Browsers

Netscape and Internet Explorer aren't the only ways to browse the Internet (Microsoft Internet Explorer can now be set up for Linux). The KDE and GNOME packages have their own browsers. Another popular Linux alternative is the Opera browser. These are graphical browsers.

If you don't have computers for all of your users, one alternative is to set up Lynx. As a text-based Web browser, Lynx does not require a lot of computer resources, which makes it practical to set up Lynx-based Internet access on inexpensive network terminals. This option is popular in public libraries where funding is often quite limited.

Mail Managers

There are several mail managers that you can use for Linux. They range from command-line interface managers, such as elm and pine, to graphical clients, such as Netscape Messenger.

Mail managers, such as Netscape Messenger, can be configured to receive mail from servers that use the POP3 or IMAP protocol. You can also configure a mail manager with filters that allow you to highlight or ignore emails based on criteria that you set. Mail managers, such as Netscape, are integrated with newsgroup readers. As discussed in Chapter 2, newsgroups are an important source of solutions when you're troubleshooting a problem in Linux.

FTP Clients

With an FTP client, you can transfer files to and from an FTP server. This is a popular option for sharing files over long distances; the chapters written for this book were shared through an FTP server.

There are a full range of text-based and graphical user interface (GUI) FTP clients. You can use the text-based **ftp** command to connect to any available FTP server. Once you connect, type "help" for a list of commands. You may notice similarities to Linux command-line commands. Alternately, if you want a graphical interface, you can use clients like gFTP.

Although you can use most Web browsers to look through and download from FTP servers, they are only "one-way." You can't upload to an FTP server through a Web browser, which means that you can't share your files using this method.

Telnet

You can use the **telnet** command to connect to any Linux computer. When you connect, you can log in just as you would to any local Linux command-line interface. Once the connection is made, you can access any username for which you have the password on the Linux computer. You can review an example in Figure 12.2, which is a Telnet session for administering Linux from a Microsoft Windows computer.

Figure 12.2   Remote access by Telnet.

Practice Questions

Question 1

Which of the following is an internet?

- ○ a. Five computers connected by a hub
- ○ b. Two separate LANs connected together
- ○ c. A computer connected to an ISP
- ○ d. Two computers in geographically distant countries networked
  together

Answer b is correct. An internet is any two LANs that are connected together. Because computers connected by a hub can be set up in a LAN, answer a is incorrect. Although a computer that's connected to an ISP can be considered a network, it doesn't mean that you're connecting two networks together. Therefore, answer c is incorrect. The same rationale applies to answer d; because you're not connecting two networks, you're not setting up an internet. Therefore, answer d is incorrect.

Question 2

Which of the following is not a valid IP address?

- ○ a. 192.66.133.54
- ○ b. 2.33.98.253
- ○ c. 254.36.18.1
- ○ d. 163.54.256.3
- ○ e. All of the noted IP addresses are valid

Answer d is correct. IP addresses consist of four numbers between 0 and 255. All of the other answers contain valid IP addresses. Therefore, answers a, b, and c are incorrect.

Question 3

You're assigning IP addresses to your network. Your network address is
10.123.55.0. Your network mask is 255.255.255.0. Which of the following
IP addresses can't be assigned to a computer on this network?

○ a. 10.123.55.1

○ b. 10.123.55.254

○ c. 10.123.55.255

○ d. 10.123.55.127

Answer c is correct. Based on the network as defined, the range of available IP
addresses is 10.123.55.0 through 10.123.55.255. The first address is the network
address. The last address in this range, which corresponds to answer c, is the
broadcast address for this network. Because answers a, b, and d are all in the
defined range, all three of those answers are incorrect.

Question 4

Your computer has a fully qualified domain name of linux44.mommabears.com.
Your computer has also been assigned to an IP address of 192.168.55.34.
The network mask is 255.255.0.0. Which of the following IP addresses cor-
responds to the network address?

○ a. 192.168.0.0

○ b. 192.168.55.34

○ c. 192.0.0.0

○ d. 192.168.55.0

Answer a is correct. The 255s in the network mask define the numbers that
describe the network address. Because the network mask includes two 255s, the
network address corresponds to the first two numbers of the IP address. Because
valid IP addresses for a computer don't correspond to network addresses, answer
b is incorrect. Answer c would be correct if the network mask was 255.0.0.0.
Answer d would be correct if the network mask was 255.255.255.0.

*Note: This explanation is an oversimplified description of how network masks help
you define network addresses.*

Question 5

> Which of the following is a hardware address?
>
> ○ a. 192.168.0.1
>
> ○ b. 1B-35-DF-23-A6-68
>
> ○ c. linux1.mommabears.com
>
> ○ d. eth0

Answer b is correct. Hardware addresses consist of 12 numbers in hexadecimal notation. Because 192.168.0.1 is an IP address, answer a is incorrect. Because linux1.mommabears.com is a fully qualified domain name, answer c is incorrect. Because eth0 represents a network card, answer d is incorrect.

Question 6

> Where would you assign a gateway address if you wanted to connect the computers inside your network to the Internet? Note that the computer that connects your network to the Internet has two network cards: One is connected to your network, and the other is connected to the Internet.
>
> ○ a. On any computer inside your network
>
> ○ b. On a computer connected to both your network and the Internet; to the network card that's directly connected to the Internet.
>
> ○ c. On a computer connected to both your network and the Internet; to the network card that's directly connected to your network
>
> ○ d. To the IP address of the computer at your ISP

Answer c is correct. A gateway address belongs on a computer that connects one network to another. The gateway address should be assigned to the network card that's connected to your internal network, so other computers can reach it. If you assign a gateway address to any computer inside your network, you may assign it to a computer that is not connected to the Internet. Therefore, answer a is incorrect. If you assign the gateway address to the network card that's directly connected to the Internet, the other computers won't be able to reach this card. Therefore, answer b is incorrect. Because your ISP generally uses a different set of IP addresses, your computer won't be able to reach it. Therefore, answer d is incorrect.

Question 7

Which of the following is usually the fastest way to install Linux?

○ a. Through a telephone modem

○ b. Via a high-speed Internet connection

○ c. Through an Ethernet network

○ d. From a local CD-ROM

Answer d is correct. Generally, the fastest way to install Linux is from local media, such as a CD-ROM. Because telephone modems are the slowest of the list, answer a is incorrect. High-speed Internet connections are generally slower than any form of Ethernet; therefore, answer b is incorrect. And because data transmission over Ethernet is generally slower than current CD-ROMs, answer c is incorrect.

Question 8

Based on the following network address and network mask, how many IP addresses do you have available for different computers in this network? The network address is 172.168.65.0, and the network mask is 255.255.255.0.

○ a. About 16 million

○ b. About 65,000

○ c. 256

○ d. 254

Answer d is correct. Because IP address numbers range from 0 to 255, the possible IP addresses range from 172.168.65.0 to 172.168.65.255. But the first address (172.168.65.0) is the network address, and the last address is the broadcast address. Therefore, there are 254 addresses available for individual computers, and answer c is incorrect. Although answer a corresponds to a network mask of 255.0.0.0, that is not the case; therefore, answer a is incorrect. Although answer b corresponds to a network mask of 255.255.0.0, that is not the case; therefore, answer b is incorrect.

Question 9

If you see an IP address of 16.52.33.235 and the network mask is 255.255.0.0, which of the following are the network and host addresses?

○ a. Network address=16.52.33.0; host address=235

○ b. Network address=16.52.0.0; host address=33.235

○ c. Network address=16.52.33.0; host address=33.235

○ d. Network address=16.52.0.0; host address=235

Answer b is correct. The 255s in the network mask distinguish the network address from the host address. Answer a would be correct if the network mask was 255.255.255.0. Because 16.52.33.0 is not the network address, answer c is incorrect. Because 235 is not the whole host address, answer d is incorrect.

Need to Know More?

 Hunt, Craig. *Linux Network Servers*. Sybex, Alameda, CA, 1999. ISBN 0-78212-506-9. A comprehensive guide to configuring different Linux network daemons.

 Kirch, Olaf, and Terry Dawson. *Linux Network Administrator's Guide*. Second Edition. O'Reilly & Associates, Sebastapol, CA, 2000. ISBN 1-56592-400-2. This is perhaps the Linux guru's resource to networking. It may not be suitable for beginners.

 Pfaffenberger, Bryan, and Michael Jang. *Linux Networking Clearly Explained*. Morgan-Kaufmann Publishers, San Francisco, CA, 2001. ISBN 0-12533-171-1. An introductory guide to Linux networking.

 The Web site for the Linux Documentation Project at **www.linuxdoc.org** is the central repository for Linux manuals, HOWTOs, and a number of other book length documents. Important HOWTOs for this chapter include the "DNS-HOWTO" for setting up a DNS server, the "Ethernet-HOWTO" for setting up an Ethernet network, the "IPCHAINS-HOWTO" for setting up a firewall, the "NFS-HOWTO" for setting up the Network File System, and the "SMB-HOWTO" for setting up communication with Microsoft Windows computers.

Applications

. . . .

Terms you'll need to understand:

✓ WYSIWYG

✓ nroff, groff, TeX, LaTeX, and HTML

✓ Document processing

✓ WordPerfect, Star Office, Applixware

✓ KOffice, GNOME Office

✓ Text editors, vi

✓ ispell

✓ GIMP, xfig

Techniques you'll need to master:

✓ Understanding the difference between WYSIWYG and text editing

✓ Describing the use of different markup languages in text files

✓ Listing basic features of document processors

✓ Understanding basic commands in vi

✓ Discussing various graphical applications

As there are text-based and graphical command utilities in Linux, there are text-based and graphical applications in Linux. Linux text-based applications use *markup* languages to achieve the same graphical results that you get from WYSIWYG (what-you-see-is-what-you-get) document processors. Many Linux devotees prefer markup languages because they give the user a greater degree of control of the output. In this chapter, you'll examine different graphical and text-based applications for text editing, word processing, and graphics.

The Linux WYSIWYG Debate

The comparison between WYSIWYG document processors and text-based markup languages is similar to the comparison between graphical user interface (GUI) and command-line interface (CLI) tools. In other words, although WYSIWYG processors are easier to use, text-based editors, with the help of markup languages, can theoretically do more. As with the CLI, it takes more time to learn text-based markup languages compared to learning GUI WYSIWYG document processors. There are also additional cycles of testing to check the result when you use markup language commands.

WYSIWYG Applications

The WYSIWYG document processor dominates the general market. Commercial examples of WYSIWYG processors include Microsoft Word, Corel WordPerfect, Vista Source's Applixware Words, and Sun's Star Office Write. All but Microsoft Word are currently available for Linux. With all of these applications, what you see on your screen is what you get when you print the file.

The problem with WYSIWYG applications is that you can't take full advantage of their capabilities unless you save their data files in binary format. Each of these applications has a different binary format; for example, you need a converter to transfer Microsoft Word files into Corel WordPerfect software. Because each WYSIWYG application has different capabilities, the formatting that you apply to a Microsoft Word file (fonts, underlining, bolding, and so forth) may be lost when you convert it to WordPerfect format.

If you use a WYSIWYG application to edit a Linux configuration file, you have to make sure to save it in text format. If you accidentally save a critical configuration file, such as /etc/inittab, in binary format, you won't be able to restart Linux.

If you use a WYSIWYG application on a Linux configuration file, be sure to save it in text format. Test the result with the **cat** command. Saving files in anything but text format (e.g., .doc, .wpd) causes problems for you the next time you need that file.

Markup Languages

A combination of a markup language with a text editor is a popular alternative in scientific and academic circles. With markup tools, you can manage fonts, graphics, and so on in what you print from a text file. Examples of text-based markup languages include nroff, groff, TeX, LaTeX, and HTML. With each of these languages, the text you enter is shown in one generic font. Markup commands change the appearance of your text only when printed. An example of the look of a text-based markup language is shown in the following HTML code from the Momma Bears' Bears Web site at **www.mommabears.com**:

```
<body>
<div align="center"><center>

<table border="0" cellpadding="0" cellspacing="0"
  bgcolor="#00FFFF">
<tr>
<td><p align="center"><font size="3" color="#9A30A9">
<strong>Welcome to Momma Bears' Bears... <br>
Your online source for collectible bean bag bears!</strong>
</font>
</td>
</tr>

</table>
</center></div>
```

The markup commands are shown in angle brackets <> and are applied to the text and background of the printed page shown on the Momma Bears' Bears Web site. With true markup languages, you can set up files in any text editor, such as vi or emacs. Although some older word-processing programs, such as WordPerfect versions 5.0 and 5.1, used markup languages, they also saved files in binary format.

Document Processing Managers

If you're used to Microsoft Windows, you can still have the advantages of WYSIWYG document processors, such as Microsoft Word. There are three major commercial document processors available for Linux: Corel WordPerfect, Sun Star Office Write, and Vista Source Applixware Words. These are all part of "office suites," which include graphical and spreadsheet applications. They also include converters that allow you to exchange data. Because each of these suites is also available for Microsoft Windows, it is possible to use one of these suites to help ease the transition of converting from Windows to Linux.

The advertising behind some office suites suggests that you can use their converters to work seamlessly with Microsoft Office files. Before you entrust critical files to this feature, test it out for yourself. As of this writing, the source code for Microsoft Office is not public. The capability of converters to carry all formatting between office suites is less than perfect. If you use features such as embedded comments, you may be disappointed.

There are also native Linux office suites available for the GNOME and KDE desktops, known as GNOME Office and KOffice. Because neither of these suites is available for Microsoft Windows, they are more suitable for native Linux users. Nevertheless, you can also use their importers and exporters to exchange data with the corresponding Microsoft Office applications.

WordPerfect

Corel WordPerfect for Linux is a full-featured WYSIWYG word processor that you can download from the **http://linux.corel.com** Web site free of charge. Multiuser versions can be purchased from Corel. WordPerfect for Linux also comes as part of the WordPerfect Office suite of applications, which includes a spreadsheet (Quattro Pro), presentation manager, and a database program (Paradox).

As discussed in Chapter 5, Corel also has a Linux distribution designed to be friendly to newer Linux users.

Star Office

The Star Office suite is a fully featured Linux office suite, currently owned by Sun. Among other things, it includes a word processor, a spreadsheet, presentation and mail managers, and a scheduler. Because it was originally developed in Germany, Star Office is more commonly seen with the KDE window manager, which was also developed in Germany. You can download the full office suite for Linux or Windows free of charge from **www.staroffice.com**.

Applixware

Vista Source is a Linux-based subsidiary of Applix, which also has a fairly complete package of office applications. Applixware Office includes a word processor, a spreadsheet, a presentation manager, graphics, and a mail manager as well as a database program. Its SHELF tools allow you to program different features into any of its applications. You can download the full Applixware Office suite from **www.vistasource.com**.

KOffice

The KDE Office suite of applications, known as KOffice, includes a similar package of applications to Star Office and Applixware Office. The KWord application is similar to FrameMaker. Unlike other office suites, it uses the text-based ispell spell-checking application. KOffice can be easily incorporated into the KDE window manager. You can download the full KOffice suite from **www.koffice.org**.

GNOME Office

The GNOME Office suite of applications also includes a similar package of applications to Star Office and Applixware Office. The GNU project didn't develop all of its office applications: GNOME Office incorporates Source Gear's AbiWord as its document processor. GNOME Office can be easily incorporated into the GNOME window manager. You can link the download locations for each of the components of GNOME Office through the **www.gnome.org/gnome-office** Web site.

Text Processing Managers

One of the minimum requirements for Sair Linux/GNU certification is basic knowledge of one of the major command-line text editors, such as joe, pico, vi, or emacs. These are critical tools to the Linux administrator. As text processing managers, these tools can help you edit and manage Linux configuration files seamlessly. Perhaps the most important of these editors is vi, because it's usually the only editor available when you need to use your emergency disk to recover from a system failure.

You can also use a text processing manager with a markup language to format documents. Many Linux users believe that markup languages, such as TeX, LaTeX, nroff, gruff, and HTML, provide superior capabilities when compared to WYSIWYG applications. You can apply the ispell spell checker to any text-based file created with one of these editors.

vi

There are two modes to the vi editor: command and insert. In command mode, you can move around a text document, delete, copy, paste, or move lines of text. You can also search for specific text strings and even run other text commands in the Linux shell. In insert mode, you can add text to a document.

You can edit a file with the **vi** *filename* command. If the file name you choose does not exist, vi creates it for you when you save and exit from this editor. Some vi commands are shown in Table 13.1.

Table 13.1	vi editing commands.*
Command	**Description**
cw	Deletes the current word and enters insert mode
dd	Deletes the current line
i	Enters insert mode
I	Enters insert mode at the beginning of the current line
o	Enters insert mode by starting a new line below your current position
p	Puts "yanked" text after the current cursor location; similar to "paste" in most word processors
q	Exits from vi
r	Replace; the next character that you type replaces the current character
u	Undo; reverses the last change
w	Writes the file
yy	Yanks (copies) the current line into the local buffer; works with the **p** command
Esc	Exits from insert mode
/test	Searches for the word *test* in the current file

In older versions of vi, you can't use the arrow keys on your keyboard. The only way to move the cursor around a file is with the h, j, k, and l keys, which correspond to the left, down, up, and right arrows.

The vi editor has a large number of commands and other features. The commands shown in Table 13.1 represent a fraction of what is available.

ispell

When you use a WYSIWYG document processor, you generally need a spell checker designed for that specific application. On the other hand, you can use the ispell application to check the spelling on any text file.

Using ispell is easy; if your text file is named *better*, you can start the spell check with the **ispell better** command. The ispell application compares every word in the file with its own dictionary. If a word is not found, it is highlighted; optional spellings are shown when available.

Graphical Applications

You can't edit images with text editors. Linux includes a number of graphical applications for drawing and editing graphics including GIMP (GNU Image Manipulation Program) and xfig. GIMP is more of an image manipulation program, whereas xfig is a drawing program more suitable for engineering design work.

Note: The default compression algorithm in GIF files is LZW, named after its developers, Lempel, Ziv, and Welch. Because Unisys has started enforcing its copyright on LZW, a number of Linux users actually avoid using GIFs.

Linux graphical applications certainly aren't limited to GIMP and xfig. Because Linux- or Unix-based applications are used to create, edit, and produce graphics-intensive movies, some would argue that graphical applications available for Linux are more capable than those available for any other operating system.

GIMP

GIMP is an all-in-one image editor often compared to JASC's Paint Shop Pro. You can use GIMP to draw, to manage images on different layers, to convert between graphical file formats, and to capture screen images. Most of the images for this book were captured using GIMP. As with other GNU applications, it is available free of charge, and in fact is included in the basic configuration of most current Linux distributions. You can review the GIMP editor in Figure 13.1.

xfig

As GIMP is used to manipulate images, xfig is used to create images and drawings. It is set up in "fig" files, which specify levels, lines, and locations in a series of numbers in text format. This is consistent with files used by various Computer-Aided Design programs that use "wire frame" models. Numeric data, such as that found in xfig files, is suitable for Computer-Aided Manufacturing. To use xfig, you need a three-button mouse or at least a setup that emulates a three-button mouse. You can review the xfig application in Figure 13.2.

Figure 13.1   GIMP version 1.1.13.

Figure 13.2 xfig version 3.2.

Practice Questions

Question 1

Which of the following is a reason to prefer text-based editors over WYSIWYG document processors? The appearance of the final printed document is important.

○ a. Text editors don't corrupt your screen with graphical images.

○ b. Text editors require you to insert a number of commands for the fonts and background that you see in the printed document.

○ c. Text editors allow you to edit Linux configuration files without concern for the format that you use to save these files.

○ d. Text editors are much simpler to use because they don't have all the pull-down menus associated with WYSIWYG editors.

Answer c is correct. If you use a text editor, then by definition, your files are saved in text format. Linux can only read its configuration files in text format. Although answer a is a true statement, the capability to embed graphical images in WYSIWYG documents is an advantage for these graphical document processors. Therefore, answer a is incorrect. Even though answer b is a true statement, the commands that you need to format a text document can be difficult to learn. Therefore, answer b is incorrect. Although answer d is nominally true, you have to use markup language commands to format any text file. Therefore, answer d is incorrect.

Question 2

Which of the following applications is a text editor?

○ a. groff

○ b. vi

○ c. HTML

○ d. LaTeX

Answer b is correct. The vi editor is a text editor. Because groff, HTML, and LaTeX are markup languages for formatting text, answers a, c, and d are incorrect.

Question 3

Which of the following office suites can't be used with Microsoft Windows?

○ a. KOffice

○ b. Star Office

○ c. WordPerfect

○ d. Applixware Office

Answer a is correct. The KDE Office suite, known as KOffice, can't be installed on Microsoft Windows. This is also true of the GNOME Office suite. However, because versions of Star Office, WordPerfect, and Applixware Office are available for Microsoft Windows, answers b, c, and d are incorrect.

Question 4

What is the danger of using office suites, such as WordPerfect or Star Office, to edit configuration files, such as /etc/fstab?

○ a. Binary programs, such as WordPerfect, aren't designed to edit text files.

○ b. Programs like Star Office save files at regular intervals. Once a program is saved at any interval, it isn't possible to restore configuration files.

○ c. By default, WYSIWYG office suites save files in binary mode. Linux can't read configuration files saved in binary mode, which causes failure when Linux is restarted.

○ d. There is no danger; you can use any kind of editor, WYSIWYG or text, to edit any Linux configuration file.

Answer c is correct. WYSIWYG office suites do save files in binary mode. Linux configuration files have to be saved in text format, or Linux won't be able to read these files. Because you can import text files into an office suite, answer a is incorrect. When office suites save files, they're backing up your work in temporary files, not overwriting your current file. Therefore, answer b is incorrect. Although you can export and save files from WYSIWYG editors in text mode, it is not the default. Therefore, answer d is incorrect.

Question 5

When you use the vi editor, which of the following commands changes your setup from insert mode to command mode?

○ a. Ctrl+Pg Up

○ b. **o**

○ c. **/command**

○ d. Esc

Answer d is correct. Pressing the Esc key changes the mode in the vi editor from input mode to command mode. Because the Ctrl+Pg Up key combination switches between different configured graphics modes, answer a is incorrect. The **o** command opens up editing by opening a new line; therefore, answer b is incorrect. The forward slash indicates a search in the current document for the word *command*; therefore, answer c is incorrect.

Question 6

Which of the following graphics applications is more suitable for image manipulation?

○ a. Star Office

○ b. GIMP

○ c. xfig

○ d. HTML

Answer b is correct. GIMP is loaded by default in most Linux configurations. Although there is a Star Office application that helps you manipulate images, it is not installed by default like GIMP. Therefore, answer a is incorrect. You can manipulate images with xfig; however, it is not nearly as capable as GIMP for image manipulation. Therefore, answer c is incorrect. Because HTML is a markup language, answer d is incorrect.

Question 7

How would you check the spelling of a document edited through the vi editor? The name of your document file is important.txt.

- a. Open vi. Go into command mode. Type the **s** command to start the spell checker.

- b. Open vi. Go into command mode. Type the **ispell** command to start the spell checker.

- c. Go to your command-line interface. Type the **ispell important.txt** command.

- d. Go to your command-line interface. Type the **vi important.txt | ispell** command.

Answer c is correct. The **ispell** command works on any text file and is independent of the editor. The **s** command in vi deletes the current character and brings vi into insert mode; therefore, answer a is incorrect. The **ispell** command is used at the command-line interface; therefore, answer b is incorrect. Because the **vi** command opens that editor, the "pipe" (|) has nothing to send to the **ispell** command. Therefore, answer d is incorrect.

Need to Know More?

 Gratzer, George. *First Steps in LaTeX*. Springer-Verlag, New York, NY, 1999. ISBN 0-81764-132-7. This book is a primer to the LaTeX typesetting system with enhancements for mathematical and scientific formulas.

 Muster, John. *Unix Made Easy*. Osborne/McGraw-Hill, Berkeley, CA, 1996. ISBN 0-07882-173-8. This beginners' book on Unix includes extensive lessons and detail on the vi editor. This book is commonly used in classroom settings with Linux terminals.

 Rackus, Phillip, Kate Wrightson, and Joe Merlino. *WordPerfect Office 2000 for Linux: The Official Guide*. Osborne/McGraw-Hill, Berkeley, CA, 2000. ISBN 0-07212-238-2. This book is the Corel endorsed guide to the WordPerfect Office 2000 suite for Linux.

 For more information on WordPerfect for Linux, review Corel's Linux Web site at **http://linux.corel.com**. At this time, you can download only the word processor and picture editor free of charge.

 For more information on GIMP, look over its home page at **www.gimp.org**. GIMP is part of the GNU project as well as the GNOME Office suite.

 For more information on the GNOME Office suite, look over its Web site at **www.gnome.org/gnome-office**. If you choose to use GNOME Office, monitor this site frequently, because Linux applications like this are under constant development.

 For more information on groff and ispell, review the applications area of the GNU Web site at **www.gnu.org**. The groff markup language is the GNU clone of the nroff document formatting system. The ispell program is the GNU spell checker for text documents.

 For more information on the KOffice suite, look over its Web site at **www.koffice.org**. If you choose to use KOffice, monitor this site frequently, because Linux applications like this are under constant development.

For more information on Star Office, look over its Web site at **www.staroffice.com**. You can also download a personal copy of Star Office from this Web site. News releases related to this suite are available through its parent company's Web site at **www.sun.com**.

 For more information on the Applixware Office suite, look over its Web site at **www.vistasource.com**. You can also download a demonstration copy of Applixware from this Web site.

 For more information on xfig, review its home page at **www.xfig.org**. You can find examples of xfig use in the Web sites listed on its links page.

Troubleshooting

Terms you'll need to understand:

✓ System message logging

✓ /etc/syslog.conf

✓ Read error

✓ Archive error

✓ Device full error

✓ **badblocks**

✓ Rescue disk

✓ Login and boot errors

✓ Keyboard repeat rate

✓ **setleds**

✓ Network Time Protocol (NTP)

Techniques you'll need to master:

✓ Finding shortcuts

✓ Mastering systematic analysis

✓ Understanding system log files

✓ Addressing installation errors

✓ Using rescue disks

✓ Solving boot errors

✓ Troubleshooting printer problems

✓ Updating system clocks

✓ Addressing memory issues

✓ Modifying keyboard parameters

When you want to solve a problem, you troubleshoot it. Sometimes you can use shortcuts that are at your fingertips; other times you need to diagnose problems systematically. Linux has extensive log files that can help you in the trouble-shooting process. Log files, however, do you no good if you encounter errors when you try to install, start, or log in to Linux. There are a number of techniques available to address installation and startup problems, including the use of the Linux boot floppy disk.

Troubleshooting is a topic almost as extensive as Linux itself. The topics covered in this chapter are limited to the topics that are addressed on the Sair Linux/ GNU Installation and Configuration exam.

Problem-Solving Philosophy

Almost every problem in Linux has a "simple" solution. But only the most experi-enced administrators know all of the simple solutions. If you can't find an easy way to diagnose and address your problem, you need to think about your problem systematically, using the basic scientific method.

Quick Tools

There is no substitute for experience when you need a quick solution. If you don't have the experience, you can lean on others with experience. If you don't have direct access to Linux experts, you do have access to documentation from a num-ber of Linux experts. As you have seen in previous chapters, the documentation supporting Linux is extensive. If all else fails, you can usually contact those Linux experts who virtually prowl the newsgroups looking for problems to solve. Gen-erally, if you have a problem, use the following steps to look for a quick solution:

1. Check applicable help switches. Almost every command includes extensive help switch output, which is available by typing --**help** after a command.

2. Study man pages. Every command, and a large number of configuration files, include manuals that help you understand the objectives of each com-mand and switch.

3. Look through the HOWTOs and FAQs of the Linux Documentation Project at **www.linuxdoc.org**.

4. Examine knowledge or troubleshooting databases for your Linux distribu-tion. Several distribution Web sites include a database of problems and solutions.

5. Search through newsgroup archives. Linux users share their experience through newsgroups. As discussed in Chapter 2, the easiest way to search through newsgroup archives is through the **www.deja.com** site.

6. If all else fails, ask for help on the appropriate Linux newsgroup. Be sure to document the work that you've done so far on the problem. If you don't get an answer to your question, you may need to clarify your situation further or try a different newsgroup.

Depending on your level of experience with Linux and knowledge of your particular problem, you may want to follow these steps in a different order.

If you need to ask a question on a newsgroup, be prepared. Experienced Linux users want to know that you've checked all available documentation. They'll want to know what else you've done to try to address your problem as well as the relevant portions of your configuration and log files. Providing this information is no different than what you would do when presenting your problem to an experienced Linux consultant.

Scientific Method

You can ask for help on newsgroups, but answers take time. And if you're a Linux administrator with a problem, your users want immediate solutions. If you don't have a quick solution, your other option is to examine your problem using the scientific method.

There are three basic steps in the scientific method: analyze, theorize, and test. In other words, analyze your problem with all available data, theorize about the cause, and test your theory with a solution.

When you analyze a problem, you need to think systematically. For example, if you're having trouble sharing information with a Microsoft Windows computer, you might have a problem with your Samba daemon. But in general, you're more likely to have a problem with your basic network configuration. Furthermore, the most probable cause is a problem with your physical connections.

Systematic solutions require "bottom-up" thinking. For most unknown problems, you might check your system in the following order:

1. Check physical connections. Are the cables properly plugged in? Is each component getting power?

2. Check Linux connections. Does Linux recognize your problem hardware? Did Linux load your driver when you booted your computer?

3. Review applicable system logs. Are there errors or other information relevant to your problem?

4. Check basic software. Can you connect to problem hardware? Did Linux start the applicable daemon?

5. Check higher-level software. Can you actually communicate with key hard-ware components with various commands? What kind of error messages do you see when you use your software?

These are general steps to problem analysis. You can theorize about a cause at any point in the process. Most of the time, when you identify a cause (e.g., the network card is not connected), you can easily determine a solution (e.g., con-nect the network card). The actual steps you take depend on your problem and experience.

System Logs

You can set up system logs in a number of categories including kernel, printer, mail, other daemons, and security (also known as *auth*). Messages are available in the following eight categories, listed in descending order of importance:

➤ emerg (emergency)

➤ alert

➤ crit (critical)

➤ err (error)

➤ warning

➤ notice

➤ info

➤ debug

Log Locations

Whenever something happens in Linux, information is sent to system logs as defined in your /etc/syslog.conf configuration file. Perhaps the best organized /etc/syslog.conf file is from the Corel distribution, shown in Figure 14.1.

As shown in Figure 14.1, messages are divided in categories and subdivided by order of importance. Messages in each area are sent to a specific log file.

System logs are organized in a *facility.level* format, where *facility* corresponds to a category, usually a daemon, and *level* corresponds to the importance of the log file.

Review the /etc/syslog.conf and the log files available for your distribution. The contents of these files should help you understand the function of each log file.

```
#  /etc/syslog.confConfiguration file for syslogd.
#
#             For more information see syslog.conf(5)
#             manpage.
#
# syslog.conf changed by Brian

# auth and authpriv are combined
authpriv, auth.=debug                     /var/log/auth/auth.debug
authpriv, auth.=info                      /var/log/auth/auth.info
authpriv, auth.=notice                    /var/log/auth/auth.notice
authpriv, auth.=warning                   /var/log/auth/auth.warning
authpriv, auth.=err                       /var/log/auth/auth.err
authpriv, auth.=crit                      /var/log/auth/auth.crit
authpriv, auth.=alert                     /var/log/auth/auth.alert
authpriv, auth.=emerg                     /var/log/auth/auth.emerg

cron.=debug                        /var/log/cron/cron.debug
cron.=info                         /var/log/cron/cron.info
cron.=notice                       /var/log/cron/cron.notice
cron.=warning                      /var/log/cron/cron.warning
cron.=err                          /var/log/cron/cron.err
cron.=crit                         /var/log/cron/cron.crit
cron.=alert                        /var/log/cron/cron.alert
cron.=emerg                        /var/log/cron/cron.emerg
```

Figure 14.1   Excerpt from the /etc/syslog.conf message log configuration file.

System Log Messages

System log messages can help you solve problems. Understanding which log file to use or review in each situation comes with experience. Take a look at Figure 14.2, which shows information messages in the daemon category (daemon.info). The last two messages shown indicate that Linux had a problem installing sound drivers for this particular computer.

You can find another useful set of messages with the **dmesg** command, which shows the sequence of events when you booted Linux on your computer.

Installation Issues

There are a number of errors that you may encounter when installing Linux. In several cases, you may also have these problems when running Linux. These issues are related to problems with files or storage media.

```
Oct 11 08:48:07 laptop cardmgr[202]: starting, version is 3.1.2
Oct 11 08:48:07 laptop cardmgr[202]: watching 2 sockets
Oct 11 08:48:07 laptop cardmgr[202]: initializing socket 0
Oct 11 08:48:07 laptop cardmgr[202]: socket 0: Serial or Modem
Oct 11 08:48:07 laptop cardmgr[202]: executing: 'insmod /lib/modules/2.2.12/pcmcia/serial_cs.o'
Oct 11 08:48:07 laptop cardmgr[202]: executing: './serial start ttyS0'
Oct 11 08:48:08 laptop cardmgr[202]: + cat: /var/state/pcmcia/scheme: No such file or directory
Oct 11 08:48:08 laptop cardmgr[202]: initializing socket 1
Oct 11 08:48:08 laptop cardmgr[202]: socket 1: 3Com 3c589D Ethernet
Oct 11 08:48:08 laptop cardmgr[202]: executing: 'insmod /lib/modules/2.2.12/pcmcia/3c589_cs.o'
Oct 11 08:48:08 laptop cardmgr[202]: executing: './network start eth0'
Oct 11 08:48:09 laptop cardmgr[202]: + cat: /var/state/pcmcia/scheme: No such file or directory
Oct 11 08:49:00 laptop modprobe: can't locate module sound-slot-0
Oct 11 08:49:01 laptop modprobe: can't locate module sound-service-0-3
```

Figure 14.2   Sample system log messages.

Read Errors

Common problems with floppy disks include *read* or *file not found* errors. Possible causes include a flaw in the floppy disk or a format that Linux can't read.

As floppy disks age, their capability to hold data diminishes. Floppy disks sent through the mail commonly fail when reformatted for Linux. Also, if you try to read data written to a floppy from an incompatible system, like Apple Macintosh, you will get one of these errors.

In either case, you should get a new floppy disk, reformat it, and reinstall your data.

Archive Errrors

New programs in Linux are most commonly available in archives known as tar. For example, you might download the latest version of Apache (the Linux Web server) from a Web site in a file such as apache_2.0.1.tar.gz. Downloads don't always go smoothly. If you receive an error like the following, try downloading the file again, perhaps from a different Web or FTP site:

```
Tar:read error or gzip: not in gzip format while installing Linux
```

Also, one or more archives on your Linux installation CD may be corrupt. If you can identify the specific problem archive, you may be able to download and install it separately. Otherwise, you may have to obtain a new Linux installation CD.

Not Enough Space

If you receive a message like *device full*, you've run out of room on one of your Linux volumes. If you get this message when running Linux, you need to delete some files. Normally, this error is fairly rare, because Linux can still run efficiently when volumes are over 90 percent full.

You may also get this message when you're installing Linux. In either case, you can reconfigure your disk volumes. This is a more difficult process, because it involves backing up current files, repartitioning, and reinstalling. If this error occurs while you are installing Linux, the best course of action is to stop the installation, reallocate space to your volumes, and try the installation again.

When you're installing Linux, you can review the progress of your installation, including error messages in some of the first four virtual consoles. One of these consoles is set up for the command-line interface (CLI) in single-user mode. As mentioned previously, you can access different virtual consoles with the Alt+Ctrl+F*x* command, where *x* represents the number of the virtual console.

Bad Hard Disk Blocks

Linux volumes are set up in units of memory known as *blocks*. Depending on your situation, you may have 512, 1024, 2048, or 4096 bytes of information in each block. If you have problems with your hard disk, you may get an error message similar to the following:

```
Read_intr: 0x10 error
```

You can get this error in two situations. Either you have a physical defect on your hard drive, or you're trying to format a volume that's larger than what's physically available on your hard drive.

One way to check for bad blocks on your hard drive is with the **badblocks** command. It marks and sets aside any blocks that can't be read.

*Note: The **badblocks** command is similar to Microsoft's **chkdsk** command. Other commands used to check for bad blocks are **mke2fs -c** and **e2fsck -c**.*

Other Installation Issues

There are two other errors that may occur, especially when you're installing Linux over a network. If you see a message like *file not found* or *permission denied* while installing Linux, you have a problem with your Linux distribution. You may have a Linux installation CD or download that's missing some files, or it may be set with improper permissions. In either case, you'll need to try downloading the distribution again, try the installation from a different CD, or try a different distribution altogether.

When you're installing Linux over a network, such as through FTP, you need to download a series of files. A common FTP command for downloads is **mget**, which copies specified files from the current FTP server directory to the current directory on your local computer. The differences between the commands used to download files can create a problem. For example:

```
mget *.*
mget .
```

If you're using the MS-DOS version of FTP, the effect of these commands are identical; they copy all files from the current directory on the FTP server to the current directory on the local computer.

However, these commands have a different effect in Linux. Many Linux files don't have a dot (.) to divide a filename from its extension, such as chapter14.doc. So when you run FTP from Linux and run the **mget *.*** command, the only files copied are the files set up in the "dot" format.

Rescue Disk Help

If your Linux system ever fails in a way that keeps you from booting or logging in, you'll need a boot disk and a backup of your /etc/passwd file. Errors in this area include problems with your hard drive's Master Boot Record (MBR), your /etc/passwd file, or a specific dynamic program library.

If you don't have a boot disk and don't have any rescue utilities on your Linux installation CD, you may be stuck installing a fresh copy of Linux and overwriting all current data on your computer.

One possible "last resort" solution is to use a Linux installation CD to upgrade the current distribution, which sometimes preserves the data created by your users.

Creating a Boot Floppy

When installing Linux, you should accept the option to create a boot disk. Alternately, the following command extracts needed files from the boot.img boot image file to a floppy drive. If the appropriate files are on different directories, substitute accordingly:

```
dd if=/mnt/cdrom/images/boot.img of=/mnt/floppy
```

Other useful floppies that you might create, depending on your distribution, include network files (bootnet.img), PCMCIA files (pcmcia.img) and drivers (drivers.img).

As a last resort, you may be able to create a boot floppy using the *expert* or *rescue* mode on your Linux installation CD, if it is available. You might also use the rescue mode as you would a Linux boot floppy. The result depends on your distribution CD.

Components of the Boot Floppy

There are two parts of the boot floppy: a compressed version of your Linux kernel and a set of utilities and files, known as *initrd*, to help you recover from most problems. When you boot from this floppy, your computer loads the Linux kernel, and then it decompresses the initrd image into a set of files on your RAM. These files appear to be on a hard drive, but they're actually on a *RAM disk*, which is an area of your RAM that's set up like a hard drive volume.

Problems with the Master Boot Record (MBR)

If your MBR is corrupt, your computer won't be able to find Linux (or any other operating system). Once you've mounted the normal root directory from your hard drive, you can use the **/sbin/lilo** command to write the contents of your current /etc/lilo.conf configuration file to your MBR.

Note: The /sbin/lilo command in Linux is almost functionally equivalent to the fdisk /mbr command in MS-DOS; both commands replace the MBR. But the fdisk /mbr command overwrites any lilo.conf boot loader on your MBR and therefore would prevent you from accessing Linux.

You know your MBR is corrupt if you see an error message like the following:

```
Drive not bootable - Please insert system disk
```

Incorrect Operating System

You can set up several operating systems to boot based on information in your /etc/lilo.conf configuration file. If this file is somehow corrupted, you may end up with the wrong operating system (e.g., you boot into Windows when you choose Linux).

The solution is the same as in the last section. You need to reinstall the lilo.conf file on your MBR.

Shell Problems

If you can't get to your default shell or command-line interface (CLI), you may have a problem with permissions or your passwords.

To run Linux, everyone needs at least read and execute permissions on the root directory (/). To check current permission on /, run the **ls -la /** | **more** command. The permissions associated with the file named "." (dot) are the permissions of your root directory. If everyone doesn't have at least read and execute permissions on this directory, go into root or superuser mode and run the **chmod 755 /** command.

If that doesn't work, you may have a problem with your /etc/passwd file, which may be addressed by solutions discussed in the following two sections.

Restoring Passwords

If you have access to Linux without resorting to your boot floppy, you can also boot Linux in single-user mode. When you boot your computer, at some point, you'll see the Linux Loader (LILO) prompt as shown:

```
LILO boot:
```

Type "linux single" at this prompt, and Linux automatically boots into single-user mode. You then have access to all Linux commands in superuser mode without having to log in to Linux.

 If you forget the password for the root or superuser, you can use this technique to delete the root password. Don't forget to set a new password once you've rebooted into Linux without the boot disk.

If you need your boot floppy to start Linux, review the technique discussed in the next section.

Restoring Passwords with a Boot Floppy

One disaster that can happen with Linux is when nobody can log in to the computer. A common cause of this problem is a corrupt or deleted /etc/passwd file. A Linux boot floppy allows you to start Linux as the root user without requiring a login. Once you've mounted your hard drive, you can then restore the password file from a backup.

If you don't have a backup password file, you need to create a new version of this file. Every user on your system then has to log in again and set up passwords of their choice.

Dynamic Library Modules

Dynamic libraries are a convenience for developers, because they allow the reuse of the same code, or programming instructions, for different commands. If you can't run some basic commands in your shell, you may have a problem with one or more dynamic library modules.

When you start Linux from the boot floppy, you gain access to some of these critical shell commands. You can then restore the appropriate dynamic library module from a different source, such as the Linux installation CD.

Printer Problems

If you're having trouble printing, there are several steps that you can follow to troubleshoot your problems. These steps include checks on physical connections, logical connections, system logs, and configuration files. You can try to print again after each of these steps:

1. Always check physical connections first. In other words, check power to your printer as well as the cable that connects the printer to the computer. If your printer is located on another computer, check your network connections as well.

2. Check for error messages. If you have an error on a currently running print job, you'll be able to find an error message in the /var/spool/lpd/lp/status file. (You can review other errors in the lp system log file as defined in your version of /etc/syslog.conf.)

Note: If you have more than one printer, each printer should have a different name. Substitute accordingly for lp in each of the following steps.

3. If your physical connections work, check for a lock file. If you have a file like /var/spool/lpd/lp/lock, you can't print on the lp printer. If you don't currently have a running print job, delete this file. Lock files are temporary devices designed to keep more than one program from printing simultaneously.

4. If you don't have a lock file, check for a control file (cf) and a data file (df) in your /var/spool/lpd/lp directory. When you print a job, the request is sent to the spool directory associated with your printer. The line printer daemon (**lpd**) creates a cf with information on the print job and a df with the information to be printed.

5. If you don't have any of the files discussed in the previous steps, check the main printer configuration file, /etc/printcap. Make sure it still conforms to the parameters you need for your printer, as discussed in Chapter 9.

6. Check basic output to your printer. Run the **lptest** > /dev/lp command. (If your printer goes by a different name than lp, substitute accordingly.) The **lptest** command sends a generic "ripple test" pattern to your printer.

7. Check text output to your printer. Select a text file of your choice and send it to your printer device using the **cat** *file* > /dev/lp command. Substitute for *file* and lp accordingly.

8. If you have a serial port printer, check the devices linked to each serial port with the **ls -l** /dev/tty0* command. Make sure your printer still has control of the appropriate serial device.

9. Check your environment variables with the **env** command. Make sure there are no environment variables, such as PRINTER, redirecting output to another file or printer.

Other Problems

There are a number of other problems that you can solve fairly easily. You can address keyboard issues related to graphics, repeat rate, and the Num Lock key. You can synchronize your clock with a site on the Internet. You can also address memory problems, including those related to the X Window.

Weird Characters

Before the development of graphics adapters, Unix used *pseudographics mode* to simulate simple pictures, such as lines and letters to illustrate the squares and pieces in a chess game. If you can't start the graphical user interface (GUI) from a CLI, you're sent to a strange mode where you see strange characters on a CLI screen. You can type the **reset** command to switch out of this graphics mode, or you can switch to another virtual console and **kill** the shell associated with the pseudographics mode console.

Num Lock

By default, the numeric keypad is off when you install Linux. This is probably preferred if you're using a laptop computer without a dedicated numeric keypad. When you turn on the Num Lock key on a laptop, numbers supersede several letters on your keyboard.

On the other hand, many people use the numeric keypad on a standard keyboard. If you want the Num Lock key to be set on by default when you boot Linux, set up the following shell script, make it executable, and copy it to the /etc/rc.local or another /etc/rc.d directory associated with booting Linux:

```
for n in 1 2 3 4 5 6 7
do
        setleds +num < /dev/tty$n > /dev/null
done
```

This script activates the Num Lock key for all virtual terminals associated with the variable *n*, using the setleds utility.

Keyboard Repeat Rate

When you press a character key on your keyboard and keep it pressed in a CLI, the character eventually repeats itself. The rate of repetition is known as the *keyboard repeat rate*. You can set this rate with some BIOS menus, or you can set it using the **kbdrate** command. For example, if you want to set a repeat rate of 20 characters per second, run the following command:

```
/sbin/kbdrate -r 20
```

Synchronizing Time

The time reported on your computer may not be accurate. Some BIOS clocks run fast. Alternately, if the battery associated with your BIOS does not have enough power, your BIOS clock may be slow.

If you're running several computers on a network, you may have applications where it's important that all of your computers report the same clock time. The TCP/IP protocol suite includes a Network Time Protocol (NTP), which allows you to synchronize the time on all of your computers. For example, if you want to synchronize with the time server at the Internet Software Consortium (ISC), run the following command:

```
ntpdate clock.isc.org
```

Other "official" NTP time servers are available worldwide. For more information, refer to the time WWW server Web page at **www.eecis.udel.edu/~ntp**, sponsored by the University of Delaware.

X Window Thrashing

When you don't have enough RAM, your computer spends a lot of time exchanging information between RAM and the swap partition on your hard drive. (The swap partition is your virtual memory, which extends the amount of "RAM" available to Linux.) This phenomenon is also known as *thrashing*, which characterizes constant activity on a hard drive.

One common cause of thrashing is the demands of the X Window. If everything slows down when you start the X Window, you probably have a memory problem and should follow the guidelines discussed in Chapter 3 for RAM requirements.

Problem Opening the X Window

If you try to open the X Window and Linux doesn't bring you into the GUI, you may receive an error message like the following:

```
cannot open display:0.0
```

In this case, you need to configure the DISPLAY variable. DISPLAY can be either an environment variable or a shell variable. DISPLAY is an environment variable if you see it in the output to the **env** command; it is a shell variable if you see it in the /etc/profile configuration file. If DISPLAY is an environment variable, you need to set it. If it is a shell variable, you should export it so it works with other shells.

In either case, you need to set this variable to *localhost:0.0*, which sets up the local computer to work locally or with remote clients. You can set DISPLAY to this value with the following command:

```
DISPLAY=localhost:0.0
```

Practice Questions

Question 1

You want to copy files from an FTP server to your computer. When you start FTP from MS-DOS and access the directory with your files, you download these files using the **mget *.*** command. Some of the file names on this FTP server directory are readme.txt, schedule, chapter2.doc, and syslog.conf. What happens if you run the same command when you start FTP from Linux?

○ a. You download all of the files from the FTP server directory.

○ b. You download some of the files from the FTP server directory including readme.txt, schedule, and syslog.conf.

○ c. You download some of the files from the FTP server directory including readme.txt and chapter2.doc.

○ d. None of the files in the FTP server directory are downloaded.

Answer c is correct. The listed command downloads only those files with a dot embedded in the file name. Although answer c is not complete (this command would also download the syslog.conf file), it is the only correct answer among the choices listed. Not all of the files in the FTP server directory include a dot. This command leaves out the schedule file; therefore, answers a and b are incorrect. Because this command does download some files, answer d is incorrect.

Question 2

> You have a computer with a dual boot configuration. In other words, both Linux and Microsoft Windows are installed. For some reason, you don't see any LILO **boot**: prompt when you boot your computer, and your system locks up when you try to boot. You suspect that your MBR is corrupt or missing. Which of the following options would restore your MBR?
>
> ○ a. Boot Linux into single-user mode. Use the **/sbin/lilo** command to restore the contents of the lilo.conf file to your MBR.
>
> ○ b. Start your computer with an MS-DOS boot disk. Use the **fdisk /mbr** command to restore generic settings to your MBR.
>
> ○ c. Start your computer with any Linux installation CD. Go into restore or recovery mode. Access the lilo.conf file on your hard drive. Use the **/sbin/lilo** command to restore the contents of the lilo.conf file to your MBR.
>
> ○ d. Start your computer with a Linux boot disk. Access the lilo.conf file on your hard drive. Use the **/sbin/lilo** command to restore the contents of the lilo.conf file to your MBR.

Answer d is correct. These steps would restore the contents of your original lilo.conf file to your MBR. Because you aren't getting a LILO **boot**: prompt, you can't go into single-user mode normally. Therefore, answer a is incorrect. Because the MS-DOS **fdisk /mbr** command installs an MS-DOS MBR, you then would not be able to access Linux. Therefore, answer b is incorrect. Although some Linux installation CDs do have a restore or recovery mode, this is not true of all installation CDs. Therefore, answer c is incorrect.

Question 3

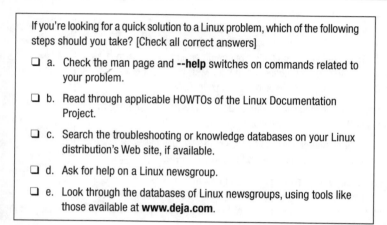

If you're looking for a quick solution to a Linux problem, which of the following steps should you take? [Check all correct answers]

❑ a. Check the man page and **--help** switches on commands related to your problem.

❑ b. Read through applicable HOWTOs of the Linux Documentation Project.

❑ c. Search the troubleshooting or knowledge databases on your Linux distribution's Web site, if available.

❑ d. Ask for help on a Linux newsgroup.

❑ e. Look through the databases of Linux newsgroups, using tools like those available at **www.deja.com**.

Answers a, b, c, and e are correct. Each of these answers are things that you can do quickly to look for a solution. The man pages and --**help** switches are easily accessible on Linux. HOWTOs of the Linux Documentation Project and trouble-shooting databases for your distribution are easily available online. You can quickly search through questions and answers within Linux newsgroups through the **www.deja.com** Web site. However, you can't expect a quick answer when you pose a question on a Linux newsgroup. Therefore, answer d is incorrect.

Question 4

One of your Linux administrators has forgotten his root password on his Linux computer. Which of the following answers is the easiest way for him to set up a new password?

○ a. Start Linux. Go into the CLI. Look through the /etc/inittab file to find the run level associated with single-user mode. Go into that mode with the **init** command, and restore a backup of the original /etc/ passwd file.

○ b. Boot your computer. When you see the LILO **boot:** prompt, enter the **linux single** command. When Linux starts, run the **passwd** command to set a new password for the root user.

○ c. Boot your computer with your Linux installation CD. Select the applicable upgrade option. When prompted, enter new passwords for the root and other users on that computer.

○ d. Boot your computer. When you see the LILO **boot:** prompt, enter the **single** command. When Linux starts, run the **passwd** command to set a new password for the root user.

Answer b is correct. The **linux single** command, when entered at the LILO **boot:** prompt, starts Linux in single-user mode. Your administrator can then use the **passwd** command to set up a new password for the root user. Only the root user can run the **init** command; because your administrator has forgotten his root password, the option shown in answer a is not possible. Although you can upgrade Linux and set up new passwords for all users, it is not the easiest thing to do, especially if the administrator is the only person who has lost his password. Therefore, answer c is incorrect. Unless your administrator has set up *single* as an option in the lilo.conf file, answer d will not start any mode of Linux and is therefore not correct.

Question 5

> If you try to install a new program and receive the following message, which of the following answers most accurately describes your problem?
>
> ```
> Tar: read error or gzip: not in gzip format while
>      installing Linux
> ```
>
> ○ a. You have a corrupt compressed program on your installation CD.
>
> ○ b. You are having trouble restoring from a backup.
>
> ○ c. You can't finish installing Linux.
>
> ○ d. You need to download the program that you're trying to install again.

Answer a is correct. This error is indicative of corruption in a tar archive. Although Linux backups are also restored from tar archives, the error message suggests an installation issue. Therefore, answer b is incorrect. Because you're installing a program and not Linux, answer c is incorrect (the error message is misleading). Although downloading the program again may help solve the problem, it does not describe the problem. Therefore, answer d is incorrect.

Question 6

> Which of the following commands changes the keyboard repeat rate to 15 characters per second?
>
> ○ a. **/sbin/keyboard -a 15**
>
> ○ b. **/sbin/kbdrate -r 15**
>
> ○ c. **/sbin/kbdrate -s 15**
>
> ○ d. **/sbin/kbd -r 15**

Answer b is correct. The command is **kbdrate**, and the -r switch specifies the rate to be used in characters per second. Because **keyboard** is the wrong command, answer a is incorrect. Because -s is the silent option, it does not change the keyboard repeat rate; therefore, answer c is incorrect. Because **kbd** is the wrong command, answer d is incorrect.

Question 7

Which of the following commands turns on the Num Lock option on your keyboard for only the fourth virtual console? Note: *x* is a variable set from 1 through 6.

○ a. **setleds -num < /dev/tty$x > /dev/null**

○ b. **setleds +num < /dev/tty$x > /dev/null**

○ c. **setleds -num < /mnt/tty4 > /dev/null**

○ d. **setleds +num < /dev/tty4 > /dev/null**

Answer d is correct. This command turns on the Num Lock only on the fourth virtual terminal. Answer a turns off the Num Lock; therefore, answer a is incorrect. Because answer b turns on the Num Lock for all virtual consoles from 1 through 6, answer b is incorrect. Answer c turns off the Num Lock on the fourth virtual terminal; therefore, answer c is also incorrect.

Question 8

You're currently unable to print to your printer, which is attached to your local computer. Among others, you have the following printer-related files: /etc/printcap, /var/spool/lpd/lp2/status, /var/spool/lpd/lp2/lock, /etc/syslog.conf, and /var/log/lpr/lpr.info. Among the following choices, where would you look first for a problem with your printer? (The name of your printer is lp2.)

○ a. Look at the messages inside the /var/log/lpr/lpr.info file.

○ b. Look at /var/spool/lpd/lp2/lock and delete it.

○ c. Look at /var/spool/lpd/lp2/status to identify your problem.

○ d. Look at /etc/printcap and make sure the settings for the lp2 printer have not been changed.

Answer b is correct. The purpose of the lock file is to keep other print jobs from interfering with the current print job. As long as it exists, other print jobs will not run. Although the messages in the /var/log/lpr/lpr.info file may help you identify the problem, the problem could be shown in a different log file. Therefore, answer a is incorrect. Although the /var/spool/lpd/lp2/status file may include error messages for your printer, it is not as clear-cut an issue as the lock file. Therefore, answer c is incorrect. Although a change to the /etc/printcap file could redirect your information to a different printer, the lock file still blocks data from reaching your local printer. Therefore, answer d is incorrect.

Question 9

> If you try opening the X Window over a network connection, and all you get is the following error, which of the following actions would you take?
>
> cannot open display:0.0
>
> ○ a. Use the **reset** command to clear the screen of display problems.
>
> ○ b. Set the DISPLAY environment variable to localhost:0.0.
>
> ○ c. Reconfigure your X Window settings.
>
> ○ d. Use the XF86Setup utility to start the X Server.

Answer b is correct. This is the proper response to the error message, which directs the display locally. The **reset** command applies to a similar situation where you see pseudographics in a CLI simulating actual graphics. Because it is not directly related to any X Window functions, answer a is incorrect. Although reconfiguring your X Window settings might work with a tool like XF86Setup, it is not as easy a solution as setting the DISPLAY variable. Therefore, answer c is incorrect. Although starting the XF86Setup utility does start a generic X Server, you can't run any other programs in that X Server, which makes it less than useful in this case. Therefore, answer d is incorrect.

Question 10

You're running different computers on the same e-commerce Web site. The computers are located in several different time zones to optimize data transfer speed with your customers. How would you synchronize the time between your computers? Hypothetically, assume you can set up a time server on a computer on your network at time.ilikemynetwork.com or on a remote network at time.asc.org.

- ○ a. Set up an NTP time server on one of your computers. Set up each of your computers to synchronize time with your NTP server. Run the **ntpdate time.asc.org** command on each computer to complete the synchronization.

- ○ b. Set up each of your computers to synchronize from a remote network. Run the **ntpdate time.ilikemynetwork.com** command on each of your computers to complete the synchronization.

- ○ c. Set up an NTP time server on one of your computers. Set up each of your computers to synchronize time with your NTP server. Run the **ntpdate time.ilikemynetwork.com** command on each computer to complete the synchronization.

- ○ d. Set up each of your computers to synchronize from a remote network. Run the **ntpdate asc.org** command on each of your computers to complete the synchronization.

Answer c is correct. If you set up an NTP time server on one of your computers, you need to apply the **ntpdate** command to that server. Answer a directs you to set up a local NTP server, and then directs the **ntpdate** command on a remote computer; therefore, answer a is incorrect. Because answer b directs you to synchronize from a remote network, and then apply the **ntpdate** command to a local computer, this solution won't work. Therefore, answer b is incorrect. Because answer d does not use **ntpdate** to contact the correct computer, answer d is also incorrect.

Need to Know More?

 Johnson, Dwight. ed. *SuSE Linux 6.0 Installation, Configuration and First Steps*. SuSE GmbH, Nürnberg, Germany, 1998. This manual for S.u.S.E. Linux provides excellent descriptions of problems and potential solutions, which are applicable for all distributions.

 Welsh, Matt, Lar Kaufman, and Matthias Kalle Dalheimer. *Running Linux*. O'Reilly & Associates, Sebastapol, CA, 1999. ISBN 1-56592-469-X. Possibly the key resource book on the Linux operating system. Although much of the information in this book is based on older versions of Linux, the basic data is concise, well written, and applicable today. Much of the writing in this book is not suitable for the novice user. If you can understand the points in this book, you have a better chance of learning troubleshooting shortcuts quickly.

 If you want more information about time servers worldwide, review the **www.eeics.udel.edu/~ntp** Web site.

 Explore the Web site for the Linux Documentation Project at **www.linuxdoc.org**, which is the central repository for Linux manuals, HOWTOs, and a number of other book-length documents. Many HOWTOs include troubleshooting sections. One important HOWTO is Howard Mann's Online Troubleshooting Resources HOWTO.

 Another important document is the Linux System Administrators' Guide at **www.tml.hut.fi/~viu/linux/sag**. This guide is written for newer administrators. You can also find a copy of this guide through the Linux Documentation Project at **www.linuxdoc.org**.

Sample Test

This chapter provides pointers to help you develop a successful test-taking strategy. These helpful tips include how to choose proper answers, how to decode ambiguity, how to work within the Sair Linux/GNU testing framework, how to decide what you need to memorize, and how to prepare for the test. At the end of the chapter, I include 50 questions on subject matter pertinent to the Sair Linux/GNU Installation and Configuration Level 1 certification exam 3X0-101. In Chapter 16, you'll find the answer key to this test. Good luck!

Questions, Questions, Questions

There should be no doubt in your mind that you are facing a test full of specific and pointed questions. Each exam includes 50 questions. You are allotted 60 minutes to complete the exam.

Remember, questions will belong to one of three basic types:

➤ Multiple choice with a single answer

➤ Multiple choice with multiple answers

➤ Statement with a choice of true or false

You should always take the time to read a question at least twice before selecting an answer. Not every question has only one answer; many questions require multiple answers. Therefore, you should read each question carefully, determine how many answers are necessary or possible, and look for additional hints or instructions when selecting answers.

Choosing Proper Answers

Obviously, the only way to pass any exam is to select enough of the right answers to obtain a passing score. However, Sair's Linux exams are not standardized like the SAT and GRE exams; they are far more diabolical and convoluted. In some cases, questions are strangely worded, and deciphering them can be a real challenge. In those cases, you may need to rely on answer elimination skills. Almost always, at least one answer out of the possible choices for a question can be eliminated immediately because it matches one of the following conditions:

➤ The answer does not apply to the situation.

➤ The answer describes a nonexistent issue, an invalid option, or an imaginary state.

➤ The answer may be eliminated because of information in the question itself.

After you eliminate all answers that are obviously wrong, you can apply your retained knowledge to eliminate further answers. Look for items that sound correct but refer to actions, commands, or features that are not present or not available in the situation that the question describes.

If you're still faced with a blind guess among two or more potentially correct answers, reread the question. Try to picture how each of the possible remaining answers would alter the situation. *Be especially sensitive to terminology*; sometimes the choice of words (*remove* instead of *disable*) can make the difference between a right answer and a wrong one.

Only when you've exhausted your ability to eliminate answers and remain unclear about which of the remaining possibilities is correct should you guess at an answer. An unanswered question offers you no points, but guessing gives you at least some chance of getting a question right. Just don't be too hasty when making a blind guess.

Because this is not an "adaptive" exam, you can wait until the last round of reviewing questions (just as you're about to run out of time or unanswered questions) before you start making guesses. Although guessing should be a last resort, you should answer every question. You don't lose any credit if you answer a question incorrectly.

Decoding Ambiguity

Sair Linux/GNU exams have a reputation for including questions that can be difficult to interpret, are confusing, or are ambiguous. In my experience with numerous exams, I consider this reputation to be completely justified. The Sair Linux/GNU exams are tough, and they're deliberately made that way.

The only way to beat Sair at its own game is to be prepared. You'll discover that many exam questions test your knowledge of things that are not directly related to the issue raised by a question. This means that the answers you must choose from, even incorrect ones, are just as much a part of the skill assessment as the question itself. In other words, the more you know about the operating system, the easier it is for you to tell right from wrong.

Questions often give away their answers, but you have to be Sherlock Holmes to see the clues. Often, subtle hints appear in the question text in such a way that they seem almost irrelevant to the situation. You must realize that each question is a test unto itself, and that you need to inspect and successfully navigate each question to pass the exam. Look for small clues, such as the mention of times, group permissions and names, and configuration settings. Little things such as these can point to the right answer if they're properly understood; if missed, they can leave you facing a blind guess.

Another common difficulty with certification exams is vocabulary. You may see some utilities and features named in obvious ways in some cases and completely inanely in other instances. Be sure to brush up on the key terms presented at the beginning of each chapter of this book. You may also want to read the glossary at the end of this book the day before you take the test.

Working within the Framework

The test questions appear in random order, and many elements or issues that are mentioned in one question may also crop up in other questions. It's not uncommon to find that an incorrect answer to one question is the correct answer to another question, or vice versa. Take the time to read every answer to each question, even if you recognize the correct answer to a question immediately. That extra reading may spark a memory or remind you about a Linux feature or function, which may help you on another question elsewhere on the exam.

Because this is not an "adaptive" exam, you can revisit any question as many times as you like. If you're uncertain of the answer to a question, check the box that's provided to mark it for easy return later on. You should also mark questions that you think may offer information you can use to answer other questions. On fixed-length tests, I usually mark somewhere between 25 and 50 percent of the questions. The testing software is designed to let you mark every question if you choose. Use this framework to your advantage. Everything you'll want to see again should be marked. The testing software can then help you return to marked questions quickly and easily.

 For the exam, I strongly recommend that you first read the entire test quickly, before getting caught up in answering individual questions. Doing this will help to jog your memory as you review the potential answers and can help you identify questions that you want to mark for easy access to their contents. You can also identify and mark the tricky questions for easy return. The key is to make a quick pass over the territory to begin with—so that you know what you're up against—and then survey that territory more thoroughly on a second pass, when you can begin to answer all questions systematically and consistently.

Deciding What to Memorize

The amount of memorization you must undertake for an exam depends on how well you remember what you've read and how well you know the operating system by heart. The exam stretches your abilities to memorize product features and functions and interface details as well as how they all relate to Linux as a whole.

At a minimum, you'll want to memorize the following kinds of information:

➤ Linux benefits and costs

➤ Basic command-line interface commands

➤ The structural components of Linux

➤ Run levels

➤ Filesystem Hierarchy Standard

➤ Graphics modes

➤ Troubleshooting solutions

➤ Documentation resources

If you work your way through this book while sitting at a machine with Linux installed and work with the files and commands as they're discussed throughout, you should have little or no difficulty mastering this material. Also, don't forget that The Cram Sheet at the front of the book is designed to capture the material that's most important to memorize. Use this Cram Sheet to guide your studies as well.

Preparing for the Test

The best way to prepare for the test—after you've studied—is to take at least one practice exam. One has been included in this chapter for that reason. The test questions are located in the pages that follow. (Unlike the questions in the preceding chapters in this book, the answers don't follow the questions immediately. You'll have to flip to Chapter 16 to review the answers separately.)

Give yourself 50 minutes to take the exam, and keep yourself on the honor system—don't look at earlier text in the book or jump ahead to the answer key. When your time is up or you've finished the questions, check your work in Chapter 16. Pay special attention to the explanations for the incorrect answers; these can also help to reinforce your knowledge of the material. Knowing how to recognize correct answers is good, but understanding why incorrect answers are wrong can be equally valuable.

Taking the Test

Relax. Once you're sitting in front of the testing computer, there's nothing more you can do to increase your knowledge or preparation. Take a deep breath, stretch, and start reading that first question.

You don't need to rush, either. You have plenty of time to complete each question and to return to the questions that you skipped or marked for return. If you read a question twice and you remain clueless, you can mark it and come back to it later. Both easy and difficult questions are intermixed throughout the test in random order. Don't cheat yourself by spending too much time on a hard question early in the test, thereby depriving yourself of the time you need to answer the questions at the end of the test.

One strategy is to read through the entire test, and then, before returning to marked questions for a second visit, figure out how much time you've got per question. As you answer each question, remove its mark. Continue to review the remaining marked questions until you run out of time or complete the test.

That's it for pointers. Good luck!

Question 1

Which of the following statements best describes "free software" in the context of the General Public License (GPL)?

- ○ a. When you sell "free software," you can set a price that includes the cost of the media, shipping, and a profit.

- ○ b. "Free software" involves the freedom to make changes. Your public release of the software can come with or without the source code.

- ○ c. "Free software" includes anything that you can download from the Internet for free.

- ○ d. When you modify "free software," you can change the source code or incorporate other proprietary products. You can then sell the package as a proprietary product.

- ○ e. None of the above.

Question 2

You want to use your HISTORY feature. How do you find a command that you used previously that started with a *w*? [Hint: You may have used several commands that started with a *w*.]

- ○ a. Press the down arrow until you reach the command that you want.

- ○ b. Enter the **!w** command.

- ○ c. Press the up arrow until you reach the command that you want.

- ○ d. Enter the **w** command.

Question 3

Jacques already has a dual boot on his computer consisting of Linux and Microsoft Windows. He is experimenting with Linux; he wants to set up a second version of Linux on his computer. During this process, Jacques accidentally deletes the MBR. Jacques has both a Linux and an MS-DOS boot floppy (with fdisk), but he's currently having trouble booting his computer. Which of the following steps should he take to resolve the problem?

○ a.   Boot the computer with the Linux boot floppy. Restore the /etc/mbr.conf file from a backup with the **/sbin/lilo** command.

○ b.   Boot the computer with the MS-DOS boot floppy. Restore the /etc/lilo.conf file from a backup with the **/sbin/lilo** command.

○ c.   Boot the computer with the Linux boot floppy. Restore the /etc/lilo.conf file from a backup with the **/sbin/lilo** command.

○ d.   Boot the computer with the MS-DOS boot floppy. Restore the /etc/lilo.conf file from a backup with the **fdisk /mbr** command.

Question 4

Which of the following commands can you use to exit a command-line interface session? [Check all correct answers]

❑ a.   **exit**

❑ b.   **logout**

❑ c.   **logoff**

❑ d.   Ctrl+D

Question 5

You're building a history of memos to another supervisor in a file named bigmemos. Which of the following commands allows you to add other memos to the end of the bigmemos file?

○ a.   **cat file >> bigmemos**

○ b.   **cat file 2> bigmemos**

○ c.   **cat file > bigmemos**

○ d.   **type file >> bigmemos**

Question 6

Assume you have one hard drive on your computer. Its size is a little over 40GB. You currently have Microsoft Windows installed. The files associated with Microsoft Windows as well as your installed programs and data take 15GB of space. Which of the following methods is the best way to set up your hard drive for Linux?

○ a. Use the **fdisk** command to split your current partition. Use the **fips** command to allocate 100MB for a swap partition and 10GB for the root volume.

○ b. Use the **fips** command to split your current partition. Use the **fdisk** command to allocate 100MB for a swap partition, 15GB for the root volume, and 10GB for the boot volume.

○ c. Use the **fips** command to split your current partition. Use the **fdisk** command to allocate 100MB for a swap partition and 15GB for the root volume.

○ d. Use the **fdisk** command to delete all partitions. Continue by setting up a 25GB partition for Windows, 15GB for Linux, and100MB for a swap partition.

Question 7

Why does the GNU development process result in higher quality software? [Check all correct answers]

❑ a. All interested developers, not just those in a single company, work together to help develop the software.

❑ b. Linux users continue to work on the software after it is released. Improvements are frequently added online.

❑ c. Linux users are motivated by prestige, not profit. The prestige associated with creating higher quality software is a greater motivator than money.

❑ d. Linux does not use developers like those who would work at proprietary software companies like Microsoft.

Question 8

You have the following network address: 192.168.33.0. You're using a network mask of 255.255.255.0. The gateway address is 192.168.33.1. Which of the following is the range of IP addresses that can be assigned to computers on your network?

○ a. 192.168.33.0 through 192.168.33.255

○ b. 192.168.33.1 through 192.168.33.254

○ c. 192.168.33.2 through 192.168.33.255

○ d. 192.168.33.2 through 192.168.33.254

Question 9

You have an older computer that you want to convert to Linux, which includes an older CD-ROM connected to your computer through a sound card. What drivers do you need to install that CD-ROM in Linux?

○ a. A sound card driver

○ b. A sound card driver and a CD-ROM driver

○ c. An updated CD-ROM driver

○ d. A combined driver that works for both your sound card and the CD-ROM

Question 10

You want to change run levels to single-user mode. Which of the following steps should you take to go into that mode?

○ a. Run the **init S** command.

○ b. Check your /etc/inittab file for the run level associated with single-user mode. Run the **init** command with the number or letter associated with single-user mode.

○ c. Check your /etc/inittab file for the run level associated with single-user mode. Go into root or superuser mode. Run the **init** command with the number or letter associated with single-user mode.

○ d. Go into root or superuser mode. Run the **init 1** command.

Question 11

You're setting up Linux on a gateway computer, so you need to install two network cards. When you start Linux, it is able to recognize only one of the cards at memory address 0x320. This card has been assigned to device eth0. What can you do to get Linux to recognize your other card? Assume you know that IRQ 12 and memory address 0x280 are available.

○ a. Enter the following command in your /etc/lilo.conf file:
   append="ether=12,0x280,eth1"

○ b. Enter the following command at the LILO **boot:** prompt:
   append="ether=12,0x280,eth1"

○ c. Enter the following command in your /etc/lilo.conf file:
   append="ether=12,0x320,eth1"

○ d. Enter the following command at the LILO **boot:** prompt:
   eth1=12,0x320

Question 12

You've logged on as the user rt. You have the appropriate privileges to mount the CD-ROM drive. You create a subdirectory called cdrom for that purpose. If you run the **mount /dev/cdrom cdrom** command, where will you find the files from your CD? You're still in rt's home directory.

○ a. /home/cdrom

○ b. /home/rt/cdrom

○ c. /cdrom

○ d. /mnt/cdrom

Question 13

You run the **ps** command and get the following output:

```
PID       TTY        TIME        CMD
682       tty1       00:00:00    bash
983       ttyp2      00:00:00    bash
1235      tty4       00:00:00    ps
```

Which of these processes is being run by a user logged in remotely?

- ○ a. PID 682
- ○ b. PID 983
- ○ c. PID 1235
- ○ d. None of the above

Question 14

Which of the following commands allows you to start a GUI login screen?

- ○ a. **startx**
- ○ b. **X**
- ○ c. **xdm**
- ○ d. **XF86Setup**

Question 15

Which of the following answers affects the resolution that you can set up for your X Window?

- ○ a. The RAM on your computer.
- ○ b. The memory in your monitor.
- ○ c. Resolution is limited by a combination of the memory in your monitor and the memory on your video controller.
- ○ d. The memory on your video controller.

Question 16

You've created a new shell called the Live Again Shell (lash). You install the files related to that shell in the bin/lash subdirectory of your home directory. Your user name is la. How would you set up other users to go into your shell by default?

- ○ a. Open the /etc/passwd file. Navigate to the line with the login information for a desired user. Substitute /la/lash for the directory shown in the last column.

- ○ b. Open the /etc/passwd file. Navigate to the line with the login information for a desired user. Substitute /bin/lash for the directory shown in the last column.

- ○ c. Open the /etc/passwd file. Navigate to the line with the login information for a desired user. Substitute /home/bin/lash for the directory shown in the last column.

- ○ d. Open the /etc/passwd file. Navigate to the line with the login information for a desired user. Substitute /home/la/bin/lash for the directory shown in the last column.

Question 17

Which of the following are the three standard channels for data in Linux?

- ○ a. stdin, stdrel, stderr
- ○ b. stdent, stdout, stdlog
- ○ c. stdin, stdout, stderr
- ○ d. stdent, stdex, stderr

Question 18

Which of the following commands deletes all files and directories from the /usr/sbin/WordProcessor directory? Assume that there are a large number of files, but only a /usr/sbin/WordProcessor/docs subdirectory, and you don't want to be prompted before each deletion. Assume you are already in the /usr/sbin directory.

- ○ a. **rm -i WordProcessor**
- ○ b. **rmdir -p WordProcessor/docs**
- ○ c. **rm -r WordProcessor**
- ○ d. **rmdir -r WordProcessor**

Question 19

You're in the X Window and have two screens open. You have a two-button mouse. You've highlighted text from one screen and want to copy it to a second screen. How do you copy the text?

○ a. Move the cursor to the desired location and press the middle mouse button.

○ b. Move the cursor to the desired location and press both mouse buttons.

○ c. Move the cursor to the desired location and right-click. When the pop-up menu appears, click Paste.

○ d. You can't use the mouse to copy and paste text in Linux.

Question 20

Assume you have a large number of users who are logged in simultaneously. Which of the following commands would you use to identify the number of times user jsmith has logged in?

○ a. **who I grep jsmith**

○ b. **who I grep jsmith I wc -l**

○ c. **who I sed jsmith**

○ d. **who I grep jsmith > logins**

Question 21

You need more information about a configuration file. Which of the following pairs of utilities can help you find the information that you need? [Check all correct answers]

❏ a. **man**, **xinfo**

❏ b. **tkinfo**, **info**

❏ c. **man --help**, **xinfo**

❏ d. **info**, **xinfo**

. . . .

Question 22

Which of the following are markup languages? [Check all correct answers]

❏ a. TeX

❏ b. emacs

❏ c. nroff

❏ d. HTML

Question 23

You have a series of shell variables set up in your /etc/profile file. You want some of these variables to apply to other shells while you're still logged in. Which of the following commands applies variables from one shell to another?

○ a. **apply**

○ b. **export**

○ c. **move**

○ d. **env**

Question 24

You just connected to an FTP server from Linux. When you run the **mget .** command, what kind of files are downloaded to your computer?

○ a. All hidden files in the current server directory

○ b. All files in the current server directory

○ c. All files with a dot embedded in the name, such as example.txt

○ d. No files are downloaded

Question 25

You're having trouble booting into Linux. When you turn on your computer, your BIOS checks your memory and basic hard drive connections. Then all you see is the following:

```
LIL
```

Which of the following might be the problem?

○ a. You have a corrupt MBR.

○ b. You're missing a secondary boot loader, /boot/boot.b.

○ c. Your vmlinuz file may be located above cylinder 1023.

○ d. Someone has changed your MBR without your knowledge.

Question 26

You're having trouble booting into Linux. When you turn on your computer, your BIOS checks your memory and basic hard drive connections, and then your computer seems to lock up. Assume that you know this is a problem with your MBR. What steps can you take to restore your MBR? [Check all correct answers]

❑ a. Use the **/sbin/lilo** command to send the contents of the /etc/lilo.conf file to your MBR.

❑ b. Boot your computer with an MS-DOS boot disk, and run the **fdisk /mbr** command.

❑ c. Boot your computer with a Linux boot disk, and type the **linux single** command at the LILO **boot:** prompt.

❑ d. Boot your computer with your Linux installation CD. Enter rescue mode if available.

Question 27

Which of the following statements is not true about GNU GPL software?

○ a. You can sell it for a profit.

○ b. You can integrate it with other proprietary software without permission.

○ c. You can modify the source code to meet your needs.

○ d. You can access documentation for it.

Question 28

Sarah, one of the administrators working with you, has forgotten her root password on her Linux computer. Because she is somewhat new to Linux, she asks you for help. Which of the following pieces of advice makes the most sense?

○ a. Start Linux, and use the **init** command to change into single-user mode. You can then change your root password.

○ b. Start Linux from a boot floppy, and use the **linux single** command to start single-user mode. You can then change your root password.

○ c. Access Sarah's Linux computer from a network connection and change into single-user mode. You can then change your root password.

○ d. Access Sarah's Linux computer from a modem connection and change into single-user mode. You can then change your root password.

Question 29

When you press the x key, you find that your keyboard repeat rate is too slow to satisfy you. It's currently about five characters per second. Which of the following commands increases this rate to 30 characters per second?

○ a. **/sbin/kbdrate -c 30**

○ b. **/sbin/kbd -r 30**

○ c. **/sbin/kbdrate -r 30**

○ d. **/sbin/krate -c 30**

Question 30

Which of the following statements best characterizes multiuser multiterminal multitasking?

○ a. One user logs on multiple times on multiple terminals to run several programs simultaneously.

○ b. Several users each log on once, each on his/her own terminal, and each running his/her own multiple programs concurrently.

○ c. One user logs on at a time and runs multiple programs simultaneously on multiple terminals.

○ d. Several users log on simultaneously. Each user can run his/her program in turn.

Question 31

Your IP address is in the format a.b.c.d. What does each of these letters represent, individually?

○ a. 4 bits

○ b. A number below 192

○ c. An octet

○ d. A dotted quad

Question 32

Which of the following directories contains processed files for your printer spool?

○ a. /var/

○ b. /var/spool

○ c. /var/spool/lpd

○ d. /var/spool/lp

Question 33

Which of the following is the standard GNU GUI tool for configuring the X Window?

○ a. Xconfigurator

○ b. xf86config

○ c. XF86Setup

○ d. **xdm**

○ e. There is no standard GNU GUI tool because they are not as reliable as corresponding command-line tools.

Question 34

You've dedicated your second virtual terminal for numeric data entry. You'd like to have the Num Lock key activated whenever you enter this terminal. Which of the following commands gets this done?

○ a. **setleds num < /dev/tty2**

○ b. **setleds num < /dev/tty2 > /dev/null**

○ c. **setleds +num < /dev/ttyx**

○ d. **setleds +num < /dev/tty2 > /dev/null**

Question 35

GPL software comes with no warranty. Which of the following can you do to make up for the lack of a warranty?

○ a. Purchase a service contract with a Linux consultant or company.

○ b. Hire people who can modify the source code of Linux to meet your needs.

○ c. Maintain the software yourself with the help of Linux documentation and newsgroups.

○ d. Download drivers as needed to keep up with your hardware.

○ e. All of the above.

Question 36

You want to find all the lines in the /etc/passwd configuration file that include the asterisk (*). You know that the **grep * /etc/passwd** command uses the file names in the current directory (not the asterisk) to search through the /etc/passwd file. What command searches for asterisks in the /etc/passwd file? [Check all correct answers]

❑ a. **grep '*' /etc/passwd**

❑ b. **grep `*` /etc/passwd**

❑ c. **grep "*" /etc/passwd**

❑ d. **grep * /etc/passwd**

Question 37

For some reason, you see a jumble of characters on your screen in the command-line interface. Which of the following commands can you use to address this problem?

○ a. **rewrite**

○ b. **reset**

○ c. **bash**

○ d. **xdm**

Question 38

Which of the following statements about environmental variables is true?

○ a. They apply from shell to shell.

○ b. Their values only work for your default shell.

○ c. You can find the current environmental value settings with the **environ** command.

○ d. Environmental variables change from shell to shell.

Question 39

You own a software company and want to get into the business of selling GPL software. You realize that you have to offer the software (and source code) as downloads free of charge. What do you have to do to make money from GPL software?

○ a. Refocus your business and advertise your expertise in the GPL software that you're selling.

○ b. Make it as easy as possible for users to download your software, and charge a fee for that privilege.

○ c. Sell rights to others to remarket and resell your software.

○ d. Distribute the software free of charge, but charge a fee to users for a copy of the source code.

Question 40

Which of the following is a limitation on the Linux Loader (LILO)?

○ a. You cannot use it to make sure Linux recognizes all of your RAM.

○ b. You cannot use it to boot more than four operating systems on any hard drive.

○ c. You cannot use it to boot multiple versions of Linux.

○ d. You can only use it if Linux is located on the first primary partition of the hard drive.

○ e. None of the above.

Question 41

Which of the following statements best describes the difference between the **ln** and **cp** commands? Assume the applicable files are on the same volume.

○ a. Any files created with the **cp** command have the same inode number as the original file. This is not true of the **ln** command.

○ b. Files created with both the **cp** and **ln** commands have identical inode numbers to the original file.

○ c. Any files created with the **ln** command have the same inode number as the original file. This is not true of the **cp** command.

○ d. Files created with both the **cp** and **ln** commands have different inode numbers than the original file.

Question 42

Which of the following statements best describes the difference between the **find** and **locate** commands?

○ a. The **find** command is faster than **locate**, but is less up-to-date because it is based on a database of your file names.

○ b. Although the **find** command works better on system files, the **locate** command works better with personal files in a user's home directory.

○ c. There is no difference: The **find** and **locate** commands are essentially the same command.

○ d. The **find** command is slower than **locate**, but it is more accurate because it searches through all of your current files.

Question 43

Which of the following run levels is dedicated to rebooting your computer?

○ a. 0

○ b. 1

○ c. 6

○ d. It depends on your distribution.

Question 44

You've created an account for a new user by modifying the /etc/passwd configuration file. Which of the following actions do you need to take before the account is ready for the new user? The user name is gsmith. [Check all correct answers]

❑ a. Use the **chown** command to pass ownership to the new user.

❑ b. Go into the new account with the **su - gsmith** command. Copy all files from the /etc/skel directory.

❑ c. Assign a new password with the **passwd gsmith** command.

❑ d. Run the **adduser** command to document the change.

Question 45

You have a program named **runaway** that doesn't seem to stop. You've logged in to a different virtual console. What do you need to do to stop the **runaway** program?

○ a. Run the **grep runaway < ps auxl** command, find the TTY associated with the runaway program, and then run the **kill** command on the TTY number associated with that program.

○ b. Run the **ps auxl > grep runaway** command, find the PID associated with the runaway program, and then run the **kill** command on the PID number associated with that program.

○ c. Run the **ps auxl I grep runaway** command, find the TTY associated with the runaway program, and then run the **kill** command on the TTY number associated with that program.

○ d. Run the **ps aux I grep runaway** command, find the PID associated with the runaway program, and then run the **kill** command on the PID number associated with that program.

Question 46

You're looking over a friend's /etc/printcap printer configuration file. Using the following excerpt, where would you find the printer?

```
lp|LaserJet:lp=/dev/lp0:sd=var/spool/lpd/lp\
:rm=rpp:rp=raw:af=/var/log/lp-acct\
:lf=/var/log/lp-errs:pl#66:pw#80:pc#150:mx#0\
:sh
```

○ a. On the local computer

○ b. On the computer named raw

○ c. On the computer named rpp

○ d. On the computer named sh

Question 47

When Linux starts the X Window, which of the following happens first?

○ a. Linux starts the X Server.

○ b. Linux starts the window manager that you previously configured.

○ c. Linux starts a login display manager such as **xdm**.

○ d. Linux looks up the programs that you had running in the X Window when you last logged out.

Question 48

Which of the following represents the first logical drive on the second hard disk on your computer?

○ a. hda2

○ b. hdb4

○ c. hdb5

○ d. hda5

Question 49

You're having trouble finding a driver that works for the time machine attached to your computer. You want to try the following driver: /lib/modules/ 2.4.11/time/machine.o. Which command would you use?

○ a. **lsmod /lib/modules/2.4.11/time/machine.o**

○ b. **insmod /lib/modules/2.4.11/time/machine.o**

○ c. **rmmod /lib/modules/2.4.11/time/machine.o**

○ d. **conf.modules /lib/modules/2.4.11/time/machine.o**

Question 50

In which directory do you normally find the Linux kernel?

○ a. /bin

○ b. /root

○ c. /boot

○ d. /usr

Answer Key

1. a	18. c	35. e
2. c	19. b	36. a, c, d
3. c	20. b	37. b
4. a, b, d	21. a, b, d	38. a
5. a	22. a, c, d	39. a
6. c	23. b	40. e
7. a, b, c	24. b	41. c
8. b	25. b	42. d
9. b	26. a, c, d	43. c
10. c	27. b	44. a, b, c
11. a	28. b	45. d
12. b	29. c	46. c
13. b	30. b	47. a
14. c	31. c	48. c
15. d	32. c	49. b
16. d	33. c	50. c
17. c	34. d	

Question 1

Answer a is correct. You can sell GPL free software for a profit. Because you need to release the source code with GPL software, answer b is incorrect. Not all "free software" downloaded from the Internet is covered by the GPL. Therefore, answer c is incorrect. Because the GPL doesn't allow you to make the software proprietary, answer d is incorrect.

Question 2

Answer c is correct. The up arrow on your keyboard is the only way to recall your history of previous commands, from newest to oldest. The down arrow moves through your history in the opposite direction; therefore, answer a is incorrect. The !w command executes the last command that you ran that started with the letter *w*. Because you don't know which command that is, answer b is incorrect. The w command is a command unto itself; therefore, answer d is also incorrect.

Question 3

Answer c is correct. Only the Linux boot floppy allows you to boot the Linux kernel. And you want to use the **/sbin/lilo** command to restore the /etc/lilo.conf file. There is no /etc/mbr.conf file; therefore, answer a is incorrect. You can't get to the **/sbin/lilo** command with the MS-DOS boot floppy; therefore, answer b is incorrect. Because the **fdisk /mbr** command restores an MS-DOS master boot record (MBR) without any boot option for Linux, answer d is incorrect.

Question 4

Answers a, b, and d are correct. You can exit from a command-line interface shell with the **exit, logout,** or Ctrl+D command. Because Linux does not recognize the **logoff** command, answer c is incorrect.

Question 5

Answer a is correct. When you want to add the contents of a file to the end of another file, you use the double arrows (>>) to redirect standard output to the end of that file. Because the **2>** redirects standard errors, answer b is incorrect. The single arrow (>) overwrites the contents of the file named bigmemos; therefore, answer c is incorrect. Because there is no **type** command in Linux, answer d is incorrect.

Question 6

Answer c is correct. It is **fips** (First Interactive Partition Splitter), that allows you to split partitions without losing data. Once split, you can then use **fdisk** to allocate space to both your swap and root partitions from the new, empty partition. The **fdisk** command can only split partitions by deleting data within a partition; therefore, answer a is incorrect. The boot directory (/boot) needs only a few megabytes of space. You do not need to set up a separate partition for this directory. In any case, allocating 10GB for this directory is not wise. Therefore, answer b is incorrect. Deleting partitions deletes data; therefore, answer d is incorrect.

Question 7

Answers a, b, and c are correct. With the GPL, all interested developers participate in the development process, even if GPL software is developed inside a single company. With the GPL, users have access to the source code, so they can work on improvements after a release. And the motivator behind many Linux users' work is prestige, not profit. However, Microsoft does hire some of the best developers in the industry. Therefore, answer d is incorrect.

Question 8

Answer b is correct. The range of IP addresses that can be assigned to a network does not include the network or broadcast address. In this case, those addresses are 192.168.33.0 and 192.168.33.255, respectively. Therefore, answer a is incorrect. Because the broadcast address (192.168.33.255) cannot be assigned to any specific computer, answer c is incorrect. Although 192.168.33.1 is your network's gateway address, it is also an address assigned to a computer on your network; therefore answer d is also incorrect.

Question 9

Answer b is correct. In this case, separate drivers are required for the CD-ROM and the sound card. An individual driver for either your CD-ROM or sound card is not enough; therefore, answers a and c are incorrect. Because a combined driver is not available for this older configuration, answer d is incorrect.

Question 10

Answer c is correct. You can only run **init** from root or superuser mode. The only way to know the right level to use to enter single-user mode is through variables defined in the /etc/inittab file. The **init S** command only works in distributions where **S** is assigned to the single-user mode run level; therefore, answer a is incorrect. You need to be in root or superuser mode to run **init**; therefore, answer b is incorrect. Because the **init 1** command only works in distributions where **1** is assigned to the single-user mode run level, answer d is incorrect.

Question 11

Answer a is correct. This option matches the format for the append command, which is **append="irq,i/o,device"**. The **append** command does not work at the LILO **boot:** prompt; therefore, answer b is incorrect. Because the address is wrong (0x320 is already assigned to eth0), answer c is incorrect. Because the format of answer d is wrong, answer d is also incorrect.

Question 12

Answer b is correct. By definition, rt's home directory is /home/rt. Because you're mounting the CD-ROM on the cdrom directory, you're mounting on a subdirectory of /home/rt. Because /home/cdrom is not a subdirectory of /home/rt, answer a is incorrect. You are not mounting on the /cdrom directory; therefore, answer c is incorrect. Although /mnt/cdrom is a fairly standard location for mounting CD-ROM drives, that is not what you're doing with the stated command. Therefore, answer d is incorrect.

Question 13

Answer b is correct. The TTY signifies the login virtual terminal. A login from a remote computer includes a *p*. The only PID on the given list being run by a remote user is 983. Because PID 682 is being run on local virtual terminal tty1, answer a is incorrect. Because PID 1235 is being run on local virtual terminal tty4, answer c is incorrect.

Question 14

Answer c is correct. The **xdm** command allows you to start a GUI login screen. The **startx** command starts the X Window without a login screen; therefore, answer a is incorrect. The **X** command works like **startx** in some distributions; therefore, answer b is incorrect. Because the **XF86Setup** command starts the X Window configuration utility, answer d is incorrect.

Question 15

Answer d is correct. The memory on your video controller limits the resolution that you can set up for your X Window. Although some computers share RAM with video controllers, that is not always the case. Therefore, answer a is incorrect. Although resolution is also limited by the number of pixels that can be shown on a monitor, a monitor itself does not have independent memory. Therefore, answers b and c are incorrect.

Question 16

Answer d is correct. The bin/lash subdirectory of la's home directory is /home/la/bin/lash. Because answers a, b, and c name the wrong subdirectory, they are all incorrect.

Question 17

Answer c is correct. The standard data channels in Linux are standard input (stdin), standard output (stdout), and standard error (stderr). Answers a, b, and d name channels that do not exist; thus, these answers are incorrect.

Question 18

Answer c is correct. The **rm -r** command recursively deletes all listed directories and subdirectories as well as all files within the listed files and subdirectories without prompting. The **rm -i** command prompts before the deletion of each file or directory; therefore, answer a is incorrect. The **rmdir -p** command works only if the appropriate directories are empty; therefore, answer b is incorrect. Because there is no **-r** switch for the **rmdir** command, answer d is incorrect.

Question 19

Answer b is correct. When properly set up, pressing both buttons on a two-button mouse emulates the functions of the middle button of a three-button mouse. There is no middle mouse button on a two-button mouse; therefore, answer a is incorrect. The right-click does not bring up a Paste option in all X Window applications; therefore, answer c is incorrect. The middle button "pastes" previously highlighted text in Linux; therefore, answer d is incorrect.

Question 20

Answer b is correct. The **who** command lists all logged on users. When piped (|) to the **grep jsmith** command, the **who** command filters for all lines with the text string *jsmith*. When piped to the **wc -1** command, it returns the number of lines with the text string *jsmith*, which also happens to answer the question. Although you can count the lines output from the **who | grep jsmith** command, the output from the command itself doesn't answer the question; therefore, answer a is incorrect. Because the **sed** command is used to perform text transformations, it does not help find the number of times user jsmith is logged on. Therefore, answer c is incorrect. Although you can open the logins file and count the number of lines to find the number of times jsmith is logged on, the output from the command itself doesn't answer the question; therefore, answer d is also incorrect.

Question 21

Answers a, b, and d are correct. The **man** and **info** commands, when combined with the name of a configuration file, can help describe that file. Variations on the **info** command, including **xinfo** and **tkinfo**, can help equally well. However, because the **man --help** command just returns the switches associated with the **man** command, answer c is incorrect.

Question 22

Answers a, c, and d are correct. TeX, nroff, and HTML are markup languages. The content is in text format. These markup languages are added to the text for formatting purposes. Because emacs is a text editor, answer b is incorrect.

Question 23

Answer b is correct. The **export** command applies variables from one shell to another. The **apply** and **move** commands are unrelated to variables; therefore, answers a and c are incorrect. Because the **env** command only lists current environment variables, answer d is incorrect.

Question 24

Answer b is correct. The dot represents all files in the current directory. Because this includes more than just hidden files in the current directory, answer a is incorrect. Because this is not limited to files with an embedded dot, such as example.txt, answer c is incorrect. Because files are downloaded with this command, answer d is incorrect.

Question 25

Answer b is correct. Linux can find your lilo.conf file, but it is having trouble finding your secondary boot loader, /boot/boot.b. Because Linux finds your lilo.conf file in your master boot record (MBR), answers a and d are incorrect. The vmlinuz file contains the Linux kernel. The Linux kernel loads after a selection is made at the full LILO **boot:** prompt; therefore, answer c is incorrect.

Question 26

Answers a, c, and d are correct. If you don't see the LILO **boot:** prompt, you have a problem with your master boot record (MBR). The **/sbin/lilo** command does restore the contents of your lilo.conf file to your MBR. Booting your computer with a Linux boot disk or installation CD can help you get to your lilo.conf file. The Linux installation CD can work as well as the boot disk if it has a rescue mode. Because the **fdisk /mbr** command restores an MS-DOS MBR, answer b is incorrect.

Question 27

Answer b is correct. You can't integrate GPL software with proprietary software unless you release the integrated package under the GPL. You can sell GPL software for a profit; therefore, answer a is incorrect. You can freely get the source code for GPL software, and you can modify it to meet your needs. Therefore, answer c is incorrect. Because you can access documentation for GPL software, answer d is incorrect.

Question 28

Answer b is correct. When you type the **linux single** command at the LILO **boot:** prompt, you start Linux in single-user mode without needing a login. You can then use the **passwd** command to change the root user password. To change into single-user mode from within Linux, you need to have root or superuser access. Because this password has been forgotten, answers a, c, and d are incorrect. You can't get to the point where you could use the **init** command, nor could you log in to Sarah's root account on her computer without her password.

Question 29

Answer c is correct. The **/sbin/kbdrate -r 30** command sets the keyboard rate to 30 characters per second. The other answers either use the wrong command, the wrong switch, or both.

Question 30

Answer b is correct. Multiple users each logging on to one terminal still means that multiple terminals are used. Each user runs multiple programs, which requires the essence of multitasking. Because one user does not demonstrate multiuser capabilities, answers a and c are incorrect. If users are required to "take turns" running programs, it is not a multitasking system. Therefore, answer d is incorrect.

Question 31

Answer c is correct. Each of the four parts of an IP address represents 8 bits, also known as an *octet*. Because an octet is more than 4 bits, answer a is incorrect. (Incidently, 4 bits is also known as a *nibble*.) Each number in an IP address is between 0 and 255; therefore, answer b is incorrect. The format of an IP address as a whole is also known as *dotted-quad*; however, because the question is about each of the numbers individually, answer d is also incorrect.

Question 32

Answer c is correct. Print files are stored in a spool in your /var/spool/lpd directory, waiting for your printer to receive them. The /var directory contains spool and log files; therefore, answer a is incorrect. The /var/spool directory contains spool files for several devices including faxes and printers; therefore, answer b is incorrect. Because there is normally no /var/spool/lp directory, answer d is also incorrect.

Question 33

Answer c is correct. The XF86Setup utility is the standard GNU GUI tool for configuring the X Window. Because Xconfigurator is included only with Red Hat Linux, answer a is incorrect. Because xf86config is a command-line tool, answer b is incorrect. Because **xdm** is the command for a GUI login screen, it has nothing to do with configuring the X Window. Therefore, answer d is also incorrect. Although GUI tools are generally considered to be less reliable than the corresponding command-line tools, XF86Setup is an exception to this rule. Therefore, answer e is incorrect.

Question 34

Answer d is correct. The second virtual terminal is represented by /dev/tty2. The **+num** switch turns on the Num Lock option on your keyboard when you go into the subject virtual terminal. The redirection to the /dev/null device helps your current terminal ignore any output from this command. Because the **num** switch is used incorrectly, answers a and b are incorrect. Because no terminal is specified in /dev/ttyx, answer c is also incorrect.

Question 35

Answer e is correct. Linux is freely available. But because it comes with no warranty, you may need help through a service contract. Alternately, people you hire can modify the source code for your special business needs. Help is available to maintain Linux through documentation and newsgroups. And new drivers are available all over the Internet to help you make Linux work with new hardware.

Question 36

Answers a, c, and d are correct. Single quotes, double quotes, and backslashes all "escape" the functionality of a single character, such as the asterisk (*). Because back quotes do not escape the functionality of a character, answer b is incorrect.

Question 37

Answer b is correct. The question indicates that you're in pseudographics mode in the command-line interface. The **reset** command restores regular input from your keyboard. Because the other commands are unrelated to pseudographics, answers a, c, and d are incorrect.

Question 38

Answer a is correct. Environmental variables apply from shell to shell. Because they work for more than just one shell, answers b and d are incorrect. Because you can find current environmental variable settings with the **env** (not **environ**) command, answer c is incorrect.

Question 39

Answer a is correct. Refocusing your business on your software expertise can get you service and support contracts for GPL software. You can't charge a fee for downloading GPL software; therefore, answer b is incorrect. You can't sell the rights to GPL software; therefore, answer c is incorrect. Because the source code must be freely available, answer d is also incorrect.

Question 40

Answer e is correct. With the **mem** command, you can use LILO to make sure Linux recognizes all of your RAM. Therefore, answer a is incorrect. There is no logical limitation on the number of operating systems that you can point to with LILO; therefore, answer b is incorrect. You can use LILO to point to more than one version of Linux; therefore, answer c is incorrect. Because you're not required to install Linux on the first primary partition, answer d is incorrect.

Question 41

Answer c is correct. When you use the **ln** command, you're creating a "hard" link between files. As long as that link is between files on the same volume, the files are functionally identical. Any change that you make to one file is also made to the other file. The link is represented by two files with the same inode number. Files created with the **cp** command do not have the same inode number; therefore, answers a and b are incorrect. (You may note that files created with the **cp -p** command *do* have the same inode number.) Files created with the **ln** command normally have the same inode number; therefore, answer d is incorrect. (You may note that files linked with the **ln -s** command do *not* have the same inode numbers.)

Question 42

Answer d is correct. Although the **find** command searches through all of your current files, directory by directory, the **locate** command uses a database file that is created periodically and therefore may not be completely up-to-date. However, the database speeds file searches with the **locate** command. Because **find** is slower than **locate**, answer a is incorrect. Because there is no difference in speed based on file types, answer b is incorrect. Because **find** and **locate** are not identical commands, answer c is incorrect.

Question 43

Answer c is correct. Run level 6 is dedicated to rebooting your computer. Run level 0 is dedicated to stopping or halting your computer without rebooting; therefore, answer a is incorrect. Run level 1 is generally (not always) associated with single-user mode; therefore, answer b is incorrect. The run level for reboot does not vary by distribution; therefore, answer d is incorrect.

Question 44

Answers a, b, and c are correct. When you create a new user by modifying the /etc/passwd configuration file, you still need to do a few things to prepare the account. The **chown** command, properly applied, allows new users to read their own directories. Copying files, as the new user (the reason for the **su -gsmith** command), from the /etc/skel directory sets up standard configuration files in your new user's home directory. The **passwd** command sets up new users with a password, which they can change after the first login. Because the **adduser** command performs all of these steps (including changing the /etc/passwd file a second time) independently, it is not the command you want to use after modifying the /etc/passwd file. Therefore, answer d is incorrect.

Question 45

Answer d is correct. You need to kill the **runaway** program by using the **kill** command on that program's PID. The **ps aux | grep runaway** command allows you to identify the appropriate PID. You can't kill a program by its virtual terminal (TTY); therefore, answers a and c are incorrect. Because the **ps auxl > grep runaway** command looks for every output line from **ps auxl** in a file named **runaway**, answer b is also incorrect.

Question 46

Answer c is correct. The computer with the remote printer is shown with the **rm** label. Because this excerpt applies to the computer with the remote printer, answer a is incorrect. The **rp** label is set to the name of the remote printer, not the name of the remote computer; therefore, answer b is incorrect. The **sh** label shown in this excerpt suppresses the printing of a header, which is unrelated to the question. Therefore, answer d is incorrect.

Question 47

Answer a is correct. Before Linux can set up anything related to the X Window, it needs to start the X Server. The window manager starts after the X Server; therefore, answer b is incorrect. If you start a login display with the **xdm** command, the X Server still starts first; therefore, answer c is incorrect. Only after starting the applicable window manager can Linux look up any programs that you previously had running in that manager. Therefore, answer d is also incorrect.

Question 48

Answer c is correct. The second hard disk is hdb, and the first four numbers are reserved for primary and/or extended partitions. Thus, the first logical drive is number 5. Because hda2 represents the second primary partition on the first hard disk, answer a is incorrect. Because hdb4 represents the fourth primary partition (or the extended partition) on the second hard disk, answer b is incorrect. Because hda5 is a drive on the first hard disk, answer d is also incorrect.

Question 49

Answer b is correct. The **insmod** command installs drivers. The **lsmod** command lists but does not install any drivers; therefore, answer a is incorrect. The **rmmod** command removes drivers; therefore, answer c is incorrect. There is no **conf.modules** command; therefore, answer d is also incorrect.

Question 50

Answer c is correct. The Linux kernel, sometimes known as *vmlinuz*, is usually found in the /boot directory. The /bin directory includes command-line commands, which do not include the Linux kernel. Therefore, answer a is incorrect. Although the Linux kernel is sometimes located in the root (/) directory, it is not located in the home directory of the root user (/root). Therefore, answer b is incorrect. Because the /usr directory contains small, commonly used programs, it is not an appropriate location for the Linux kernel. Therefore, answer d is also incorrect.

Appendix
GNU General Public License

Version 2, June 1991
Copyright (C) 1989, 1991 Free Software Foundation, Inc.
59 Temple Place, Suite 330, Boston, MA 02111-1307 USA

Everyone is permitted to copy and distribute verbatim copies of this license document, but changing it is not allowed.

Preamble

The licenses for most software are designed to take away your freedom to share and change it. By contrast, the GNU General Public License is intended to guarantee your freedom to share and change free software—to make sure the software is free for all its users. This General Public License applies to most of the Free Software Foundation's software, and to any other program whose authors commit to using it. (Some other Free Software Foundation software is covered by the GNU Library General Public License instead.) You can apply it to your programs, too.

When we speak of free software, we are referring to freedom, not price. Our General Public Licenses are designed to make sure that you have the freedom to distribute copies of free software (and charge for this service if you wish), that you receive source code or can get it if you want it, that you can change the software or use pieces of it in new free programs; and that you know you can do these things.

To protect your rights, we need to make restrictions that forbid anyone to deny you these rights or to ask you to surrender the rights. These restrictions translate to certain responsibilities for you if you distribute copies of the software, or if you modify it.

For example, if you distribute copies of such a program, whether gratis or for a fee, you must give the recipients all the rights that you have. You must make sure that they, too, receive or can get the source code. And you must show them these terms so they know their rights.

We protect your rights with two steps: (1) copyright the software, and (2) offer you this license which gives you legal permission to copy, distribute and/or modify the software.

Also, for each author's protection and ours, we want to make certain that everyone understands that there is no warranty for this free software. If the software is modified by someone else and passed on, we want its recipients to know that what they have is not the original, so that any problems introduced by others will not reflect on the original authors' reputations.

Finally, any free program is threatened constantly by software patents. We wish to avoid the danger that redistributors of a free program will individually obtain patent licenses, in effect making the program proprietary. To prevent this, we have made it clear that any patent must be licensed for everyone's free use or not licensed at all.

The precise terms and conditions for copying, distribution and modification follow.

Terms and Conditions for Copying, Distribution, and Modification

This License applies to any program or other work, which contains a notice placed by the copyright holder saying it may be distributed under the terms of this General Public License. The "Program," below, refers to any such program or work, and a "work based on the Program" means either the Program or any derivative work under copyright law: that is to say, a work containing the Program or a portion of it, either verbatim or with modifications and/or translated into another language. (Hereinafter, translation is included without limitation in the term "modification".) Each licensee is addressed as "you."

Activities other than copying, distribution and modification are not covered by this License; they are outside its scope. The act of running the Program is not restricted, and the output from the Program is covered only if its contents constitute a work based on the Program (independent of having been made by running the Program). Whether that is true depends on what the Program does.

1. You may copy and distribute verbatim copies of the Program's source code as you receive it, in any medium, provided that you conspicuously and appropriately publish on each copy an appropriate copyright notice and disclaimer

of warranty; keep intact all the notices that refer to this License and to the absence of any warranty; and give any other recipients of the Program a copy of this License along with the Program.

You may charge a fee for the physical act of transferring a copy, and you may at your option offer warranty protection in exchange for a fee.

2. You may modify your copy or copies of the Program or any portion of it, thus forming a work based on the Program, and copy and distribute such modifications or work under the terms of Section 1 above, provided that you also meet all of these conditions:

    (a) You must cause the modified files to carry prominent notices stating that you changed the files and the date of any change.

    (b) You must cause any work that you distribute or publish, that in whole or in part contains or is derived from the Program or any part thereof, to be licensed as a whole at no charge to all third parties under the terms of this License.

    (c) If the modified program normally reads commands interactively when run, you must cause it, when started running for such interactive use in the most ordinary way, to print or display an announcement including an appropriate copyright notice and a notice that there is no warranty (or else, saying that you provide a warranty) and that users may redistribute the program under these conditions, and telling the user how to view a copy of this License. (Exception: if the Program itself is interactive but does not normally print such an announcement, your work based on the Program is not required to print an announcement.)

These requirements apply to the modified work as a whole. If identifiable sections of that work are not derived from the Program, and can be reasonably considered independent and separate works in themselves, then this License, and its terms, do not apply to those sections when you distribute them as separate works. But when you distribute the same sections as part of a whole which is a work based on the Program, the distribution of the whole must be on the terms of this License, whose permissions for other licensees extend to the entire whole, and thus to each and every part regardless of who wrote it.

Thus, it is not the intent of this section to claim rights or contest your rights to work written entirely by you; rather, the intent is to exercise the right to control the distribution of derivative or collective works based on the Program.

In addition, mere aggregation of another work not based on the Program with the Program (or with a work based on the Program) on a volume of a storage or distribution medium does not bring the other work under the scope of this License.

3. You may copy and distribute the Program (or a work based on it, under Section 2) in object code or executable form under the terms of Sections 1 and 2 above provided that you also do one of the following:

(a) Accompany it with the complete corresponding machine-readable source code, which must be distributed under the terms of Sections 1 and 2 above on a medium customarily used for software interchange; or,

(b) Accompany it with a written offer, valid for at least three years, to give any third party, for a charge no more than your cost of physically performing source distribution, a complete machine-readable copy of the corresponding source code, to be distributed under the terms of Sections 1 and 2 above on a medium customarily used for software interchange; or,

(c) Accompany it with the information you received as to the offer to distribute corresponding source code. (This alternative is allowed only for noncommercial distribution and only if you received the program in object code or executable form with such an offer, in accord with Subsection b above.)

The source code for a work means the preferred form of the work for making modifications to it. For an executable work, complete source code means all the source code for all modules it contains, plus any associated interface definition files, plus the scripts used to control compilation and installation of the executable. However, as a special exception, the source code distributed need not include anything that is normally distributed (in either source or binary form) with the major components (compiler, kernel, and so on) of the operating system on which the executable runs, unless that component itself accompanies the executable.

If distribution of executable or object code is made by offering access to copy from a designated place, then offering equivalent access to copy the source code from the same place counts as distribution of the source code, even though third parties are not compelled to copy the source along with the object code.

4. You may not copy, modify, sublicense, or distribute the Program except as expressly provided under this License. Any attempt otherwise to copy, modify, sublicense or distribute the Program is void, and will automatically terminate your rights under this License. However, parties who have received copies, or rights, from you under this License will not have their licenses terminated so long as such parties remain in full compliance.

5. You are not required to accept this License, since you have not signed it. However, nothing else grants you permission to modify or distribute the Program or its derivative works. These actions are prohibited by law if you do not accept this License. Therefore, by modifying or distributing the Program (or any work based on the Program), you indicate your acceptance of this License to do so, and all its terms and conditions for copying, distributing or modifying the Program or works based on it.

6. Each time you redistribute the Program (or any work based on the Program), the recipient automatically receives a license from the original licensor to copy, distribute or modify the Program subject to these terms and conditions. You may not impose any further restrictions on the recipients' exercise of the rights granted herein. You are not responsible for enforcing compliance by third parties to this License.

7. If, as a consequence of a court judgment or allegation of patent infringement or for any other reason (not limited to patent issues), conditions are imposed on you (whether by court order, agreement or otherwise) that contradict the conditions of this License, they do not excuse you from the conditions of this License. If you cannot distribute so as to satisfy simultaneously your obligations under this License and any other pertinent obligations, then as a consequence you may not distribute the Program at all. For example, if a patent license would not permit royalty-free redistribution of the Program by all those who receive copies directly or indirectly through you, then the only way you could satisfy both it and this License would be to refrain entirely from distribution of the Program.

If any portion of this section is held invalid or unenforceable under any particular circumstance, the balance of the section is intended to apply and the section as a whole is intended to apply in other circumstances.

It is not the purpose of this section to induce you to infringe any patents or other property right claims or to contest validity of any such claims; this section has the sole purpose of protecting the integrity of the free software distribution system, which is implemented by public license practices. Many people have made generous contributions to the wide range of software distributed through that system in reliance on consistent application of that system; it is up to the author/donor to decide if he or she is willing to distribute software through any other system and a licensee cannot impose that choice.

This section is intended to make thoroughly clear what is believed to be a consequence of the rest of this License.

8. If the distribution and/or use of the Program is restricted in certain countries either by patents or by copyrighted interfaces, the original copyright holder who places the Program under this License may add an explicit geographical distribution limitation excluding those countries, so that distribution is permitted only in or among countries not thus excluded. In such case, this License incorporates the limitation as if written in the body of this License.

9. The Free Software Foundation may publish revised and/or new versions of the General Public License from time to time. Such new versions will be similar in spirit to the present version, but may differ in detail to address new problems or concerns.

   Each version is given a distinguishing version number. If the Program specifies a version number of this License which applies to it and "any later version", you have the option of following the terms and conditions either of that version or of any later version published by the Free Software Foundation. If the Program does not specify a version number of this License, you may choose any version ever published by the Free Software Foundation.

10. If you wish to incorporate parts of the Program into other free programs whose distribution conditions are different, write to the author to ask for permission. For software, which is copyrighted by the Free Software Foundation, write to the Free Software Foundation; we sometimes make exceptions for this. Our decision will be guided by the two goals of preserving the free status of all derivatives of our free software and of promoting the sharing and reuse of software generally.

No Warranty

11. BECAUSE THE PROGRAM IS LICENSED FREE OF CHARGE, THERE IS NO WARRANTY FOR THE PROGRAM, TO THE EXTENT PERMITTED BY APPLICABLE LAW. EXCEPT WHEN OTHERWISE STATED IN WRITING THE COPYRIGHT HOLDERS AND/OR OTHER PARTIES PROVIDE THE PROGRAM "AS IS" WITHOUT WARRANTY OF ANY KIND, EITHER EXPRESSED OR IMPLIED, INCLUDING, BUT NOT LIMITED TO, THE IMPLIED WARRANTIES OF MERCHANTABILITY AND FITNESS FOR A PARTICULAR PURPOSE. THE ENTIRE RISK AS TO THE QUALITY AND PERFORMANCE OF THE PROGRAM IS WITH YOU. SHOULD THE PROGRAM PROVE DEFECTIVE, YOU ASSUME THE COST OF ALL NECESSARY SERVICING, REPAIR OR CORRECTION.

12. IN NO EVENT UNLESS REQUIRED BY APPLICABLE LAW OR AGREED TO IN WRITING WILL ANY COPYRIGHT HOLDER, OR ANY OTHER PARTY WHO MAY MODIFY AND/OR REDISTRIB-UTE THE PROGRAM AS PERMITTED ABOVE, BE LIABLE TO YOU FOR DAMAGES, INCLUDING ANY GENERAL, SPECIAL, INCIDENTAL OR CONSEQUENTIAL DAMAGES ARISING OUT OF THE USE OR INABILITY TO USE THE PROGRAM (INCLUD-ING BUT NOT LIMITED TO LOSS OF DATA OR DATA BEING RENDERED INACCURATE OR LOSSES SUSTAINED BY YOU OR THIRD PARTIES OR A FAILURE OF THE PROGRAM TO OPER-ATE WITH ANY OTHER PROGRAMS), EVEN IF SUCH HOLDER OR OTHER PARTY HAS BEEN ADVISED OF THE POSSIBILITY OF SUCH DAMAGES.

How to Apply These Terms to Your New Programs

If you develop a new program, and you want it to be of the greatest possible use to the public, the best way to achieve this is to make it free software which everyone can redistribute and change under these terms.

To do so, attach the following notices to the program. It is safest to attach them to the start of each source file to most effectively convey the exclusion of warranty; and each file should have at least the "copyright" line and a pointer to where the full notice is found.

```
<one line to give the program's name and
a brief idea of what it does.>
Copyright (C) 19yy  <name of author>

This program is free software; you can
redistribute it and/or modify it under the
terms of the GNU General Public License as
published by the Free Software Foundation;
either version 2 of the License, or
(at your option) any later version.

This program is distributed in the hope that
it will be useful, but WITHOUT ANY WARRANTY;
without even the implied warranty of
MERCHANTABILITY or FITNESS FOR A PARTICULAR
PURPOSE. See the GNU General Public License
for more details.
```

```
You should have received a copy of the GNU
General Public License along with this
program; if not, write to the Free Software
Foundation, Inc., 59 Temple Place, Suite 330,
Boston, MA  02111-1307  USA
```

Also add information on how to contact you by electronic and paper mail.

If the program is interactive, make it output a short notice like this when it starts in an interactive mode:

```
Gnomovision version 69, Copyright (C) 19yy
name of author Gnomovision comes with
ABSOLUTELY NO WARRANTY; for details type
'show w'. This is free software, and you are
welcome to redistribute it under certain
conditions; type 'show c' for details.
```

The hypothetical commands 'show w' and 'show c' should show the appropriate parts of the General Public License. Of course, the commands you use may be called something other than 'show w' and 'show c'; they could even be mouse-clicks or menu items—whatever suits your program.

You should also get your employer (if you work as a programmer) or your school, if any, to sign a "copyright disclaimer" for the program, if necessary. Here is a sample; alter the names:

```
Yoyodyne, Inc., hereby disclaims all copyright
interest in the program 'Gnomovision'
(which makes passes at compilers) written
by James Hacker.

<signature of Ty Coon>, 1 April 1989
Ty Coon, President of Vice
```

This General Public License does not permit incorporating your program into proprietary programs. If your program is a subroutine library, you may consider it more useful to permit linking proprietary applications with the library. If this is what you want to do, use the GNU Library General Public License instead of this License.

Glossary

*

A wildcard character that represents zero or more alphanumeric characters. For example, if you were to run the **ls a*** command, you would see all files starting with the letter *a*. If you have a file named a, you would see this file in the listing as well.

.

Also known as the *dot*, this represents the current directory.

..

The double dot represents the parent of the current directory.

<

A redirection. The contents from the term to the right of this arrow is redirected as standard input (stdin) to the file to the left of the arrow. Commonly used to input several terms or data from a file to a program.

>

A redirection. Standard output (stdout) from the term to the left of this arrow is redirected to the file to the right of the arrow. If the file already exists, it is overwritten.

>>

Redirect and append. Standard output (stdout) from the term to the left of this arrow is redirected to the end of the file listed to the right of the arrow. Does not overwrite the file to the right of the arrow.

&

When used after a program name, the ampersand (**&**) instructs your shell to run that program in the background.

?

A wildcard character that represents one alphanumeric character. For example, if you were to run the **ls a?** command, you would see all files with two characters starting with the letter *a*, such as a1, ab, a6, ax, and so on.

[]

Brackets. Used to define a range of search terms.

|

A pipe. Standard output (stdout) from the term or command to the left of the pipe is redirected as standard input to the term or command to the right of the pipe.

2>

Redirect standard error. Standard error (stderr) from the term to the left of the arrow is redirected to the file to the right of the arrow. If the file already exists, it is overwritten.

/

The root directory. This is the top directory in any Linux system.

/bin

The Linux directory with essential command-line utilities.

/boot

The Linux directory with startup utilities, often including the Linux kernel.

/dev

The Linux directory with device drivers.

/dev/null

An output file that ignores output from a utility or a script. It prevents unwanted or unneeded output from affecting other systems.

/etc

The Linux directory with most basic configuration files.

/etc/bashrc

The configuration file that contains bash shell variables for all users.

/etc/environment

The configuration file with environment variables applicable to all users.

/etc/exports

The configuration file with a list of Linux directories that you make available through the Network File System (NFS).

/etc/fstab

The configuration file that lists volumes to be mounted during Linux boot and those that can be mounted after boot.

/etc/hosts

The configuration file where you can associate computer names and IP addresses on your local network. This file is an alternative to DNS on smaller networks.

/etc/inittab

The configuration file that specifies run levels as well as local and remote virtual consoles.

/etc/login

A configuration file that may contain environment or shell variables, depending on your distribution.

/etc/mtab

The file that lists current mounted or mountable volumes.

/etc/passwd

The file that lists all users that are set up on your Linux computer. Passwords are either encrypted in this file or are marked with an x. In the latter case, passwords are encrypted in the /etc/ shadow configuration file.

/etc/printcap
The printer configuration file.

/etc/profile
A configuration file with variables for all users. Whether the variables are environment-wide or specific to one shell depends on your Linux distribution.

/etc/resolv.conf
The configuration file with the fully qualified domain names or IP addresses of your DNS servers.

/etc/skel
The directory where default configuration files for individual users are located. If you want to create a new user, you can copy the files from this directory to your new user's home directory.

/etc/syslog.conf
The configuration file that specifies the location of various log files.

/etc/X11/XF86Config
The main configuration file for the Linux X Window.

/home
The Linux directory that contains home directories for regular individual users.

/lib
The Linux directory that contains program libraries referenced by the Linux kernel and command-line utilities.

/mnt
The Linux directory that contains the mount point or directory for removable media, such as floppy or CD-ROM drives.

/opt
The Linux directory that is commonly used for third-party applications, such as WordPerfect or Applixware.

/proc
The virtual Linux directory that contains currently running kernel-related processes.

/root
The home directory for the root user for the local system.

/sbin
The Linux directory containing many system administration commands.

/sbin/lilo
The command that incorporates information from the /etc/lilo.conf file in the Master Boot Record.

/tmp
The Linux directory commonly used for temporary files, such as downloads from the Internet.

/usr
A Linux directory with a number of smaller programs and applications.

/var
The Linux directory for variable data, such as print spools and log files.

absolute path
The fully defined path to a file or directory in Linux, starting with the root directory.

access.conf
An Apache configuration file where you set up directories for use by your Web server.

address classes

The term associated with the five main groups of IP addresses. By convention, there are five address classes: A, B, C, D, and E.

adduser

A command that partially automates the process of adding users in Linux.

af

Accounting filter. Associated with the /etc/printcap printer configuration file. A way to collect costs associated with printing.

AfterStep

A window manager based on FVWM code, which is designed to look like the window manager associated with the NeXTStep operating system.

alias

A Linux command used to designate a word that is equivalent to a Linux command. Commonly used to help MS-DOS users make the transition to Linux; one common alias command is **alias dir= "ls –l"**.

Apache

The Linux Web server, also known as *httpd*.

append

A LILO configuration command used to assign IRQs and I/O addresses to peripherals, such as network cards.

Applixware

Applixware Office is a Linux office suite from Vista Source. Functionally similar to Microsoft Office.

apropos

Searches through available commands. For example, **apropos ethernet** searches through the title of every available man page for the word *ethernet*. This command does not work in all Linux distributions.

archive error

An error associated with collecting or extracting from an archive file.

ARPA

The Advanced Research Projects Agency of the U.S. Department of Defense. The agency that contracted with various universities for a network that could survive a nuclear war. This ARPAnet that developed was the precursor of the Internet. It was built on university computers with the Unix operating system and a networking protocol stack known as *TCP/IP*.

ATAPI

AT Attachment Packet Interface. The most common interface for CD-ROM drives.

badblocks

A command that checks for physical defects on your disk in specific blocks. When defects are found, these blocks are set aside and marked to keep hard disks from storing files on them. Conceptually similar to the MS-DOS **chkdsk** command.

bash

Bourne Again SHell. Possibly the most common shell in use in Linux.

Basic Input/Output System (BIOS)

The first program that runs when you start your computer. It initializes your hardware and starts the process of booting.

beta

A prerelease status for software, which is not suitable for production computers. Intended for testing and debugging by developers.

bg

A command that resumes suspended programs in the background of the command-line interface. You can suspend a program with the Ctrl+Z command, and then resume it in the background with the **bg** command. After you run this command, you get a command-line interface that allows you to run another program. *See also* &.

Blackbox

A window manager designed to work in a minimum of RAM. Includes support for KDE applications.

boot.b

Also known as the *secondary boot loader*, which loads after you choose Linux at the LILO **boot:** prompt.

broadcast address

The network address used to send messages to every computer on a LAN. On a TCP/IP network, the broadcast address is the last address in the range for the LAN. For example, if the network address is 192.168.12.0 and the network mask is 255.255.255.0, the broadcast address for that network is 192.168.12.255.

bus

A communications channel inside a computer. PC buses are dedicated to PCI cards and ISA cards as well as RAM.

Caldera

A Linux distribution sometimes known as *Open Linux* or *eLinux*.

cat

The concatenate command sends the contents of a file to your standard output, usually the screen. Similar to the MS-DOS **type** command.

cd

The Linux change directory command.

chgrp

The command to reassign the group associated with a file or directory.

chmod

The command to change the permissions associated with a file or directory.

chown

The command to reassign the ownership of a file or directory.

CLI

See command-line interface.

COAS

Caldera Open Administration System. A graphical utility that allows you to administer many parts of your Linux system.

command completion

In a Linux shell, this is the ability to complete partial commands with the Tab key.

command-line interface (CLI)
The operating system interface that you control with text-based commands.

command line-interpreter
Another name for a Linux shell.

community development model
The way software is developed in Linux. In the community development model, independent developers combine their efforts to write, develop, test, and debug software.

copyleft
See General Public License (GPL).

Corel Linux
A Linux distribution that focuses on ease of use. It is based on Debian Linux.

cp
The Linux copy command.

CPU
Central Processing Unit. The main processing engine in a personal computer.

cracker
A user who tries to break into computer systems for malicious reasons.

daemon
Any program resident in your RAM that watches for signals to go into action. For example, network daemons watch for data transmitted between computers before they start.

dd
Device dump. This command is used to unpack images to other directories and is especially suited for floppy disks. Similar to the **rawrite** command.

Debian
A Linux distribution that is popular among Linux developers, which supports a large number of available software packages. Debian is one of the distributions maintained by volunteers.

Defrag
The Microsoft Windows disk defragmenter utility, which reorganizes the locations of different files on your hard drive.

Deja.com
Refers to the Web site that is a common source of troubleshooting tips and is based on the questions and answers of actual users.

device full error
An error associated with a lack of space on a Linux volume or a hard disk.

df
The disk free space command, which summarizes used and free disk space on each mounted volume.

DHCP
Dynamic Host Configuration Protocol. You can use a DHCP server to ration or assign IP addresses on your network.

dhcpd
The Linux daemon associated with DHCP.

DMA
Direct Memory Address. For peripherals with independent processing capability that can bypass your CPU.

dmesg

The Linux command that recites the messages associated with booting Linux on your computer, including installed hardware and daemons.

DNS

See Domain Name Service.

domain

A group of computers administered as a single unit. The computers in a local area network are commonly organized in a domain.

domain name

The name associated with a specific network. Examples of domain names on the Internet are linuxcertification.org, coriolis.com, and mommabears.com.

Domain Name Service (DNS)

A system that translates domain names such as coriolis.com to IP addresses such as 38.187.128.10. Usually set up as a database on a server. Sometimes also known as the Domain Name System.

DOSEMU

DOS emulator. It includes a series of commands that you can use in Linux to directly read, write, and execute MS-DOS files.

dotted-decimal notation

The standard format for IP addresses: four numbers between 0 and 255, separated by periods or dots.

dotted-quad format

See dotted-decimal notation.

du

The disk usage command. Lists the files used in your current directory and subdirectories as well as their sizes.

dual boot

A configuration where you have two operating systems installed on one computer.

elm

Electronic mail. This is a Linux email manager.

emacs

Also known as *GNU/emacs*. A text editor based on the LISP programming language.

Enlightenment

A window manager designed to be especially configurable.

environment variable

A variable that remains constant when you move from shell to shell.

Ethernet

A standard type of local area network with a maximum data transmission speed of 10Mbps. Variations on Ethernet are available for faster speeds: Fast Ethernet has a maximum data transmission speed of 100Mbps; Gigabit Ethernet has a maximum data transmission speed of 1,000Mbps.

export

When this command is applied to a shell variable, it makes that variable work for all shells.

ext2fs

The Linux second extended file system. A format for a volume; in the same category as Microsoft's File Allocation Table (FAT).

extended partition

A partition designed to contain multiple logical drives. When you need more than four volumes, you can set up an extended partition

fdisk

A utility that sets up primary and extended partitions as well as logical drives on a hard disk. Different versions of fdisk are available for MS-DOS and Linux. The **fdisk /MBR** command overwrites your Master Boot Record for MS-DOS or Microsoft Windows operating systems.

FHS

See Filesystem Hierarchy Standard.

file

A Linux command that allows you to view the type of any specific file.

Filesystem Hierarchy Standard (FHS)

The standard way to store files on different directories on Linux, Unix, and related operating systems.

File Transfer Protocol (FTP)

A protocol used to transfer files between two computers in a TCP/IP network.

find

A command that allows you to search through different directories for a specific file.

fips

See First Interactive Partition Splitter.

firewall

A computer between your network and another network such as the Internet. A firewall is designed to protect a network from the ravages of crackers

who might try to break into your network.

First Interactive Partition Splitter (fips)

The Linux utility that you run in MS-DOS to divide active partitions without deleting data.

free software

Any software that is distributed without a charge. GPL and open source software is free software in accordance with the limits as stated in the respective licenses. GPL and open source software is a subset of free software; in other words, not all free software is governed by the GPL or OSI.

Free Software Foundation (FSF)

The Free Software Foundation (FSF) is the group behind the GNU components of Linux. According to its Web site, the FSF is "dedicated to eliminating restrictions on copying, redistribution, understanding, and modification of computer programs." Because FSF's work makes up most of the Linux operating system, it is referred to as *GNU/Linux*.

FTP

See File Transfer Protocol.

fully qualified domain name

A name that uniquely identifies a computer, consisting of its hostname and the domain name of the associated network. For example, if your computer's host-name is linux and the domain name of your network is mommabears .com, your fully qualified domain name is linux.mommabears.com. Names such as **www.examcram.com** are also fully qualified domain names; *www* represents the host, which might be an Apache server.

FVWM

An older window manager with pop-up windows. FVWM and derivatives like FVWM2 and FVWM95 are designed to use less memory than other window managers.

gateway

The name given to a computer or device that transfers messages between networks. To reach other networks, you need to configure your computer with the IP address of your gateway, which is also known as the *gateway address*.

gateway address

The IP address of a computer on a LAN that is also directly connected to another network.

General Public License (GPL)

A copyright for free software, which requires a release with source code and prevents others from modifying or re-releasing the software under any license other than the GPL. Also known as *copyleft*.

getty

Another name for a console or a login port.

GIMP

GNU Image Manipulation Program. GIMP is an "all-in-one" image editor similar to JASC's Paint Shop Pro.

GNOME

GNU Network Object Model Environment. A complete window manager that includes everything from login screens to office applications.

GNOME Office

The office suite associated with the GNOME desktop.

GNU

GNU's Not Unix. Symbolizes the work of the FSF for programs and applications that clone the functionality of Unix.

graphical user interface (GUI)

An interface that uses the graphical capabilities of your computer and monitor to create a visual interface for your programs.

graphics mode

The graphical resolution that you set on your video card for display on your monitor.

grep

A command to search through a file for a text string. Outputs any matching line.

groff

The GNU troff utility. This is the GNU clone of troff, which is a system for typesetting documents by embedding commands in text files.

group

Every user in Linux belongs to one or more groups. You can assign common permissions on a file or directory to the members of a specific group.

GUI

See Graphical User Interface.

gunzip

A command that uncompresses a compressed file.

gzip
A command that compresses a file.

hacker
In the Linux world, hackers are good people who make, or *hack*, improvements for software.

Halloween documents
The reported Microsoft memos on GPL software released on Halloween eve, 1998.

halt
A command that shuts down Linux and stops your computer. Commonly associated with run level 0.

hardware address
The address assigned to a specific network card. Every network card created today is supposed to be built with a unique hardware address, which you can identify with the **/sbin/ifconfig** command. Hardware addresses are normally shown in hexadecimal notation.

head
A command that gives you a view of the first few lines of a file.

help
A switch that you can use to find more information about the switches associated with a specific command. For example, if you want more information on the **ls** command, type **ls --help**.

home directory
The starting directory for every Linux user. For standard users, the home directory is /home/*user name* (substitute the actual user name for *user name*). For the root user, the home directory is /root.

horizontal resolution
The number of pixels that a monitor can display in a line on your monitor. For example, if the resolution on your monitor is 1024×768, the horizontal resolution is 1024 pixels.

hostname
A name given to a computer. In a TCP/IP network, each computer needs a unique hostname on that network. *See also* fully qualified domain name.

HOWTOs
Manuals associated with the Linux Documentation Project. HOWTOs for many Linux topics are available on the **www.linuxdoc.org** Web site.

HTML
HyperText Markup Language. The commands embedded in text files most commonly used to create Web pages.

httpd.conf
The main Apache configuration file.

I/O
Input/output address. Dedicated locations in your RAM for peripherals to store information while waiting for service from your CPU.

IEEE 802.3
Institute of Electrical and Electronics Engineers standard 802.3. The specification most closely associated with Ethernet.

if

Input filter. Associated with the /etc/printcap printer configuration file. This variable specifies the filter to be used for every print job.

ifconfig

A Linux command used to configure network cards.

image

A parameter that you may find in the /etc/lilo.conf file, which specifies the location of the Linux kernel.

info

A utility that provides a structured way to look through different man pages.

init

The first program that starts when you start Linux. As a daemon, init starts other programs like your shell. It also watches for signals that might shut down your computer, such as a power failure signal from an uninterruptible power supply (UPS).

init.d

The directory with indirect scripts for daemons and other programs that are started or stopped at various run levels.

initdefault

A command in the /etc/inittab file that specifies the default run level when you start Linux.

insmod

The Linux command that adds drivers to your system after Linux boots on your computer.

interactivity

In a Linux shell, this is the ability to reference the HISTORY of previously used commands.

internet

Two or more LANs connected together.

Internet

The worldwide group of networks, sometimes known (not quite accurately) as the World Wide Web.

IP address

A numeric address used for computers on a TCP/IP network. IP addresses are typically formatted as four numbers between 0 and 255 divided by dots. There are 256 numbers available between 0 and 255 (inclusive). Because $256=2^8$, each number is known as an *octet*. The format is known as *dotted-decimal notation*.

ipchains

A firewall utility command commonly associated with Linux kernel 2.2.

iptables

A firewall utility command commonly associated with Linux kernel 2.4.

IPv4

IP Version 4. The standard method of IP addressing used since the development of TCP/IP in the 1970s.

IPv6

IP Version 6. The method of IP addressing that is being incorporated into the Internet today. IPv4 addresses work seamlessly in IPv6.

IRQ

Interrupt request. There are typically 16 IRQ channels in a PC for different peripherals and devices to ask for service from your CPU.

ISA

Industry Standard Association. Also the name of a standard for peripherals that you install inside a computer.

isapnp

The Linux command to reconfigure ISA adapters.

ispell

A spell checker for text documents.

joe

"Joe's own editor." A Linux text processing editor.

kbdconfig

The Red Hat Linux configuration utility for keyboards.

kbdrate

The command used to set the keyboard repeat rate.

KDE

K Desktop Environment. A complete window manager. KDE includes everything from a login screen to office applications.

kernel

The part of your operating system that translates commands from your programs to your hardware. One of the six modules of the Linux operating system.

keyboard repeat rate

When you press a character on a keyboard and keep it pressed down, it eventually starts repeating itself on the screen. The rate at which you see additional characters is the keyboard repeat rate.

kill

A command you can use to end a currently running program or process. You need the PID of the program or process in question.

KOffice

The office suite associated with the KDE desktop.

label

A parameter found in the /etc/lilo.conf configuration file that specifies the label you see associated with booting a particular operating system.

LAN

See local area network.

LaTeX

A typesetting language for text files commonly associated with scientific documents.

less

A command that allows you to view the contents of a file, one screen at a time. You can use the Page Up and Page Down keys on your keyboard to scroll through the subject file in either direction.

lf

Line filter. Associated with the /etc/printcap printer configuration file. Specifies a file that collects errors associated with printing.

LILO

See Linux Loader.

lilo.conf

The LILO configuration file.

LinuxConf

Red Hat's graphical administration utility.

Linux Documentation Project

The project that maintains the main library of Linux information including HOWTOs, book-length guides, manual (man) pages, and lists of FAQs (Frequently Asked Questions). You can find these documents on the www.linuxdoc.org Web site.

Linux Loader (LILO)

Used to boot the Linux kernel. The Linux loader is stored in your hard disk's Master Boot Record (MBR).

Linux Today

The daily digest of Linux information, which includes the latest developments in Linux software and security. You can find its Web site at www.linuxtoday.com.

LISA

Linux Installation System Administration. A semigraphical configuration utility for Caldera Linux.

ln

The link command. Creates a second file that is linked to the first. When you edit one linked file, the changes are also seen in the other file. When you run a file linked to a script or a program, Linux runs that script or program.

local area network (LAN)

A group of two or more computers connected together for data exchange.

locate

A command that searches through a database of files on your computer. This database may not reflect the latest changes that you've made to your system.

logical drive

A division of a extended partition set up as a volume. You can set up a Linux directory to mount on a logical drive.

login

A category of user mode programs. Associates a user's ID with a shell and other personalized settings.

login shell

The shell or command-line interpreter that starts by default when a user logs in to a Linux account.

lpc

The line printer control command allows you to manage communication between Linux and your printer.

lpd

The line printer daemon is an application resident in memory that awaits print related commands.

lpf

A text filter that you can specify in your /etc/printcap printer configuration file.

lpq

The line printer query command returns your current print queue or the jobs that are currently waiting for other jobs to be completed on your printer.

lpr

The line printer request command is a print client that requests print service from the line printer daemon.

lprm

The line printer remove command allows you to remove jobs currently stored in your print queue.

ls

The command used to list the contents of a directory.

lsmod

The command that lists drivers currently loaded on your system.

major.minor.patch

The standard format for Linux kernel release version numbers. Currently, Linux is on its second major release. "Minor" releases are also significant. An odd numbered minor release of a kernel is beta software, and is not suitable for production. The patch number reflects minor changes to the kernel.

man

The command that calls up manual pages. For example, if you want to see the manual page for the **cd** command, type **man cd**.

MAN

See metropolitan area network.

Mandrake

A Linux distribution based on Red Hat Linux.

map

A Linux command that specifies the location of your Linux partitions.

Master Boot Record (MBR)

The first area read on your hard disk, which locates operating systems on your hard disk by their primary partition or logical drive.

MBR

See Master Boot Record.

mcopy

A Linux command that allows you to copy files to or from an MS-DOS directory. The syntax and output matches what you would get from the MS-DOS **copy** command. You can even use this on an unmounted floppy drive.

mdir

A Linux command that lists files in an MS-DOS directory. The output is what you would get from the MS-DOS **dir** command. You can even use this on an unmounted floppy drive.

metropolitan area network (MAN)

Two or more LANs, connected in a fairly small geographic area, that are administered as one unit.

mget

An FTP command for copying files from a server.

Minix

An operating system developed by Andrew Tannenbaum in 1986 as a clone of Unix.

mmove

A Linux command that allows you to move files to or from an MS-DOS directory. The syntax and output matches what you do with the MS-DOS **move** command. You can even use this on an unmounted floppy drive.

mkdir

The Linux make directory command.

mke2fs

The Linux command to format volumes to the second extended file system; also known as *ext2fs*.

mkswap

The Linux command to format a swap partition.

more

A command that allows you to view the contents of a file, one screen or "page" at a time.

mount

The Linux command that's required before you can access any storage device. For example, you can mount a CD-ROM on some Linux distributions with the **mount -t iso9660 /dev/cdrom /mnt/cdrom** command.

mount point

The directory where a certain partition or logical drive is to be mounted.

mouseconfig

The Red Hat Linux configuration utility for your mouse.

multitasking

The ability to run more than one program or process simultaneously.

multiterminal

The ability to access a single Linux computer from more than one terminal. The multiterminal characteristic of Linux enables multiple users to log on simultaneously.

multiuser

A run level where more than one user can run programs in Linux at the same time.

mv

The Linux move command that effectively changes the name and possibly the location of a file.

nameserver

A computer with a database of names and IP addresses. Also known as the *Domain Name Service (DNS) server.* It is based on the Berkeley Internet Name Daemon (BIND).

network

Any group of two or more computers set up to exchange information. Network modules set up the communication. Because network modules are located in the same area as the kernel, their failure can mean that you have to reboot Linux.

Network File System (NFS)

The Network File System is the standard protocol to connect two or more Linux or Unix computers in a network.

network mask

An IP address that helps you define a range of IP addresses on a single local area network. Also known as a *subnet mask.*

Network Time Protocol

The TCP/IP protocol associated with synchronizing the time between computers.

newusers

A command designed to process a large number of users and passwords from a batch file.

NFS

See Network File System.

nice

A command that allows you to start a program with a specific priority level.

nroff

A Linux formatting tool where commands are embedded in text files. Linux manual (man) pages are created with this tool.

of

Output filter. Associated with the /etc/printcap printer configuration file. Specifies the filter to be used for the first in a series of print jobs.

open source

A method and a license for releasing software. Open source software is freely redistributed and includes the source code. Modifications to open source software must be made by "patch" to preserve the integrity of the original software. The open source license is not specific to any product.

Open Source Initiative (OSI)

A group started by Eric Raymond in 1998 to defend "free software." The OSI has its own license that is slightly less restrictive than the GPL. *See also* open source.

other

A parameter found in the /etc/lilo.conf file that specifies a non-Linux operating system.

partition

A logical part of a hard drive.

password

The combination of letters and numbers that you use for a specific user name. Passwords that are a combination of numbers and upper-case and lowercase letters are strongly encouraged.

$PATH

A Linux variable that specifies the directories where Linux automatically looks for a command. If a directory is not located in your $PATH variable, you need to specify the absolute path to run a program or script from that directory.

PCI

Peripheral Component Interconnect. A standard for peripherals that you can install inside your computer.

PCL

See Printer Control Language.

pico

Pine composer. A text editor for Linux.

PID

Process identifier. If you want to kill a program, you need its PID. You can find PIDs with the appropriate **ps** command.

pine

Program for Internet News and Email. A Linux email reader developed at the University of Washington.

pipe

A Linux command construct that uses the |, where the standard output to one command is directed as standard input to a second command.

Plug-and-Play

The capability of a computer BIOS and/or operating system to automatically assign or configure communication channels with various components and peripherals.

PostScript
The printer language developed by Adobe for communication with printers.

primary partition
A partition that can include a Master Boot Record. You can set up a Linux directory to mount on a primary partition. Each hard disk can be configured with up to four primary partitions.

Printer Control Language (PCL)
The language developed by Hewlett Packard for communication with printers.

printtool
Red Hat's printer configuration utility.

private IP addresses
The range of IP addresses that cannot be assigned on the Internet. Private IP addresses are intended for use on private LANs that are connected to the Internet.

ps
The process status command that shows currently running programs and utilities. Commands such as **ps aux** return all programs and daemons currently running on your Linux computer. It also outputs PIDs, which you can use to identify and kill programs of your choice.

pseudoterminal
A virtual console that you can access from a remote computer over a network connection.

pwd
The Linux command that returns your present working directory.

RAM
Random access memory. The main memory inside your computer.

rawrite
An MS-DOS based Linux utility. The rawrite utility is primarily used to unpack the files from Linux images, such as boot.img, to a floppy disk.

Raymond, Eric
The founder of the Open Source Initiative, which is the group behind the open source license.

rc.d
The directory containing various files and scripts to be loaded at different run levels. These scripts are usually divided by run levels linked to actual scripts in the init.d directory.

read error
An error associated with poor media, such as a defective floppy disk.

reboot
The reboot command halts current programs before rebooting your computer. Commonly associated with run level 6. When you run the **reboot** command, Linux initializes the halt run level (0) before restarting your computer.

Red Hat
Perhaps the most widely known Linux distribution.

refresh rate
The number of times information is resent to your monitor every second.

relative path
The path to a Linux file or directory that is relative to your current working directory.

renice

A command that allows you to raise or lower the priority associated with a currently running program.

rescue disk

A disk, usually a 1.44MB floppy, that you can use to boot your computer into Linux. Often used when you have problems with your LILO or Master Boot Record.

restorrb.exe

A utility that you can use to restore a Master Boot Record from a backup stored in a rootboot.00x file (x is typically a number between 0 and 9).

rm

The Linux remove command that deletes files. Depending on the switch you use, this command can also delete directories. In the /etc/printcap printer configuration file, rm is a parameter that specifies the hostname or IP address of the computer with a remote printer.

rmdir

The remove directory command. This command does not work if the directory that you are trying to delete is not empty.

rmmod

The command that removes drivers currently loaded on your system.

rootboot.00x

A backup file for your Master Boot Record (MBR), where x is a number between 0 and 9. You can set up fips to create this file from the information on your MBR. If you need to restore

your MBR for any reason, you can then use the **restorrb.exe** command.

run level

A parameter defined in the /etc/inittab file that defines different processes and daemons. Different run levels are associated with different conditions in Linux, such as single- or multiuser mode.

Samba

The network program that allows computers running Linux to communicate with computers running Microsoft Windows.

SaX

The S.u.S.E. GUI configuration tool.

ScanDisk

The Microsoft Windows utility for checking for errors on hard disks.

SCSI

Small Computer Systems Interface. A type of connector for disk drives and other peripherals.

sd

Spool directory. Specifies the location of spool files prior to processing by your printer. Associated with the /etc/printcap printer configuration file.

sendmail

The Linux-based mail transport agent, which allows you to set up mail servers.

setleds

The command to set keyboard defaults, such as Num Lock, for different virtual terminals.

shadow

The /etc/shadow file is the encrypted password file.

shell

A command interpreter. The most commonly known Linux shell is known as *bash*, which was developed from the original Unix Bourne shell.

shell variable

A variable that may change from shell to shell.

shutdown

A command that shuts down Linux. Depending on the switch you use, this command can halt or reboot your computer.

single sequential user system

An operating system where only one user can log on at a time. The system is limited to a single terminal.

single user

A run level where only one user can run programs in Linux. Commonly associated with run level 1 or S. If you boot into single-user mode, no login is required, and you have root privileges.

Slackware

A Linux distribution with a ZipSlack package option for the Zip drive.

srm.conf

The Apache configuration file that defines subdirectories used by people who browse your Web site.

Stallman, Richard

The founder of the Free Software Foundation and the GNU General Public License (also known as *copyleft*).

Stampede

A Linux distribution that focuses on ease of use and the newest processor hardware.

Star Office

A suite of office programs owned by Sun Microsystems. It is available for free download for Linux.

startx

The command that starts the Linux graphical user interface (GUI); also known as the *X Window*.

stderr

Standard error, usually to the monitor.

stdin

Standard input, usually from the keyboard.

stdout

Standard output, usually to the monitor.

stty

Standard Linux terminal line settings.

subnet mask

See network mask.

sudo

See superuser.

SuperProbe

A command that detects key parts of your video controller.

superuser

When a regular user wants root privileges on a Linux computer, he or she can log on as a superuser with the root user's password. Also known as *sudo*.

S.u.S.E.

The best selling Linux distribution in Europe. Depending on the version, S.u.S.E. Linux includes up to six CDs.

SVGA

Super VGA or Super Video Graphics Adapter. A type of generic video server.

swap partition

A volume on your hard disk that is set up for overflow from RAM. If the RAM in your computer is not sufficient, less-used information is moved to the swap partition.

swapon

A Linux command to activate a file as a swap file.

system message logging

The process of collecting messages about one or more daemons.

table

A parameter associated with the /etc/lilo.conf configuration file. Defines a logical volume, such as hda1, associated with an operating system.

tail

A command that gives you a view of the final few lines of a file.

tar

A command that collects (or extracts) a series of files into a one file archive.

telnet

An application available on many operating systems including Linux and Microsoft Windows, which allows you to log in remotely to a Linux server.

TeX

A typesetting language based on macros embedded in text files.

thrashing

What you hear when Linux spends a lot of time exchanging information between your RAM and a swap partition on your hard disk. Thrashing is the sound made by the constant motion of a hard disk. This is characteristic of insufficient RAM.

tkinfo

An X Window version of the **info** command.

top

This command lists the programs and utilities in order of their load on your system resources, especially CPU and RAM.

Torvalds, Linus

The main developer of the kernel at the core of the Linux operating system.

Trojan horse

A malicious program that is usually set up to look like a regular program or command.

umask

The command used to set up default permissions for any files and directories that you subsequently create.

umount

This Linux command unmounts any directory that you may have previously mounted.

uninterruptible power supply (UPS)

A power source that starts when you have a power failure. It supplies temporary power to your computer. The /etc/inittab file is normally configured to shut down Linux in a short number of minutes after receiving a signal from your UPS.

Universal Serial Bus (USB)
A type of peripheral. Support for at least USB mice and keyboards is being incorporated into Linux kernel 2.4.

Unix
The operating system developed in the late 1960s and early 1970s at AT&T's Bell Labs. The functional ancestor to Linux.

UPS
See uninterruptible power supply.

USB
See Universal Serial Bus.

useradd
A command that automates the creation of users in Linux based on the defaults shown when you run the **useradd -D** command.

userdel
A command that deletes a specific user including his or her home directory and entry in the /etc/passwd configuration file.

user mode
User mode programs and applications communicate with the kernel. The kernel then communicates requests to your hardware. If a user mode program fails or crashes, Linux still runs, and you need not reboot your computer.

user name
The name that you use at the **login:** prompt to access an account.

utilities
Commands used inside a shell.

vertical resolution
The number of horizontal lines shown on a monitor.

VFAT
Virtual File Allocation Table. A system used to format volumes to be read by Microsoft operating systems.

vi
A basic Linux text editor.

video controller
A computer card with independent processing capability that manages graphics for display on your monitor.

video memory
The memory on your computer that is dedicated to graphics. Usually resident on a video controller.

video RAM
See video memory.

video server
The type of video controller resident on your computer.

virtual console
Every terminal where a user can log on to Linux, locally or remotely, is a virtual console.

virtual display
Hidden GUI screens where you can open and store other applications.

vmlinuz
A common file name for the Linux kernel.

VMware
A third-party application that allows you to run Microsoft Windows operating systems inside a Linux X Window (or vice versa).

w
A command to show currently logged on users and their current activities.

WAN
See wide area network.

wc
A command that allows you to count the lines, words, and characters in a file.

Webmin
A graphical installation utility for Caldera Linux, which you can use in a Web browser.

who
A Linux command to show currently logged on users.

wide area network (WAN)
Two or more geographically separate networks connected together.

Wide Open News
The electronic magazine of Linux sponsored by Red Hat. You can find its Web site at **www.wideopen.com**.

widget
A library program often associated with Linux window managers.

WindowMaker
A GNU window manager designed to be similar in feel to AfterStep.

WINE
Windows Is Not an Emulator. The WINE project is developing an emulator that you can run in Linux that runs various Microsoft Windows programs.

winmodem
A modem that substitutes Microsoft Windows driver libraries for some modem hardware controllers. Because this takes CPU resources, some Linux developers believe that it would be wrong to create Linux drivers for winmodems.

wildcard
A character such as * or ? that can represent other characters.

WordPerfect
A Corel WYSIWYG word processor that is available for Linux.

WYSIWYG
What-you-see-is-what-you-get. Used mainly in reference to graphical word processors.

X11
Another name for the X Window.

X Window
The Linux GUI.

Xconfigurator
The Red Hat GUI configuration tool.

xdm
The command that starts a GUI login screen.

xf86config
A text-based GUI configuration tool.

XF86Setup
The main GUI configuration tool from the XFree86 project.

xfig

An image editor used to create drawings. It is consistent with computer-aided design requirements.

XFree86

The group that creates Linux drivers for video adapters. It also creates and maintains the XF86Setup program, which is the main utility for configuring the Linux GUI.

xinfo

An X Window version of the **info** command.

.xinitrc

The default startup script for the X Window. Normally stored in users' home directories.

Xinu

An operating system developed by Douglas Comer in 1983 as a Unix clone to help teach operating system structures in the classroom.

xman

An X Window version of the **man** command.

YaST

Yet another Setup Tool. The S.u.S.E. graphical administration utility.

YaST2

Yet another Setup Tool Number 2. The next S.u.S.E. graphical administration utility. Works together with YaST to administer a system for the S.u.S.E. distribution.

Index